THE HIDDEN FACE OF JESUS

Dedicated
with love and gratitude
to
the peoples of Africa
in whom
so often and so searchingly
I have encountered
Jesus.

MARGARET MAGDALEN CSMV

THE HIDDEN FACE OF JESUS

Reflections on the Emotional Life of Christ

Foreword by Desmond Tutu

First published 1994 by
Darton, Longman and Todd Ltd
1 Spencer Court
140–142 Wandsworth High Street
London SW18 4JJ

ISBN 0–232–51996–X

A catalogue record for this book is available from the British Library

Phototypeset in 10/12pt Raleigh by Intype, London
Printed and bound in Great Britain
at the University Press, Cambridge

CONTENTS

ACKNOWLEDGEMENTS

As always with a book, there are many people who have helped me along the way as I have reflected and prepared to launch into the writing of *The Hidden Face of Jesus*. Some people with whom I have talked have fed me ideas or suggested lines of approach but, in this respect, my very particular thanks go to Sister Valerie CSMV with whom I have had many enriching, brainstorming sessions which have been stimulating and fun. Her valuable insights have been largely incorporated into this book and I am especially grateful to her for help with Chapter 5 and parts of Chapter 4. Over a period of four years, she has given generously of her time on each of her visits to the Convent and has shared with prodigality much wisdom from her own field of psychotherapy and counselling.

I also owe an enormous debt of gratitude to Bishop David and Carol Beetge of the Diocese of South-East Transvaal who offered me the use of their guest house as a place to write, but who also opened their home and hearts in incredibly generous hospitality. My time with them at Springs will remain with me as a lifelong and cherished memory. They provided the silence, space and solitude (apart from the constant and delightful companionship of their two dogs!) necessary for a month of intensive writing. The daily worship in the Bishop's Chapel gave me the privilege of sharing in the office of the Church of the Province of South Africa, and of entering more deeply than ever before, through intercession, into the terrible suffering of the black peoples of that beautiful country. David and Carol will never fully understand just how significant for me that month in their home was, nor how inadequate this expression of thanks is.

I am deeply grateful, too, to Mother Muriel Grace and the CSMV Sisters in South Africa for their love, encouragement and support in this venture; to Bishop Michael Nuttall of the Diocese of Natal for allowing me to use him as a sounding board and for his generosity of time and ideas; to the Revd Jean Cornell (CSMV Oblate and Deacon on the Ecumenical Parish of Bishop's Cleeve, Cheltenham) for her helpful literary criticisms, suggested emendments and affirming theological comments; to Sister Mildred Rebecca CSMV for the daunting task of checking most meticulously all the Biblical references; to Sister Frances Mary CSMV for the long and tedious job of making photocopies of the manuscript (and I should like to emphasise my thanks to those two Sisters very especially, for both are over 90!); to Peggy Haynes for her speedy typing and patience in working from a handwritten and often much altered script, and to David, Alexis and Annika – her long-suffering family – who have been willing to 'spare' her from family demands for this work. I am very grateful to her for being so unruffled and good-natured at all times; to Ann Orbach for her helpful comments and suggestions on Chapter 5, most of which I have been able to incorporate; to all the Sisters, Oblates and friends who have prayed for me regularly as I have been engaged in the writing of this book; and to Morag Reeve, editor of DLT, for her unfailing support and consistent encouragement in the whole enterprise, particularly when my faith in it all has been at a low ebb.

One of the problems of a good memory is the ability not only to absorb and retain what one reads but at times to quote phrases or sentences without always being aware of doing so. All writers would, I think, agree that one so internalises what one reads that it is often difficult to trace back the origin of a thought. If it has a familiar ring it is difficult sometimes to know if it has been encountered in reading or stems from one's own previous writing.

If I have erred in any such way, I apologise and can only claim that it is unintentional.

FOREWORD

One of the lessons I learnt in England was that you were more likely
to impress Westerners by understatement than by hyperbole. I also
found that they were allergic to anyone who was dogmatic. This
latter trait was illustrated for me when I was a student at King's
College, London. We had superb teachers among whom was my Old
Testament teacher, Professor Peter Ackroyd. You could safely predict
that at some point in his lecture he would use his pet phrase 'It is
not unreasonable to suppose . . .'

All this is a preamble, for *The Hidden Face of Jesus* also soft-
pedals where dogmatism is concerned. It is a quite remarkable book
that will richly deserve the accolades it receives. It is an outstanding
tour de force, which persuasively describes the inner life of Jesus, his
psychological make-up and development. It is speculative theology at
its best, restrained and sober but wonderfully profound in the
insights that it produces.

I suppose it is true to say that many of us think we accept that
Jesus Christ was 'like unto us in all things, sin excepted', as the
Epistle to the Hebrews describes the nature of the incarnation – that
he is God of God, but more importantly, that he is fully and truly
human as we are human, that is, a creature of flesh and blood. But,
in reality, many of us perhaps believe that the human nature Jesus
assumed was not *really* real, that he was masquerading as a human
being. Deep down many are docetists, believing that Jesus was play-
acting and was human only in appearance. It may not be quite so
crudely stated, but we seem to have an embarrassment about our
recalcitrant human nature. I have a great deal of admiration for St
Augustine of Hippo, but I must sadly concede that his dabbling
with Manichaean dualism has had a baneful influence on Christian
theology. Most Christians have sadly unbiblical views about human
nature and are especially negative about human sexuality. Is it not

instructive that we still say 'they are living in sin', meaning that a
couple are cohabiting without the benefit of matrimony, reducing
sins of the flesh to those relating to sexual immorality, and ignoring
such 'spiritual' sins as idolatry, hatred and envy?

Sister Margaret Magdalen hopes that we will take the incarnation
seriously as meaning that Jesus became a real human being of flesh
and blood. And because that is the case, he had an inner life which
is a proper subject of study by theologians. She looks closely at the
psychology of Jesus, including his possible pre-natal psychology and
development, working on the understanding that the Fathers were
quite right when they rebuked heretics who gave our Lord an incomplete humanity by declaring that what he did not assume he did not
redeem. She brings an impressive knowledge of psychology to bear
on her study, and looks at Jesus as a real human being who had a
sexuality, and who experienced dreams and fantasies.

There is a discussion of how Jesus appeared to deal with hurts
and slights, and it is in this section that I encountered one of the
outstanding characteristics of the book. Whilst it clearly is very good
theology, I had not expected it also to be a devotional book that
affected my spiritual life. I found that in a strange way as Sister
Margaret Magdalen described what she believed must have been
how our Lord operated, she was holding a mirror up to me. I was
being challenged to engage in a searching examination of how I
was operating in my own life. I found the analogy of the washing
machine and the vacuum cleaner particularly apt. Jesus was like the
washing machine, taking in all that was thrown at him and cleansing
it, letting the evil pass out into the sewer in an appropriate manner
and so drawing the poison from, for example, the barbed remark. I
tend to be like the vacuum cleaner, soaking up dirt and keeping it
inside. I let things fester and build up, exploding some time later,
inappropriately, often, with little or no provocation at all.

It is like a breath of fresh air to be told that each of us, in a sense,
is Legion: we are potentially a community of selves as created in the
image of the triune God, and we grow into who we are as these
selves become more and more integrated. Yes – Jesus holds up to us
what it means to be truly human. The glory of God is a human being.
In a way this book sent me to my knees; I found it humbling and
yet edifying. I believe it is a remarkable book and thank God for it.

DESMOND TUTU

INTRODUCTION

Readers of this book will quickly realise that it is written from the standpoint of faith. I make no apology for that. It is not a scholarly work and makes no claim to be so. It is not intended as a contribution to the current debate about Jesus. Rather, it is the fruit of prayer and reflection upon the life of Jesus and what it means to be fully human. It seeks to go behind what is explicit in the Gospels to what may be implicit and, using contemporary insights and background information about that period, it aims to draw out a fuller picture of Jesus. It is speculative – but not speculative theology in the technical sense. It will be described as 'uncritical', and that is true in so far as it does not spring out of historical analysis or critical examination of documents, texts and manuscripts. In 1992 there were a flurry of books on Jesus which formed part of the new quest for the historical Jesus, but this book is not in that line.

I sincerely hope that I have been sufficiently sensitive in the use of imaginative insights and loyal to biblical truth in so far as I have apprehended it. Some chapters tread on holy ground and tackle what, in many respects, are extremely delicate subjects. I hope that no one will judge this to be a blasphemous intrusion into the personal and emotional areas of Christ's life, or merely wishful thinking. Much of what I have written is in the form of suggestions for further reflection in the hope that it will make Jesus more immediate and accessible to many readers.

Some scholars believe that it is impossible to reconcile the Jesus of faith with the Jesus of history. I think it is perilous to separate them. We cannot have a Christ of faith divorced from the Jesus of history. Who Jesus is for us now *must* be rooted in history. For that reason, although I have used imaginative reflections as a way of encountering Jesus through the Gospels, I have tried to set him squarely in the context of first-century Judaism, to earth him in his own culture, at the same time drawing out possible insights for the contemporary community of the new humanity. Whilst Jesus cannot be understood apart from his cultural setting, it must also be said that historical analysis is not the only test of authenticity. Faith has other criteria by which it discerns truth. In addition, we must never underestimate the power and reliability of the oral tradition which lies behind the Gospels.

This is not a theological treatise but, agreeing with Nikos Kazantzakis in his view that, 'that part of Christ's nature which was profoundly human, helps us to understand him and love him and to pursue his Passion', it is an attempt to draw together theological and imaginative insights in such a way that ordinary lay members of the Church with little or no theological training, and possibly a minimum of Christian teaching, may yet be able to understand the substance of this book and ponder its questions. It is intended for those who, after a busy working day, want to take up some spiritual reading and feel stimulated and nourished by it, but whose energies cannot reasonably stretch to more academic work.

It is my earnest prayer that everyone who reads *The Hidden Face of Jesus* written as it has been with personal devotion, will 'more than ever before, better than ever before'[1] find themselves loving him.

Margaret Magdalen CSMV
Wantage 1993

1

'FULLY HUMAN'

Pre-natal Influences

Recent researches into the development of the unborn child have produced some illuminating and fascinating discoveries. The 1960s gave us new insights into a post-birth system of mother-child communication called 'bonding', and in many ways, more recent researches are a logical extension of these earlier findings. They move the communication system back a step and place it in the womb.

> The single most gratifying aspect of our new knowledge is what it reveals about the pregnant woman and her role in shaping and guiding her unborn child's personality. Her tools are her thoughts and feelings, and with them she has the opportunity to create a human being favoured with more advantages than previously thought possible.[1]

It cannot, of course, be claimed that everything that happens to the mother in those critical nine months irrevocably shapes her baby's future. So many things go into the moulding of a new life. 'Maternal thoughts and feelings are just one element in the mix, but what makes them a unique element is that unlike givens such as genetic inheritance, they are controllable. A woman can make them as positive a force as she wishes.'

These discoveries are by no means undisputed and would not be held by all psychologists, but, if there is any truth in them, we may well ask what Mary's influence was upon Jesus whilst he grew in her womb. What did he pick up from her – what moods, what emotions, what feelings towards him, all of which might have gone into the shaping of his character? For, if he was fully human, born into the world as any other child is born, we need to acknowledge the possible profound influence she may have had upon him, and he upon her. According to Dr Florovsky:

> Motherhood is a personal relation between two persons ...
> Motherhood in general, is by no means exhausted by the mere
> fact of procreation. It would be lamentable blindness if we
> ignored its spiritual aspect. In fact, physical procreation itself
> establishes an intimate spiritual relation between the mother
> and child. This relation is unique and reciprocal, and its essence
> is affection and love. Mary was not merely a physical instrument,
> not just a 'channel', through which Jesus came, but 'truly the
> mother of whom he took his humanity'. Saint John of Damascus
> precisely in these very words summarises the teaching of the
> Church: he did not come 'as through a pipe but has assumed *of
> her* a human nature consubstantial to ours.'
>
> The mystery of the Incarnation was for her also the mystery
> of her own personal existence ... It was an undisturbed orien-
> tation of the whole personal life towards God, a complete self-
> dedication.[2]

Jesus was born a normal baby with the same natural limitations as
any child. He had to grow in understanding as well as stature and
through all the normal processes of learning and discovery like
other children.

I sometimes wonder if, because by faith we believe him to be the
Son of God, there is a lurking, probably unacknowledged, impression
that he was somehow born with divine omniscience, an adult mind
in a baby's body. But the joy of a truly incarnational theology is that
he had to begin where we all began our journey in life. He, too, had
to grow in the normal and often painful ways that we have to
experience. There was no skipping of certain stages to put him ahead
of other children – which would have made him a freak. That it was
clearly not so is revealed by the fact that, when as a young man, he
was invited to preach in the synagogue and did so with astonishing
eloquence, insight and authority, the congregation at Nazareth was
up in arms at the implication of what he was saying. 'Isn't this the
son of Joseph, the carpenter?' they cried (implying that he was no
more nor less than that). 'Isn't this the boy we have watched grow
up along with our own children? How dare he stand there and make
such exalted claims about himself.' From their reactions it seems
pretty conclusive that there had been nothing so extraordinary about
his childhood that the villagers of Nazareth had thought him destined
for great things.

If then we consider a few of the insights into the development of a child that researchers such as Thomas Verny, John Kelly, and Frank Lake have proposed, what can they suggest to us of Mary's part in the moulding of her son's character?

At the Annunciation she received the news, through angelic communication, that she would conceive in her womb and bear a son. Obviously that came as a mighty shock. 'Then gentle Mary meekly bowed her head' says the hymn,[3] but that surely wouldn't have been her immediate response. Indeed, we know that she questioned the announcement – which was a perfectly proper thing to do. 'How *can* there be a conception?' she asked. 'I have never had intercourse with a man.' 'And,' she might have added, 'I would never even entertain such a thought until I marry Joseph, my betrothed.'

I can't help feeling that Mary's acceptance, her 'Be it unto me according to your word', was given only after wrestling with this startling and indeed terrifying news. She must have realised immediately some of the implications, including the possibility of death by stoning, for if a woman had sexual relations with another man during the year of her betrothal, it carried the same penalty as adultery after marriage.

Inevitably her mind would have raced to such thoughts as, 'What will the neighbours think? What do I tell my parents? How can I break this to Joseph?' She would rightly have anticipated how he would find it almost impossible to accept seemingly wild, exaggerated stories about angelic messengers and supernatural conception which left her still a virgin. Despite being very untypical of the Mary he knew, Joseph could have assumed this to be a story invented to explain her pregnancy and cover up her guilt.

Moreover, she would not have been human had she not worried about the inevitable divorce (even if she were spared execution) which would leave her totally responsible for the support of the child. Other unmarried mothers and young widows with families to feed, were forced into prostitution out of desperate need for money. 'Will I be driven to join their ranks?' she might have wondered.

One can imagine that like her predecessors who had been called by God to very special vocations, she sought refuge in excuses. 'I'm too young for such a mighty responsibility.' That had been Jeremiah's fearful response to his call. 'I am not worthy' might have been another – shades of Isaiah's reaction to his vocation. 'I'm not an outstanding person nor a natural leader' – which echoes Moses' initial objection to God's choosing him. (See Jeremiah 1:6; Isaiah 6:5; Exodus 3:11, 4:10ff.)

Some, if not all, of these thoughts must have raced through Mary's mind as she tried, in a state of stupefaction, to cope with the import of the announcement. 'Who am I', she must have asked, 'that God should choose *me*? Is this just a sudden delusion of grandeur, a fit of megalomania, or a moment of wild fantasising about status?'

Was it as she pondered the message in her heart that she was able, after much struggle and self-doubting, to recall that God is always on the side of the poor and lowly. That was clear from all she knew of history. Wasn't it typical of him to put down the mighty and exalt the humble and meek? Wasn't he especially concerned to fill the hungry with good things? Those who regarded themselves as rich and self-sufficient in every way, who were unaware of their own desperate needs in spiritual and emotional respects, whose self-knowledge was obscured by their material wealth and corresponding status in society, would continue to feel a deep inner emptiness. Only when people came to acknowledge that they were poor in spirit and needed help would he lift them up.

Only then, as she saw the announcement of God's action to be wholly in keeping with his often strange reversals of human standards, part of a pattern in his way of choosing people for special tasks, could she bow her head and in acceptance and trust of phenomenal magnitude say, 'Let it be to me according to your word'. This was no mere passive acquiescence or, worse still, resignation to God's call. She was not silent – she responded in humility and faith, without knowing in advance all the consequences of her total acceptance.

When does an unborn child start to react to its mother's feelings? In the opinion of one group of investigators, from the moment of conception onwards. Precisely at what point the brain cells acquire the ability to sense large undifferentiated emotions such as love and hate, but also more shaded complex feeling states like ambivalence and ambiguity, is not certain. But it is believed that something like consciousness exists from the very first moments of conception. As evidence of this belief, researchers point to the thousands of perfectly healthy women who repeatedly have spontaneous abortions. They speculate that in the very first weeks of a baby's life – perhaps even hours – after conception, the fertilised ovum has enough self-awareness to be able to sense rejection and has enough will to act on this knowledge. (The researchers understand that although this theory has very strong support, it is not, as yet, a fully proven fact. What does have real authority – because it has been confirmed by psychological studies – is what is known about the child from the sixth month *in utero* onwards. 'By almost any standard, he is a fascinating human being at this point. He can already remember, hear, even learn.)[4]

Did Jesus, then, even in that embryonic state, sense Mary's deep shock and her initial anxiety? Did Mary's wholly understandable ambivalence but ultimate acceptance of God's will, lay a foundation whereby, well into adult life, he could accept the seemingly outrageous will of God? Surely her struggle to say 'Yes' to God's choice of her and her final and total fiat embedded in his unconscious a pattern of response which gave him additional strength when he himself was in the same position, struggling in a garden to say *his* 'Yes' to God's will? Mary's 'Let it be to me according to your will' would have been there as a memory, part of his inner resource, to bring him to the point where *he* bowed his head and said, 'Nevertheless, not my will, but yours be done'.

One cannot believe that all Mary's anxieties and ambivalence evaporated at the moment of her 'fiat', never to return. There must have been other times in the nine months when she was worried and perhaps even had to do battle with fear. But a child's future happiness doesn't hinge on the mother's ability to banish all fear and think bright thoughts for 24 hours a day – which would be wholly unrealistic. Occasional doubts, ambivalences and anxieties are a normal part of any pregnancy. What seems clear, though, is that an expectant mother has at her disposal an active way of affecting her baby's emotional development for good; definite moments of choice which influence the child's responses to life.

This all highlights the enormously important part the father has in the months of pregnancy. A relationship with a loving, sensitive man provides a woman with a sense of ongoing emotional support. Just how important emotional security and nurturing are, not only to the woman, but to the unborn child, could not be measured, as Dr Verny points out, until the father's rightful place in the whole process of pregnancy and birth began to be acknowledged and restored to him.

Though Joseph was not yet the husband of Mary, nor the father of Jesus, we know that he was just, kind and sensitive. Far from stoning Mary to death, he made plans for her to go into seclusion at the home of her kinswoman Elizabeth, to spare her from becoming the subject of speculation and gossip in the village. He knew well enough what agony she would experience as she faced the pointed finger of self-righteous critics and saw their disapproving looks and meaningful glances. He genuinely loved her – enough to protect her from that pain and humiliation. Nor, of course, did he want them speculating about his own part in it all. Inevitably he too risked accusations – of anticipating their wedding and causing a premature pregnancy. He was fully aware that this kind of situation was meat and drink to the gossips and a potential source of much trauma and ultimate ostracism.

Joseph's understanding, his truly astonishing willingness to believe the divine disclosure (how many men would have done so in his position?) and his deep concern for Mary's welfare and that of the child, would have vanquished immediately some of her own fears about the future – how she would cope with criticism and at the same time support her son.

The fact that she had in no way lost Joseph's respect, but rather that he felt personally called by God to share the responsibility for the upbringing of this special child, might have eased any residual anxieties Mary had. Perhaps she wondered if Joseph would wait until the baby was born and then quietly divorce her. But when she realised, and was assured, that he accepted this birth as part of his vocation, that God's call was in a sense to them both, she must surely have been able to relax and perhaps even begin to enjoy the prospect of this miracle. (Though I do not agree with them, I have to acknowledge that there are other writers who see the birth as a source of perpetual tension between Mary and Joseph.)

Through various experiments and studies into the unborn child's capabilities, researchers reckon they now know more about the ways personality characteristics and traits begin forming in the womb. Likes and dislikes, fears and phobias and all the distinctive behavioural characteristics that go to making a child uniquely his or her self are, in part, the product of conditioned learning. The womb is where the first stage in that learning process begins. Dr Michael Lieberman gives one particular contemporary example of this in the area of anxiety – that created by smoking. An unborn child can become very emotionally agitated each time his mother so much as thinks of smoking – before ever a cigarette touches her lips or is lit. Smoking causes a drop in oxygen and the child associates the very distressing physical sensations caused through the lowering of the oxygen content in the mother's blood which passes through the placenta, with the smoking habit. This is physiologically harmful to the baby but even worse are the psychological effects. It thrusts the child into a state of chronic fear and anxiety, and because of the unpredictability of the smoking and its associated acute discomfort, predisposes the child to a deep-seated conditioned anxiety complex.[5] A foetus can also become very distressed indeed by raised voices in angry exchanges between the parents, and will often kick and struggle in its anxiety.

Other researches have shown happier forms of learning – for example, speech. We each have our own idiosyncratic speech rhythm. It may go unnoticed by others on the whole, but it can be picked up in a sound analysis test. Our speech pattern is as unique and distinct as our fingerprints. The source of such uniqueness comes from the mother. Children learn their speech (on the whole) by copying their mother (or their father if their mother goes to work and he is taking care of them). Even if the father takes over after birth, the baby has been developing a distinct speech rhythm from the mother during the months in the womb. Dr Truby in his studies was able to show that the foetus hears clearly from the sixth month *in utero*, and even more amazingly is able to move bodily to the rhythm of the mother's speech.

Given the baby's acute hearing, it isn't surprising that unborn children are capable of learning something about music. At four or five months, a foetus can definitely respond to sound and melody – and even be quite discriminating. For example, a tape of Vivaldi's music is almost always guaranteed to calm a child down. But put on Beethoven and even the calmest child will start kicking. Goodness knows what effect rock music has!

Personality is, of course, much more than the sum of learning situations and experiences in or out of the womb, but these researches by paediatricians have identified some of the traits and characteristics that are shaped by very early experiences. They lead us to believe that a woman can begin actively to influence her child's life well before birth. Hence the need to talk to the child soothingly, tell him/her how much he/she is loved and wanted, to croon to the child, to stroke the abdomen – in other words to provide as many auditory and tangible signals as possible to convey to the child a real sense of well-being, a basic approach to life that says, 'It's good to be alive and to be me.'

There are probably thousands of people who have been deeply scarred by destructive pre-natal experiences, people whose disorders and afflictions can be explained only in terms of what happened to them in the womb or at birth. Knowledge in this area of pre-natal psychology is vitally important in terms of preventing such tragedies from repeating themselves in the future, from possibly even establishing a pattern, like a chain reaction, within a family. There is hope now of improving future generations' chances of starting life free of the corrosive mental and emotional disorders that have blighted children in the past.

With these contemporary insights perhaps we can conjecture a little as to what Jesus might have heard and experienced in the womb? Certainly he would have heard the chanting of prayers both in the home and in the Synagogue. Mary may well have sung to and crooned over her unborn baby. Perhaps he picked up some of the tensions that he heard in the voices of Joseph, Mary and their friends as they discussed aspects of Roman oppression. Galilee in particular produced many rebels and was a sharp thorn in the side of the Romans. Rebels who were captured were crucified in their hundreds. As we imagine Mary shuddering at the very thought of such mass execution, did her child within move in response to her horror? Was he in some way aware of his mother's terrible anguish and compassion as she listened to and tried to comfort other mothers whose sons had been subjected to a terrible death by crucifixion?

If indeed she had suffered with such women, she must have searched within herself wondering, 'How does any mother cope with the sight of her son, her own flesh and blood, the child of her love whom she has nurtured, hanging in agony on a cross, suffering death by slow torture? How would a mother's broken heart ever be healed after such unspeakable trauma? Could she ever recover? Would she not go out of her mind with the mental and emotional agony?' Being, as I imagine, a highly sensitive person, Mary would no doubt ache with the depth of her sorrow for them, and grieve for those sons whose lives had been cut off in their prime, with all their hopes and aspirations shattered. And that ache would surely have communicated itself to the foetus in her womb unable, of course, to understand why such sorrow flooded his little world, but nevertheless sensing it deeply. Adults, and even children after a certain stage, are able to build up defence mechanisms that enable them to soften or deflect the impact of a painful or distressing experience. But an unborn child cannot. And it is all the more traumatic because the child is quite literally 'in the dark'. What affects an unborn child does so 'neat' as it were, which is why maternal emotions have the power to etch themselves deeply on the memory and psyche and continue to exercise a strong pull in later life.

Mary's quiet trust and faith would most certainly have affected her baby. He would have sensed her strong confidence in God. He would, I am sure, have felt himself surrounded by positive feelings and a certainty of being loved and revered as he grew in her womb. If initially she communicated fear to him – fear at the awesome vocation she had been given – later he would have sensed her gentle acceptance and indeed, in the end, her eager expectation at his coming. Subconsciously he would surely have been aware of the depth of her radical obedience expressed in her song: 'My soul magnifies the Lord, and my spirit rejoices in God my Saviour, for he has looked with favour on the lowliness of his servant. Surely from now on all generations will call me blessed' (Luke 1:47–8).

A child could scarcely be given a better start in life!

Birth and Babyhood

For Joseph and Mary the decree that all Jews were to go to their family town for a census could not have come at a worse time. Mary was nearing the date when the baby was due to be born and Joseph, descended as he was from the lineage of David, was obliged to make the long journey to Bethlehem and take Mary with him. Not only must they have been alarmed at the prospect, given Mary's condition, but there would be other hazards to face such as very rough terrain and the threat from bandits who frequently attacked travellers, robbed them of whatever valuables they carried and, more often than not, left their victims half-dead.

That, plus the fear that perhaps the baby would arrive before they had reached shelter, must have sent ripples of fear through the foetus too. Mary could scarcely have failed to be worried about where she would actually have the baby. Neither she nor Joseph appear to have had relatives actually living in Bethlehem, had that been so, they would not have been contemplating staying at the inn.

On top of all those anxious feelings, which might well have communicated themselves to Jesus, came the bumping, jolting movements as Mary rode on the donkey led by Joseph. It must have been an appallingly uncomfortable journey for her and hardly less so for the baby – but at least the amniotic fluid in which he floated, cushioned him from some of the discomfort.

Then came the shock of finding the inn full with no hope of a room there. All the signs of imminent birth must have left Joseph almost demented. Was he going to have to deliver the baby himself by the roadside? Although none of the Gospels actually states that they were offered accommodation in a stable, the mention of placing the baby in a manger has given rise to the belief that it was there that Jesus was born.

No details are given as, for example, whether it was a hard birth or whether, in the end, the arduous journey actually brought the birth on rather suddenly ahead of time. It would seem quite possible; otherwise, surely Joseph would have sought refuge at an earlier village.

A birth in a stable would seem to Western eyes to be horrifically unhygienic. In such conditions there would surely be an enormous risk of infection. In actual fact, the chances are that the conditions made the birth a far less daunting experience for Jesus than it is for many other babies.

Imagine the stable dimly lit by lamps but warm with that amazing heat given off by cattle. A cowshed on a winter's night can be as hot, if not hotter, than a centrally heated room. There would have been familiar animal smells rather than disinfectant, and the softness of straw rather than a delivery table. It would have been a warm, reassuring, gently lit environment which is very important. For the child is very much aware of how he/she is born. None of us forgets our birth, even if we no longer have access to those memories. Under hypnosis or certain forms of primal therapy people can relive their birth experiences very vividly. Often they are illuminating and give important clues to problems that arise in adulthood but stem from as far back as the birth experience itself.

A baby at birth will feel comfortable with a soft glowing light and will sense softness and a caring touch. He will respond to them much as he senses and responds (in a totally different way) to the bright lights, the clinically white walls, the electrical bleeps and cold impersonal atmosphere that are so often associated now with hospital deliveries.

When the birth was over and one imagines the baby lying contentedly in Mary's arms feeling still her heartbeat and nestling into her soft, warm body, there must have come a very strong bonding. The immediate fears and anxieties were over. Now she had the freedom and emotional space to absorb the wonder of this miracle. For although it would seem the gestation and growth of the foetus had been normal, and he had been born naturally, she could hardly forget that his conception had been quite other. Here were the words of the angelic message coming to fruition. She had indeed given birth to a son and in obedience to the divine intimation, they called him Jesus.

Someone, it appears, offered them more suitable accommodation shortly after this, for Matthew's Gospel records the arrival of wise men from the East who followed an unusually bright star in which

they read the portents of a royal birth. They had come to bring
offerings to the royal infant, and we are told it was after 'going into
the house' (Matthew 2:11) that they had their first view of the young
child and his mother, and presented the gold, frankincense and
myrrh – though admittedly, stables were often considered an integral
part of an actual house in the Palestine of that day.

Whether the census took a long time, or whether Joseph felt the
little child was too young for the long journey back to Nazareth, it
seems that by the time the wise men came looking for the 'new-
born king', Jesus was no longer a new-born baby. For Herod's decree
had specified that all male children *up to the age of two* were to
be slaughtered.

As I write, the funeral is taking place of little James Bulger – a
two-year-old child who was abducted in Bootle in Liverpool and
beaten to death with an iron bar by two ten-year-old boys. The
whole British nation has been shocked to the core by this death.
The outrage and horror of it have gripped the entire country and the
reactions of the people of Liverpool have not unnaturally been violent. They had nowhere to place their anger and sheer sickness of
heart that this could happen to an innocent two year old. In fact,
the ripples of horror have spread out to the whole world, undoubtedly due in part to the fact that this murder was committed *by*
mere children.

Imagine then for a moment, what it was like in Bethlehem that
day when soldiers swarmed into the houses and killed the male
children of two years old and younger with swords. Probably as
many as forty children lost their lives because of Herod's insane
jealousy. The sheer horror of it would have made it a city of inconsol-
able grief and sorrow made all the worse by the unbelievable brutality
of it all as mothers had their children wrenched from their arms
whilst trying to run for safety. Maybe they even saw them bayonetted
or hacked to pieces before their very eyes. There were no sedatives
in those days to give a degree of merciful, if only temporary, relief
from such unbearable emotional pain. It is almost impossible to
conceive of bearing that kind of suffering without going out of
one's mind.

Warned in a dream of impending danger – and some of those who
have studied dream psychology will be familiar with the kind of
intuitive knowledge given Joseph in dream form – he left Bethlehem
taking Mary and the child down to Egypt to escape from the treachery
of Herod.

No more information is given as to how they fared in that foreign land – for them a land of exile, even though ever since the destruction of Jerusalem by Nebuchadnezzar there had been a

> ... considerable Jewish colony which had continued to expand after Palestine became a Greek province, until it became nearly a million strong. Jewish colonists had even built at Leontopolis a temple said to rival that of Zion. The majority of these Jews remained faithful to Palestine and in constant relation with their compatriots there. It was in Alexandria, where the Jews formed two-fifths of the population, that their servants had made for the library of the Pharaoh Ptolemy II that translation of their sacred books which we call the Septuagint. Since the Holy Family had to flee Palestine as refugees, it was fairly natural that Joseph should escape to Egypt.[6]

In all probability they would have hugged the coastline following the caravan route. The interior of the country was inhospitable in the extreme. 'All the armies of history which have traversed this hostile land have met with misfortune, from Gabinus and Titus in 55 BC and AD 70 down to Lord Allenby in 1918.'[7]

It is strange to think that the one born to save his people should follow in the footsteps of his illustrious, patriarchal forbear who also went down into Egypt – not of his own volition – and 'saved' a whole people in time of famine. Interestingly, Jesus may have spent as many as four of his early years in the land in which Moses the Lawgiver had been brought up. What might have been the lasting effects, even emotional damage, of these traumatic events upon him – events, which had they happened to us, would need deep healing of the memories to reverse the damage?

Did he in later years ever suffer from a 'Survivor Syndrome'? There are plenty of modern examples of those who have so suffered, as for example, Eli Weissenfelt, burdened with a sense of guilt because he survived the concentration camps where thousands upon thousands went to the gas chambers. He believed the reason he survived was to tell others what happened and so absolve his guilty conscience. Special counselling facilities had to be set up after the sinking of the *Marchioness* in the Thames and the *Herald of Free Enterprise* cross-channel ferry, not so much to help those in shock after the experience, but those who felt deep guilt that they had somehow survived whilst being powerless to save others who eventually drowned. Their sense of impotence only compounded their guilt.

And what of those who will survive 'the éliticide' in Bosnia? Will they view life with greater awe and a sense of having been saved for a purpose? Or will their guilt be so intolerable that all joy in life will be driven out?

What must Jesus have felt when, perhaps as a teenager or even earlier, he had to come to terms with the fact that his life had been saved at the expense of so many others? He was the reason for a wholesale slaughter and the terrible anguish it brought to the city of Bethlehem. Did he ever ask himself, 'Why me? Why did I escape?'

When told of the massacre in his youth, did he ever struggle against the feeling that he had to live up to some wonderful ideal? If so, at what stage in his maturation was he able to let go of 'the ideal' and make the transference to 'responding to his Father's will'? Nothing that we read of Jesus in the Gospels gives any hint whatso- ever that he was trapped in guilt feelings about the past, rather that increasingly he grew in discernment about his vocation – the destiny for which he was born.

Nor do we hear of his going back to visit his birthplace or to preach to the people there. Apart from the fact that Jerusalem seems to have been as far south as he ever went as an adult, perhaps he simply couldn't return to the city where he would be a visible reminder of their appalling loss – for there would have been no other young men of his age there.

Being the sensitive person we will later see him to be, did he ever suffer the terrible weight of compassion overload, particularly in respect of those babies who had died in such cruelty? Deeply as he must have felt the horror of it, I would suggest that he neither felt guilty about the children being killed, nor suffered from 'Survivor Syndrome'. That horrendous act was Herod's doing, the vileness that came from *his* inner being, and Jesus refused to take responsibility for other people's guilt. He would unquestionably have felt a searing pain, but not guilt. M Scott Peck[8] says that the neurotic accepts responsibility and therefore the guilt for what is not his own fault. The one with a character disorder won't take responsibility for his own wrong-doing. Jesus falls into neither of those two categories.

How was it, we may ask, that as an adult, Jesus could choose to re-live some of those traumas of early childhood that would have left others of us emotional cripples for life? If we suffered homelessness, refugee status, becoming a 'wanted' person, an exile, rejection by virtue of being a member of a despised minority group, even as an adult, let alone a child, there would be deep and indelible scarring –

so much so we would probably be thrown into depression, childish or anti-social behaviour by any adult experience that resonated with our early experiences and opened up scar tissue. But as Jesus grew from adolescence to manhood, he was so in touch with his feelings and memories as to be able to appropriate his past and integrate it in such a way into the present that he could use it creatively.

For example, as a child on the point of being born, there was no room in the inn. He entered this life homeless, in great uncertainty (and anxiety on the part of his parents). Probably, as we have seen, Mary's own deep trust in God's goodness and provision enabled both her and the baby to cope with the situation without the excessive panic many would feel. However it was, he was free enough in himself later on to adopt a lifestyle where he often had 'nowhere to lay his head'. He could face once more, being a member of a minority group – i.e. the disciples – quite often a despised minority. Certainly that is implied in the way the servant taunted Peter during Jesus' trial before the High Priest. 'This man is one of *them*. You also were with Jesus the Galilean.'⁹ Other bystanders said to Peter, 'Certainly you are one of them; for you are a Galilean' (Mark 14:69–70; Matthew 26:69–71, 73).

He followed a path where, once more, he would be a 'Wanted Man' hounded by the authorities (Roman and Israelite, state and religious). His life was under constant threat towards the end. And, at the last, he was able steadfastly to set his face towards Jerusalem and the death he once escaped as a baby, leaving Barabbas perhaps with a 'Survivor' complex.

Boyhood

◆◇◆◇◆◇◆◇◆◇◆◇◆◇◆◇◆◇◆◇◆◇◆◇◆◇◆◇◆◇◆◇◆◇◆◇◆◇◆

Practically nothing is told us in the Gospels about the boyhood of
Jesus other than the fact that after Herod died and Archelaus (one
of his sons) came to power, Joseph deemed it safe to take the family
back to Nazareth. It cannot be established with certainty whether or
not there were more children by then. Matthew's Gospel mentions
four brothers of Jesus – all with interesting names: James (an alternative form of Jacob) and Joseph (after two great patriarchs) and Simon
and Judas (after two heroes of the Maccabean revolt);[10] and at least
two sisters (Matthew 13:55ff). This is a delicate subject and a point
of basic disagreement between the Catholic wing of the Church,
which has always held to the belief of Mary's perpetual virginity, and
Protestants, who have real problems with that view because of its
implications that sex is somehow unholy or an indication of inferior
spiritual status.

The expression 'brothers of the Lord' requires elucidation. In Aramaic *aha*, in Hebrew, *ah*, it can signify brother, half-brother, cousin
or even a close connection. There are a number of examples in the
Old Testament of this loose usage of the word translated as 'brother'.
For example, Abraham says to Lot, who happened to be his nephew:
'We are brothers' (Genesis 13:8) and Laban uses the word to his
nephew Jacob. In 1 Chronicles 23:21, 22, the sons of Kish are referred
to as the 'brethren' of the daughters of Eleazar, although it transpires
in the next verse that they are in fact cousins. It cannot be established
with certainty whether these were cousins of Jesus or half-brothers
and sisters. If the latter, it seems odd that tradition has held that Jesus
took over the carpenter's shop when Joseph died, and supported his
mother in widowhood. It is strange too, that on the cross, Jesus
commends his mother to the safe-keeping of John. Where were her
other children at that point, and wouldn't they have expected to
take responsibility for their mother?

Maybe the cousins lived close by, or the families even shared one house (which was not unusual) so that the children grew up together. If that were so, in all probability there would have been much discussion where feelings ran high for, the names given to the boys imply an enthusiastically nationalist family. Not surprisingly, since in Galilee, nationalist feelings were stronger and more militant than in Judea, the people bitterly resented the Roman occupation and, along with other Galileans, would have nurtured a growing hope of speedy deliverance through the coming of a Messiah. His arrival would bring them liberation from domination and oppression, and establish peace and prosperity.

The failure of the uprising of Judas the Galilean and his followers in 6 AD must have left an indelible impression on the sensitive adolescent Jesus – especially as he could hardly not have seen the crosses that lined the road out of Nazareth on both sides 'as far as the eye could see' we are told. One wonders whether, as the respected owner of the town's carpentry business, Joseph was actually forced to make the crosses for their execution? Under the Roman system of impulsion, he may not have had any choice. In which case, did Jesus as a young apprentice have to assist him in the grisly task?

The home itself, in which Jesus grew up, would certainly not have been rich, but it is unlikely that it was abjectly poor either. Carpentry was a respectable and respected trade. E P Sanders[11] points out that the occupations of Palestinian Jews were the same, on average, as those in other Mediterranean countries. He says that, in discussing the rules for Sabbaths, the Mishnah very helpfully lists 39 classes of work. The first seven have to do with agricultural work outside; the next four with the preparation of food inside (from grinding to baking); the next 13 with producing textiles; the next seven with hunting, slaughtering and butchering; two with writing; three with construction; two with fires; and one with carrying.

Many people made their living by agricultural work tending the olive trees, the cereal crops, the pulses, the vines, the date palms and fruit trees. There were many flocks and herds that needed tending. The people were known to be 'good graziers and stock breeders, and kept flocks and herds of goats, oxen and sheep.'[12] Josephus describes Galilee as one of the most fertile parts of the country. Certainly simple country things impressed themselves on Jesus' mind as he grew up and he called upon them readily when he spoke in parables.

Carpentry would come under the heading of construction or artisan work and might also have included stone-masonry, which didn't depend upon rainfall at the right seasons or the terrible consequences of drought to quite the extent of the agriculturalists. There must therefore have been a degree of financial security in the home but doubtless seeds of his compassion for the poor must have been sown in early days when perhaps some of his school friends had a more precarious existence. It wasn't only the weather that could ruin crops. If a plague of locusts happened to descend on fields, crops could be totally devoured within half an hour leaving the farmers devastated and destitute. There would be no celebration of harvest in times like that, and much anxiety among parents with young children to feed.

Nazareth was considered an uncouth village and had a bad reputation. Aramaic was spoken with a distinctive dialect (cf. Matthew 26:73). It was a much despised town – hence Nathaniel's astonished remark: 'Can anything good come out of Nazareth?' (John 1:46).

Jesus would have received the same kind of education as any young Jew of his time, which would chiefly have consisted of learning Torah – reciting it until long passages of it were known by heart. It was considered of prime importance that children should have intimate knowledge of the Law both in theory and in practice.

Philo wrote:

> Since the Jews consider their laws to be divine revelations and are instructed in them from their earliest youth, they bear the image of the Law in their souls. Even before any instruction in the holy laws and unwritten customs, they are taught, so to speak, from their swaddling clothes by parents, teachers and educators to believe in God, the one Father and Creator of the world.[13]

Clearly this education was primarily the duty of the parents, and we can imagine that Mary and Joseph would have been scrupulously conscientious in this respect. They would have taught him by word of mouth, and more importantly, by their example. They would surely have lived out the precepts of the Law in their fidelity to it.

It seems that by the time of Jesus, the village community also provided instruction for their children by the establishing of primary schools. It would have been at one of these *beth-hasepher* that Jesus, sitting on the ground, around the scrolls of the Law, would with the other children have repeated the verses in unison until they had memorised them. In Hebrew the same word is translated 'repeat' and 'learn'.

That there were such schools is attested by the Mishnah – from which we know that elementary schools did exist in the second century AD. There were legal rulings with regard to the minister of the congregation teaching the children to read on the Sabbath. It was also decreed that an unmarried man must not teach children. It seems reasonable then to accept the later tradition that claimed that Joshua ben Gamla (an alternative form of Jesus, son of Gamaliel) ordered school teachers to be appointed in every province and in every town, and children to be brought to them from the age of six or seven. The only Jesus, son of Gamaliel, known to history is the High Priest of that name who flourished in about AD 63–5. It seems probable then that this information refers to him. As Joshua ben Gamaliel's order presupposes that boys' schools had already existed for some time, it is reasonable to assume they were operating in the time of Jesus.

Instruction then centred almost exclusively on Torah. And all this zeal in providing schooling for the young was aimed at impressing Torah on their minds – not at providing children with a general education. Only interest in Torah made the teaching of reading desirable. For in public worship, it was important for a Jew to be able to read the Law. He could be called out (without forewarning and it was and still is considered a wonderful privilege) to read from the Scrolls as Jesus did on the occasion when he so offended his countrymen. The teaching of writing was far less general. Could Jesus write? We hear of only one occasion when he wrote anything – when accusers brought the woman taken in adultery to Jesus for him to pronounce judgement on her. We are told that, while her accusers one by one sheepishly dropped their stones and backed off, he bent down and wrote something in the sand. Sadly, nobody thought to record whether or not it was anything of significance or merely an aimless scribble.

Although small children were not expected to fulfil Torah, nevertheless they became familiar with it from their very earliest days. They were expected to observe the Sabbath rest. They were gradually introduced to the strict fast kept by the Jews on the Day of Atonement, taking part in it one or two years before it became obligatory. Certain things were compulsory though, even for children. For example, they were not expected to recite the *Shema* or to wear the phylacteries, but they were required to be able to recite the *Shermoneh Esrah* and grace at table.

Any young boy living in Jerusalem was expected to go up to the

Temple mount to the feasts as soon as he could walk, without having to ride on his father's shoulders or hold his hand. A boy living some distance from Jerusalem, it seems, began to take part in the pilgrimage when he reached his twelfth birthday. As soon as he began to show signs of puberty he was obliged to fulfil the whole Torah, whereupon he would take on all the responsibilities and rights of an adult.

A later ruling fixed the date when a young Jew attained legal majority – on his thirteenth birthday – which made it all far less invidious, and less embarrassing for the physical late developers. When therefore Jesus went up to the Temple at the age of twelve, he would already have been well versed in Torah and able to recite large portions of it. This knowledge of the Scriptures clearly stayed with him and grew throughout his life enabling him to quote freely not only the Law but the Psalms and Writings too. However, at the time when he first went up to the Temple, he was still a minor, awaiting his *bar-mitzvah*.[14]

I cannot imagine that Jesus was a precocious child though he was probably very bright, intelligent and high spirited, quick to learn and hard working. But surely he was not the objectionable little sorcerer that A N Wilson cites in *Jesus* in his chapter 'His Wondrous Childhood.'[15] Quoting from the Gospel of Thomas, the Arabic Gospel and Syriac History, he suggests Jesus used his divine powers to play capricious tricks – deliberately sending people mad, deaf or blind and then making them better again. He was even supposed to have struck people dead in order to raise them to life. When children ran from him and hid in a cellar, he turned them into goats till the parents of 'the goats' implored Mary and Joseph to use their influence to get him to turn them back into children.

If these legendary stories grew up to show how Jesus had practised his 'magic' as a child before trying out miracles as an adult, they couldn't be more wrong. The Jesus who resisted temptation to satisfy his hunger by turning stones into bread, who taught his disciples that the power to heal only came through prayer and fasting, who could do no mighty work in one place 'because of their unbelief' and who ultimately resisted the most searching temptation of all – to save himself and come down from the Cross – would hardly have been able to practise such reverent discipline over his divine powers as an adult had he been accustomed to using them for fun. God would surely not have colluded with such nonsensical misuse of his gifts. And Mary, I am convinced, would have put a stop to it. She must have watched him closely for any signs of growing self-aware-ness that he was 'different' from other boys.

Throughout his adult ministry he made it clear that he could do nothing were it not for his Father's power, and that would surely apply, perhaps particularly so, to his power to perform miracles?

The Emerging Vision

◆◇◆

We can imagine the excitement of Jesus when, for the first time, he was eligible to join the other pilgrims going up to Jerusalem for the Passover Festival. So much of what he had learned of the history of his people and their worship was focused there, in the Holy City. Other, older boys and his parents, must have tried to describe the magnificent Temple buildings – the like of which was seen nowhere else in the world at that time – the scenes of crowds gathering, the busy Temple officials going about their duties, the learned doctors of the law and supremely, of course, the High Priest in his gorgeous robes.

There may have been an additional reason why Jesus looked forward eagerly to this first visit. His education up to the age of ten years would have been exclusively the teaching of the Old Testament, and from then, the Mishnah (or traditional law) as well. At the age of 15 onwards a pupil passed on to higher studies involving theological discussion. One wonders whether Jesus was ahead of his years at school and already into the over-fifteen stage. Perhaps his questions to the local rabbi at the Synagogue school had been so searching that the poor man was floored. In which case he might well have said to Jesus, 'Why don't you save that question for one of the learned doctors at the Temple?' Maybe it was the rabbi who put into his head the idea of asking them for their interpretation of puzzling passages or their explanation of aspects of worship or Jewish history etc. Possibly then, Jesus arrived at the Temple with a prepared agenda of subjects for discussion.

It would seem that he didn't tell Mary and Joseph of his intentions, or might they not have guessed what had happened when they discovered him missing from their homeward bound party? Indeed, Jesus himself must have wondered how, in view of the huge crowds and the awesome magnificence of the Temple, he would ever get a chance to consult even one learned scholar let alone several – he, a mere lad and still a minor. Could he possibly claim individual attention from such eminent people at one of the busiest times of the year?

And what kind of questions *did* he ask that could hold not just one scholar, but a whole group of them, utterly rivetted? It would have been quite exceptional for any 12-year-old to be able to hold his own in theological discussion with men of their learning – and to do so without embarrassment, pride or appearing to over-reach himself. He would hardly have done so if his questions had been trivial or irrelevant. This makes me wonder if he had already begun the stage of theological discussion at school. The scholars showed the true humility of the learned in welcoming his thoughts and reflections. But they would have discouraged him if he had seemed to be merely a precocious, attention-seeking youngster who was showing off.

One subject which had long been a matter of speculation – even among religious leaders – was that of the identity of that enigmatic figure of Isaiah's prophecies, the Suffering Servant. Might Jesus perhaps have been searching for answers as to who he was and whether he had lived and died unrecognised, or was still to come? Was he an individual, or was the Servant to be the whole nation Israel? Had Jesus begun, even at this stage to wonder about connections between the Servant of Isaiah and the Messiah of their hopes? And did he puzzle over the seeming contradiction between the popular under-standing of Messiah – a liberator from Roman oppression – and this *Suffering* Servant? Both were destined for salvific roles but in conflicting ways. Whatever happened, something seemed to have shifted for him in his thinking that, in response to Mary's remon-strances, he could reply, 'But didn't you know that I must be busy with my Father's affairs?' (cf. Luke 2:49).

This may have been the first intimation Mary and Joseph were given that Jesus was beginning to discern his vocation. Had he given any prior hint that he had burning questions to ask?

Perhaps there was far more to discuss by the end of the Feast than had been on his original 'agenda'. What, for instance, were his reactions to this first visit to Jerusalem? Did it match up to his expectations? Was he even more awed than he had anticipated at the sheer magnificence of the Temple, and the very size of the huge slabs of stone Herod the Great had used for this building which was such a personal triumph?

Possibly his second impression was one of ambivalence. On the one hand there was all the excitement of a market and on the other a sense of shock and disappointment at the noise, bustle and dirt that confronted a visitor entering the Temple precincts. This was the place above all places where a devout Jew longed to worship and pray. But the noise, the smell, the droppings of the birds, the bleating of the lambs destined for sacrifice, the cacophony of men haggling over the exchange rate (which was extortionate and naturally foreigners seeking to exchange their money were not going to be swindled blatantly without a fight) – all conspired to make it anything but conducive to prayer. Voices would inevitably have been raised in heated argument, and the sharp eyes and ears of an intelligent 12-year-old would have taken all this in.

Did he feel the injustice of it all even then? Was something of his later outrage conceived at that first visit, only to be fuelled by every subsequent one? The account of the cleansing of the Temple in Mark's Gospel (Mark 11:15) reads as though Jesus entered the Temple for the express purpose of ridding it of the malpractices and unscrupulous traffic that had been going on for years. But possibly something occurred on that occasion that was like a spark to the kindling of his cumulative anger, which had been building up, and created a blaze. Perhaps he had reached the point where he could no longer tolerate the injustice of those who cheated their own countrymen and deprived Gentiles of their only rightful praying space. Whatever it was, his rage boiled over into violent action. Could it have been during this or a previous visit that he actually saw a Gentile standing with bowed head, beating his breast in deep humility and praying, 'Lord, be merciful to me, a sinner'? And did his heart go out to this man who genuinely longed for God's mercy and forgiveness? It must have been impossible not to contrast his behaviour with the strutting stance of some of the Israelites he had observed glancing at the Gentile with withering scorn, before going on into the inner Court of the Israelites, heads held high and their whole body language shrieking, 'Lord, thank goodness we are not like that benighted Gentile, but Israelites and people of God entitled to draw closer to him than any other people and enjoy the special privileges of his chosen ones' (cf. Luke 18:9ff).

I wonder, too, what impression that self-same inner court left on the youthful Jesus? He would have known what to expect by way of prayers and, being a country boy, would undoubtedly have seen animals slaughtered for meat. But had anything or anyone prepared him for the sight that would meet his eyes at a Passover feast? Far from being a place of lofty worship, it must have resembled an abattoir. So great was the slaughter, there were special channels by which the blood ran down from the Temple into the Brook of Kedron which, we are told, became thickened almost solid as the blood congealed. Local farmers came and dug it out to sell as fertiliser – the proceeds going to the Temple.

Since most Palestinian Jews would have been in Jerusalem for the Festival there would have been an estimated 250,000 to 500,000 pilgrims present, plus a large number ('tens of thousands') of pilgrims of the Diaspora. One lamb was slaughtered for every family or group of ten people – which gives us some idea of the number slain.

Where did all the pilgrims sleep? An inscription from a synagogue in Jerusalem indicates that it contained rooms for foreign visitors, and many inhabitants rented space for temporary accommodation.[16] Many would have found lodgings in the villages around.

Maybe it was fairly early on that Joseph and Mary found the household of Lazarus, Mary and Martha, and perhaps their parents too, and stayed with them on that and subsequent visits to Jerusalem. In which case, it could have been that the children grew up together and were good friends before their adult years, so that Jesus gravitated there quite naturally whenever he was in the environs of Jerusalem. It was obviously one place where he felt 'at home', assured of an understanding and sympathetic reception and the freedom to relax completely.

Journeying to Jerusalem, the pilgrims would have sung pilgrim songs. Pilgrims on foot always travelled in companies both as protection from bandits and also to enjoy the mounting excitement as they approached the goal of their journey. It must have been rather like present day football supporters travelling in groups to matches, singing and shouting support for their teams. Perhaps crowds gathering for Spring Harvest or Green Belt would be more appropriate comparisons, with coach-loads arriving, their passengers singing choruses and spiritual songs in a fever of excitement.

Some of the songs sung by the Jewish pilgrims would have been secular ones, and they would have told jokes to one another and enjoyed more wine at night than usual. It was a holiday for most of them – the only kind they would ever get. The atmosphere would therefore have been very festive – a happy blend of fun and laughter together with piety. There would have been dancing, good food and chatting round the fire at night.

The celebration began on the road and built up in intensity the nearer the pilgrims got to the Holy City. For the final stage of their journey, they would surely have reserved some of the gradual psalms:

> How lovely is your dwelling place, O Lord of hosts!
> My soul longs, indeed it faints for the courts of the Lord;
> my heart and my flesh sing for joy to the living God.
> (Psalm 84:1f.)

> O send out your light and your truth;
> let them lead me,
> let them bring me to your holy hill
> and to your dwelling
> Then I will go to the altar of God,
> to God my exceeding joy;
> and I will praise you with the harp,
> O God, my God. (Psalm 43:3f.)

> I was glad when they said to me,
> 'Let us go to the house of the Lord!' (Psalm 122:1)

Familiar words – but if we can picture ourselves as pilgrims fervently longing for our first glimpse of the city and the Temple in all its splendour – they may take on a more colourful and contextual significance. When you were a child travelling excitedly to the seaside, did you ever crane your neck to catch your first sight of the sea, and, having caught it, feel you couldn't wait to rush down to the beach? So the youngsters amongst the pilgrims must have felt the urge to race ahead of their parents who, weary from the long journey, probably seemed to travel at an unendurably slow pace.

Then, after all that, imagine the scene that greeted Jesus – the market place and the slaughter house with squawking, the crying of animals, the smell of roasting, and the hubbub of loud conversations. The priests would have been dispersed around the inner courtyard at different points to receive the animals from the men of the families who would have ensured that they had previously been examined for any impurity. The priest would hold back the head of the lamb but the man himself actually slit the throat whilst the priest collected the blood in a basin. He would then have to find hanging space on one of the walls where the animal would be flayed and its skin returned to the worshipper. The fat was then burned on the altar, the priest's portion taken and the worshipper received back the carcass (the wives having watched all this from the gallery of the women's court). The family would then roast and eat the animal with the other food included in a Passover meal.

With so many thousands of lambs being slaughtered, there was sometimes no more room on the walls to hang the lambs for flaying. Poles were therefore provided and held by two men from which a lamb would be suspended and flayed.

To Western eyes it would be a revolting scene likely to induce fainting or vomiting. But such sacrifice was, of course, a natural part of worship in the ancient world in all religions (though not always on such a scale). It was as natural as hymns and prayers are for most worshippers today, and was not viewed as a barbaric act. Nevertheless, there was no avoiding the sheer quantity of blood shed and splashed around, or the sheer number of carcasses that would cover every inch of the walls.

Before offering a sacrifice, worshippers had to undergo proper preparation and cleansing of any ritual impurity. They were required to abstain from sex the night before and to bathe in immersion tanks. As the lamb was offered, the man laid his hand on its head and confessed his sins – if it was a guilt offering; or his cause for thanks – if it was a thank offering.

Did Jesus, watching all this, wonder about the people who could not make the journey to the Temple – the old and infirm, those too poor to have a 'second tithe' (the money set apart for such a visit, which could *only* be spent in Jerusalem)? What of those who found the weight of their sin too awful to bear, and yet, maybe, had to delay for a year or even years before they could off-load their guilt on to a sacrificial lamb and know for certain that they had received forgiveness?

Somewhere along the line, and it may even have been at this first visit that such questions began to formulate in his mind, Jesus must have wondered with concern about those who were cut off for one reason or another from this cleansing and release from guilt. Did he already begin to see the inadequacy of a system that barred so many from experiencing God's mercy through this tangible sign? Was it right that the whole matter of forgiveness should be so much in the control of the priests?

In his book *The New Testament and the People of God*, N T Wright says:

One cannot go to Jerusalem to offer sacrifices on a regular basis if one lives in Babylon or Rome, in Athens or Alexandria, as a large number of would-be observant Jews did. Observance of key Torah Commandments will do instead. 'Spiritual sacrifices' are thus offered when one gives alms, or prays, or studies Torah or fasts. It is difficult to tell how far this had been taken by the time of Jesus, but Jews came to believe that in the presence of the Torah one was in the presence of the covenant God. Thus what became true for all Judaism after 70 and 135 was anticipated in the necessities of Diaspora life.[17]

Although the study of the Torah could be a replacement for Temple worship, it did not eliminate the sense of it being a second best substitute.

In some respects it could be compared to the sense of loss Christians would feel (and *do* feel in some isolated parts of the world) if their worship consisted solely of the ministry of the Word and they were denied the sacraments. Whilst God is not limited by rituals or sacraments, and can be encountered richly through the written word, nevertheless, the sheer externalism of the sacraments is important as objective assurance of his presence, his acceptance, his forgiveness, his healing.

If Jesus pondered the inner meaning of it all, recognising that all the butchery and bloodshed had to be repeated year after year, would his main concern perhaps have been to know if a man really felt released from guilt when he made a guilt offering? Did a woman really feel herself flooding with thanks when she made a thank offering? Was there a truly corresponding inner change in their lives as a result of the outward actions? However dimly comprehended and embryonic the questions, might he not have recalled the Scriptures:

> For you have no delight in sacrifice; if I were to give a burnt offering, you would not be pleased. The sacrifice acceptable to God is a broken spirit; a broken and contrite heart, O God, you will not despise. (Psalm 51:16–17)

> For I desire steadfast love and not sacrifice, the knowledge of God, rather than burnt offerings. (Hosea 6:6)

> 'With what shall I come before the Lord, and bow myself before God on high? Shall I come before him with burnt offerings, with calves a year old? Will the Lord be pleased with thousands of

rams, with ten thousands of rivers of oil? Shall I give my first-
born for my transgression, the fruit of my body for the sin of
my soul?'

He has told you, O mortal, what is good; and what does the
Lord require of you but to do justice and to love kindness, and
to walk humbly with your God? (Micah 6:6–8)

With his thorough training in the Scriptures and his desire to
uncover their inner meaning, Jesus would have come to appreciate
how futile ritual could be, indeed, how offensive the outer act could
be to God, if it were not accompanied by an inner reality. The
inner reality that clearly pleased God was a passion for justice, an
overflowing mercy that reflected his own, a heart broken for the
injustice and oppression practised so widely, and an ear attuned to
his word for his people. Only such attitudes would qualify a person
to bring sacrifices to the Lord.

Perhaps because of his own inner purity, his perceptions were
far more acute than average. Discernment was almost unavoidable.
Holiness in an adult and innocence in a child can confer a natural
intuitive power that sees straight through sham. Without sitting in
judgement on others, had Jesus somehow been disturbed by any
unreality or inconsistencies in the worship as he had observed and
taken part in it?

Could this then have been a further area of discussion with the
doctors of law? How, for instance, did they see the inner reality and
the outward ritual matching up? Did they ever feel at times that
people were 'using' sacrifice as a kind of 'automatic grace dispenser',
in order to absolve their guilt feelings and to rid themselves of the
burden of an uneasy conscience, when there seemed little evidence
of true penitence? 'Might there not be other ways', Jesus may have
asked, 'whereby people could know their guilt purged and their sin
removed "as far as the east is from the west"?' (cf. Psalm 103:12).

I believe that, increasingly, as the years of boyhood passed into
manhood, he became deeply convinced that the only true worship
of God was in spirit and in truth; that the only valid sacrifice was
that accompanied by a broken and contrite heart. Any incompatible
behaviour made sacrifices worse than useless in the eyes of God.

When Mary and Joseph found Jesus in the Temple and rebuked
him, his reply might well have seemed off-hand and rude. But could
it not have been simply one of genuine surprise? For he had probably
made a very long inward journey, as well as the outward one, during

that first Passover, moving forward very rapidly in his thinking and understanding as he pursued meanings which up to that point had eluded him. He might not however have allowed for the fact that Mary and Joseph would not necessarily have realised the extent of his sudden leap in faith and knowledge. Doubtless for some while he would have been questioning all sorts of things at home, and we can imagine Mary trying to lead him gently but surely towards a fuller self-knowledge. But the experience of being at the very heart of Israelite worship in solidarity with all his people down through the history of the nation, must have opened up unimagined vistas for him.

Nevertheless, he was obedient and returned with his parents (however costly it must have been) to Nazareth where he grew 'in stature and in favour', with God and with all those around him. He too had to grow – in knowledge, in character, in understanding, through relationships, through the circumstances and vicissitudes of life, through pain – for inevitably he had his share of disappointments, sadness, misunderstandings and being misunderstood, through betrayals, and the rough and tumble of school life.

I also see him as the kind of boy who would step into the middle of a squabble and try to defuse it. He would champion the weaker or more backward ones. Even at a very early age, I believe, he would have begun to realise where real power lay as he observed the pseudo-power which the bully, inwardly insecure but physically tougher, assumed over the smaller and weaker boys. But he would also have known the power of inner authority.

In all of this Mary would have played an important part, her mothering, I am sure, the complete opposite of parents who try to push their children forward, who spot talent and seek to nurture it as genius, who possibly work out their own frustrated ambition through their children, encouraging them – indeed driving them – to attain dizzier and dizzier heights of success, without regard for what it may do to them emotionally, socially or spiritually.

Mary, one can imagine, would surely have exercised great caution and discretion to ensure that Jesus did have a normal upbringing, that he didn't stand out from among his peers as being so different that he was ostracised by them. Nor would she have sought to make him an extension of herself. As Charles Lamb once said, 'A child's nature is too serious a thing to admit to its being regarded as a mere appendage to another being.'[18]

All parents must at times feel awed, if not terrified, at the responsibility that is theirs. 'Parentage is a very important profession', wrote George Bernard Shaw (though I prefer to call it a vocation), 'but no test of fitness for it is ever imposed in the interests of the children'.[19] In Mary's case, however, she was, we believe, 'highly favoured' and very especially chosen *because* of her unique fitness, in the eyes of God, for a vocation more demanding and daunting than that given to any other mother.

Adolescence and Puberty

Although the teenage years of Jesus are most definitely 'hidden' years for us, there is a certain amount that we can learn of his upbringing simply by studying cultural patterns and norms of home and family life at that time.

In a home of Jewish piety, there would be an emphasis on correct action in every sphere of life, which was technically called orthopraxy. Fundamental to Jewish life and worship – the daily worship in the home – was the Shema, the central statement of Jewish belief, which begins: 'Hear O Israel, the Lord is your God; the Lord is one. You shall love the Lord your God with all your heart, and with all your soul, and with all your might' (Deuteronomy 6:4–5). The passage continues by saying that the Commandments are to be 'upon the heart', spoken of in the home and taught to the children, remembered before sleep and on waking. They are to be bound upon the hand, placed 'as frontlets' between the eyes, and fixed to the doorpost or gate (vv. 6–9).

The practice was, then, to recite the Shema and the Ten Commandments morning and evening, write other passages from the Commandments and post them on the door in *Mezuzah* (little cylindrical containers) and fix *tefillin* (phylacteries in Greek) to the left arm and forehead. The Mishnaic rabbis took it for granted that every Jew said the Shema, together with daily prayers twice a day, and did not deem it necessary even to enquire whether or not this was so.

These practices prescribed in Deuteronomy 6:6–9 were clearly still widespread during the lifetime of Jesus for in Matthew 23:5, the Pharisees were criticised for making their *tefillin* too ostentatious – but not for wearing them, showing that the wearing of them was general. Presumably Jesus wore them himself on the appropriate occasions.

In addition to the common practices of praying twice a day in the morning and in the evening (either at bedtime or at the hour of evening sacrifice in the Temple), many devout Jews also recited the Eighteen Benedictions which blessed God for giving his people the opportunity to repent and receive forgiveness. Although a communal prayer, it was often prayed privately and, as it was thematic in structure, it could be prayed in part or as a whole. Inevitably the prayers twice a day became mere routine for some, but a great many Jews sincerely recalled the passages contained in the *tefillin*.

This would have been the pattern in Jesus' home at Nazareth, where one would imagine adherence to the law to have been a discipline of love, springing out of reverence and devotion. No wonder Jesus later sought so hard to free the law from the legalism in which it had often become shackled, making it a heavy burden to many. That was a travesty, for the law had always been regarded as one of the key places where the Covenant God had agreed to meet his people.[20]

Such then would have been the gentle and joyful piety of Jesus' home life – a life steeped in Scripture, prayer and Sabbath observance, homely rituals and purity laws which began their symbolic teaching long before the infant could understand their full implication. It was not an unnatural background, nor would it have been a 'spiritual hothouse' atmosphere compared to that of other families of his time. It was (and still is in orthodox Jewish homes) the norm – a life which revolved around God and his law; a life of obedience, prayer and worship, all of which interpreted and gave meaning to life itself. It also maintained their God-given distinctiveness over and against the pagan nations and preserved a definite social and cultural identity.

What of aspects of Jesus' maturation other than his developing understanding of the Law and his immersion in the Scriptures? Did he have to suffer those 'awkward' years that can be so difficult for parents and teenagers alike?

Part of the turmoil of adolescence for any boy is his curious ambivalence towards his mother. In this respect Jesus would surely have had to cope with the turbulent emotions typical of teenage years and the struggle to harmonise his natural and increasing longing for independence at one minute with a continuing and contradictory need for dependence at another. Melanie Klein[21] speaks of the stage before the boy's rebellion against his mother as his 'feminine phase', in which there is rivalry with the mother and envy of her, and which is characterised by feelings of inferiority. R Stoller[22] maintains that the boy's first identification with his mother has to be repressed if he is to develop a masculine identity.

Perhaps the lingering in the Temple to talk with the doctors of law had more than a conscious motive to it. He had questions to explore, some of which, as I have already suggested, may have been on his 'agenda' as he prepared for this first celebration of a Festival at Jerusalem. But perhaps, too, there was an unconscious desire to venture into a new independence. Had he given any hint to his parents of his intentions to talk with the learned men of the Temple, they would almost certainly have discouraged him from presuming on their time and attention.

On that, his first journey to Jerusalem, they had perhaps wanted to allow him freedom to enjoy the companionship of his peer group, and so had resisted the temptation to be over directive or protective. They would probably have had the wisdom to appreciate a teenager's need for freedom from adult supervision allowing him to develop coping skills, self-esteem, a sense of identity, and responsibility – all of which are necessary for mental and emotional health. And, in any case, the people of Nazareth would have been a village family with a sense of shared responsibility for one another and the children.

What has always struck me as far more astonishing than Mary and Joseph's not discovering Jesus' absence until they had travelled such a distance, was the seemingly irresponsible behaviour of the doctors of law. Did they not question where the boy's parents were or wonder if they might be worried about him? Presumably they fed him and provided sleeping accommodation.

Would any of these same men have been among those who were later outraged by the adult Jesus when he overthrew the money-changers' tables and drove out the sacrificial animals from the Temple? If so, did they recognise in him the bright young boy from Nazareth who had challenged them all those years before with his perceptive questions? Or had they watched him with concern over the years as he came to the Temple year by year, and been deeply disturbed by the direction his life seemed to be taking, particularly in the last three years? Were they among those who indirectly sentenced him to death by sending him to Pilate for the final order of execution?

By any standards, Jesus' first visit to the Temple is an astonishing story. How, we may wonder, did Mary and Joseph explain his behaviour when eventually they caught up with the other pilgrims, all of whom would have been understandably anxious about his safety too . . . and full of curiosity as to what had happened? To have told them the real reason would have given the impression of extreme precociousness. His parents must have realised that was far from the truth. Indeed, it had been a veritable milestone in Jesus' life as he took a leap ahead in his quest for self-identity. Even if there had been something of a need for detachment from maternal ties and a normal teenage struggle to establish his masculine identity, there was a much deeper and more crucial aspect of this event. And, after all, not every teenager is in *conscious* conflict with his mother. Much depends, of course, on the kind of mothering he receives – whether it is possessive, domineering, over-protective; or caring without coddling, directive without being manipulative, disciplined without being restrictive, relaxed without being indulgent. It depends, also, on his relationship with his father and whether or not his parents have a secure loving marriage. God in his providence placed his Son in a home where, it would seem, a good relationship with his mother, a healthy flow of mutual love and respect, probably enabled him to weather, and his parents to handle, the confusing and sometimes traumatic years of adolescence. They certainly parented someone who, as an adult, showed exceptional maturity and inner security.

The adolescent Jesus could hardly have bypassed the kind of emotional upheaval that arises out of all the hormonal activity taking place in puberty either. He probably had to battle with the usual mood swings. He may have been more equitable than many teenage boys, but it seems improbable that he travelled through that stage of growth with perfect serenity and ease. To have come in human form and then be exempted from some of the more complex aspects of being human would be less than true incarnation.

> On the biological level sex is a raw power or instinct. It is at its most potent when we are least able to cope emotionally or psychologically with it. In a young adolescent male hormones are zooming around like jet fighters which the young man, unless he is powerfully motivated, is almost incapable of hand-ling well.[23]

As we have already seen, Jesus' education consisted of a very narrow syllabus, and although it could no doubt be made a peg on which to hang a good deal of knowledge, it was almost entirely a religious syllabus with no mathematics, no science, no general history or geography and no human biology. He would not, therefore, have learned the whys and wherefores of the bodily changes taking place at school. Such instruction would have been given presumably at home or through special bar mitzvah preparation for the responsibilities of adulthood and the nature and observance of purity laws – many of which had to do with bodily functions and fluids.

Whatever confusion puberty may have brought, Jesus, steeped in Scripture as he was, would have resonated deeply with the words of the Psalmist and his sense of wonder and gratitude at how fearfully and wonderfully he had been made (Psalm 139:14–16). Maybe his own sense of wonder inspired a holy and healthy fascination with the function and intricate design of the body, at the co-ordination of its different parts and interdependence between emotional and physical health. By the time he was an adult he was fully aware that whilst disorders made themselves apparent through the body they did not always originate there, nor would they always respond to normal medication.

He may not have had an academic knowledge of the human body and its working, but as one who later showed such concern and care for the bodies of others, would he not have reverenced his own as something designed and created by God? One cannot help wondering if, in praising God for his being so wonderfully made, he questioned why some of God's perfect designs and laws of the body which enabled healthy functioning and procreation should have been considered impure; why women, for whom a healthy menstrual cycle was essential for child-bearing should then be automatically rendered ritually and socially unclean for a quarter of every year.

Would he not have echoed the Psalmist's gratitude that his body had developed normally, that not one of his limbs was 'late in growing' (Psalm 139:16)? For he would inevitably have been familiar with the sight of all manner of deformities, which had created a whole industry of begging on the streets. It could well have been in childhood and adolescence, as he began to appreciate the appalling social disadvantages a physical deformity could create, that compassion was awakened in him – a compassion which, as an adult, expressed itself in a loving compulsion to heal those whose twisted or stunted limbs prevented them from leading a normal life. He would perhaps have acknowledged with even greater awe his own ability to run, walk, climb and enjoy physical activities with other children and given thanks for the normality of a body that didn't force upon him a helpless dependence on others.

Like any other growing boy he would have taken a certain pride, and begun to enjoy, his growth in stature, his increased stamina and physical prowess. He was probably thrilled when he could take on some of the heavier carpentry jobs from Joseph, and begin more skilled work involving greater co-ordination of hand and eye, more perfection in joinery or precision in, for example, fitting animals with yokes. And it must have been a source of real delight to be able to explore his creativity and stamp his work with his own originality.

There would have been pride in the obvious and outward signs of physical growth for a different reason. In some forms of Judaism of that day, a boy was allowed to celebrate his bar mitzvah at the first sign of pubic hair. Later, as we have seen, the age for 'the coming of manhood' was fixed at 13 years. Every Jewish boy would have looked forward to the first hint of a rudimentary beard and waited eagerly for the day when, in the Synagogue, he would leave the gallery of the women and be welcomed into the ranks of Israelite men as a full Jew. It is powerfully symbolic, too, of leaving his 'feminine phase', his attachment to his mother, and entering more fully into his masculine identity. The pride and joy of a boy at his bar mitzvah was, and still is, transparent as he reads the Hebrew Scriptures for the first time in public and joins the procession of the Scrolls. To become a full Son of Israel had more than a religious significance. It was of enormous social and cultural importance – similar to a coming of age, confirmation, first communion, freedom to drive and to vote all rolled into one for a young man of Western society.

The Waiting Years

◆◇◆◇◆◇◆◇◆◇◆◇◆◇◆◇◆◇◆◇◆◇◆◇◆◇◆◇◆◇◆◇◆◇◆

In his book, *The Stature of Waiting*,[24] W H Vanstone points out how in both Mark and John's Gospels there is a clear change after the 'handing over' of Jesus by Judas, to the Sanhedrin, and on to Pilate, Herod, Pilate again, and finally the executioners – from Jesus the active one, the initiator, the one who 'does' to the one who is 'done to'. The Passion, he says, is not only the suffering of pain, but suffering in the sense of allowing things to happen. 'Suffer it to be so now', he said to John at his baptism; 'Suffer the little children to come to me', he said to his disciples. So he moved from the period of active ministry to the Passion, the passive waiting, the acceptance of events of which he was no longer the initiator.

We are told that when Judas left the Last Supper table at Jesus' request, to 'go and do what he had to do – quickly', he went out and 'it was night'. This is usually interpreted by preachers as Judas entering into the terrible darkness of the sin he was about to perpetrate. Canon Vanstone claims, however, that 'night' here is not used in the sense of evil (the word normally used for that is 'darkness', as opposed to 'light'). The opposite of 'night' is 'day', and in John's Gospel, Jesus is recorded as saying that one could only do the works of the Father 'while it was day'. Now, however, the 'night' has come when 'no one can work' (John 9:4). So for Jesus, the night of his being 'handed over' brings to an end his active works. He had been the worker, moving from place to place in a breathtaking whirl (according to Mark) of social contacts, miracles, healings, teaching and preaching, confrontation and clashes with the authorities. But then . . . 'It is night' and he becomes passive, on the receiving end of what people do to him, *subject* to power and authority – of the Jews, Herod and Pilate – rather than being the one who exercises it so astonishingly.

However, I would maintain that the period *before* his active ministry was also for Jesus a time of waiting, of active patience. Rather like a sandwich, his adult life consists of two periods of waiting wrapped around his active ministry.

In that period between his bar mitzvah and his baptism, he did not move about freely and independently. He returned to Nazareth, where he was, I imagine, subject and submissive to Mary and Joseph, obediently 'honouring his father and mother' as laid down in the Law, waiting for a word and a clear sign from his Father to confirm his sense of vocation and initiate his life's ministry and purpose of establishing the Kingdom.

In contemporary life, most of the waiting is associated with frustration – the delayed bus or train, the late delivery of post, the tardy visitor, the long queue, the breakdown on the motorway and even the changing of traffic lights to red, can all arouse in us impatience, tension, anger and frustration. To be dependent on others, particularly the professional or public services, brings a certain feeling of powerlessness which we experience as an affront to our dignity – we are like those people in the 'patient' role who have to wait for things to be done for them and to them, and who therefore need to exercise a great deal of patience.

Jesus waited for years – with no sense of diminishment or loss of dignity, if his sure-footedness and authority when he began his ministry were anything to go by. We have no Gospel material to provide us with details of this period of his life, and maybe he did feel the 'patience of those who understand and the impatience of those who love',[25] and 'suffer' things to happen but not without an intensity of longing for something dimly apprehended. Very probably, however, he was content to do what he perceived to be his Father's will at that moment, without chafing, not concerning himself too much about the specific details of the future: 'Tomorrow will bring worries of its own. Today's trouble is enough for today' (Matthew 6:34). There would not have been the same pressure stemming from the pace of his life in his day and culture that we often feel in ours. It never ceased to astonish me, when living amongst Africans (both in Zaire and Botswana), how they would happily wait for hours without winding up frustrated, resentful and angry, wringing their hands, champing and swearing as most Westerners would. Sometimes we had to be out for a whole day, and would arrive home to find people sitting on our verandah, who had been there for hours – perhaps having arrived just after we had left. But they had patiently waited, slept, talked with neighbours for the entire day until we

returned . . . and were not the least bit perturbed at the apparent
waste of time. Attitudes to time were so different from those of the
West, and, in all probability, Jesus did not suffer from the pressures
we impose on ourselves in our current lifestyles where speed is
all-important.

There are so many different ways of waiting – some positive;
others negative and exhausting.

There is the waiting of resignation in the dentist's waiting room;
of dread in the waiting room of the casualty ward after an accident
or in the hospital when a loved one has undergone a critical operation; or the excited waiting in the labour ward as a baby is about
to be born; or the eager waiting of the lover at the rendezvous as
the time draws near for his beloved to arrive; or of sheer resignation
and a feeling of helplessness when waiting for exam results. Nothing
further can be done – there is only the waiting. alternately filled
with hope and fear.

There is, then, the anxious, resigned form of waiting which brings
with it a sense of powerlessness, the waiting filled with dread and
hopelessness, the eager waiting for new life and new love – in both
cases the longing must be contained for neither can be hastened to
order. But there is also the waiting of active patience.

I grew up as a small child not knowing my parents. My father had
returned to his missionary work in the Belgian Congo when I was
three months old, and my mother followed him six months later,
leaving my brother (one year older) and me in a Home for Missionar-
ies' Children in England. I was only aware of their existence through
what the staff of the Home told me and, as I grew a little older,
through letters and photos. Not surprisingly, letter-writing has always
been for me a primary form of communication, and the Scriptures –
as the written word – a fundamental revelation of God and experience of his reality. We were told, from time to time, that *one day*
mummy and daddy would return home. Naturally, we waited for it
eagerly and I devised all sorts of schemes to make it an even more
wonderful day than they could possibly anticipate. I set targets to be
achieved – I would learn to ride a bicycle, learn to read and write,
try not to get into too much trouble, to ensure that their home-
coming would not be wrecked with a recital of my misdeeds by the
staff – and there were probably other goals I have forgotten.

That waiting period for me was a busy one of preparation, partly,
as I realise now, out of an unconscious need to prove that I was a
child worthy of their love and one they could be proud of – after

all, their entire knowledge of me was dependent upon the highly selective reporting of our guardians; and how was I to trust that? Even more, however, my activity was in order to make that day of return more glorious.

That I believe is how Jesus waited at Nazareth for his 'hour' to arrive. His activities would not have been about achieving – they didn't need to be, as mine did. Nevertheless, I feel sure that as he worked in the carpentry business with Joseph he was already learning to do 'all things well' (Mark 7:37).

Perhaps it was during these years that he developed the habit of getting out on to the hillsides at night to be alone with his Father. There in nourishing silence and solitude he would discern the voice of God and learn to distinguish it from that other inner voice familiar to us all – the one that stems from either conscious or subconscious desires, the voice which can be that of the tempter, beguiling and misleading us. Maybe it was there in such times of solitude that he was preparing, quite unwittingly, for the period of testing in the wilderness that was to follow his baptism.

In that solitude, too, he would learn more of the ways of people, as he reflected upon the ordinary things of life. Some of his shrewd observations, his deep understanding of underlying human motivation and the manipulative tactics so common in relationships, may have been the fruit of this discipline. For, it is in solitude that we discover more about true community and togetherness, and learn to make a holy space within ourselves for God, but also for others – 'hospitality of the heart' as Henri Nouwen calls it.

Jesus would almost certainly have spent much time in reading and reflecting upon the Scriptures – perhaps with the local rabbi, as the only person in the village who would have any grasp of his developing understanding of their meaning for him, other than perhaps Mary. As he grappled with passages such as those of Isaiah in his prophecies concerning the Suffering Servant, Jesus may have felt that they went beyond what Mary could receive at that point. Despite Simeon's prediction, for much of the time as he grew up, she must have tried to push those dread words to the back of her conscious thinking.

Apart from the Suffering Servant Songs, would he not have steeped himself in the Torah, trying to sift out its real essence from its accretions? Would he not have been searching for its heart and his Father's revelation of himself in it, as one who 'loved the law and made it his meditation day and night' like the Psalmist?

Inevitably he would have been learning all he could about the history of his people, God's dealings with them down through the ages and where they had 'come from' in terms of tradition and culture. He would, one would imagine, have deepened in his Jewishness and his fidelity to family customs and worship, the corporate nature of village life. He would have reflected upon the underlying causes of tension between the Pharisees and Sadducees, the Jews and the Samaritans, the Herodians and the Romans. He would have needed to know the 'story' not only of his own people, but also those of others to comprehend the unhealed national and tribal memories, the prejudices and bitternesses. Possibly these areas of knowledge were those that any thinking Jew would explore in his growing years. For Jesus, they must have taken on much greater significance, for though he may not have realised it to the full, his life was going to be caught up in the web of intrigue and hatred that dominated Jewish society, in a far more personal and crucial (quite literally) way than that of his contemporaries.

Surely part of his preparation would have been a deep pondering of the nature and meaning of 'The Kingdom' – a recurrent theme in the Old Testament Scriptures which he must increasingly have recognised as a paradigm that impinged on his own generation? Would he not have wrestled with all the implications as he sought to articulate that vision which was to be the nub of his teaching and the driving passion of his whole ministry? Would he not, too, have thought long and hard about the right form of protest he should make – to the religious authorities to stir up a new understanding of the inwardness of the Law; and to the temporal authorities to open their eyes to the injustices, cruelty and oppression that crushed their subject peoples but, at the same time, dehumanised them as the oppressors? There in his contemplation of the Kingdom and its inauguration, perhaps he began to see the qualities and values that would be manifested by its members and the unique love that would be the hallmark of the new humanity.

These were certainly not wasted, frustrated years that undermined his sense of worth and dignity. They were years of essential preparation, of learning to bide the right moment in obedience to God's timing. And God is never under pressure to hurry. Each of us reflects the image of God in the way we face 'waiting times', for God is a God who waits in divine freedom in order to give freedom. He stands back in patience, sometimes sorrowful and suffering, sometimes active and eager, but his very nature precludes him from forcing his will. He chooses to wait for our co-operation.

Jesus, then, revealed that God-like quality as he watched and waited, readying himself for the 'hour' when God would call him forth from the obedience of waiting to the obedience of action.

2

<hr>

'TEMPTED
IN EVERY RESPECT'?

Fully Human, Fully Divin

and compassion

The writer of the letter to the Hebrews is both explicit and comforting on the subject of Jesus and temptation. 'For, because he himself has suffered and been tempted, he is able to help those who are tempted' (Hebrews 2:18). 'For we have not a high priest who is unable to sympathise with our weaknesses, but one who *in every respect* has been tempted as we are, yet without sin' (Hebrews 4:15).

In every respect? Can Jesus really have been tempted in all the ways in which we are tempted? When we pause to consider the nature of some temptations, the grosser and more insidious variety, it might seem almost blasphemous to pursue this thought any further. And yet, if we back off in fright and refuse even to consider his temptations, we at once lose an enormous resource of power to help us in our pilgrimage through life. For he was not only tempted in every respect – he overcame in every respect, giving us a living example of how God does, *with* the temptation, provide a way of escape.

Obviously the particular circumstances in which Jesus met temptation had an historical, social and cultural context very different from our own. For this reason, we might be tempted to dismiss the struggles he faced as irrelevant to our situation. Can it really be true that 'because he himself has suffered and been tempted, he is able to help those who are tempted', when they are coming from a very different place from his? How, for example, can his inner conflicts and temptations as a first-century Jew, impinge on the life of those in today's dehumanised, consumer society with all its responsibilities and stresses: the subtle lures to compromise that are encountered, for example, in top managerial posts, or by Members of Parliament with all the pressures to violate personal integrity, or by executives in vast, multi-national corporations spending hours travelling all over the world attending conferences and consultations that determine international policies affecting the lives of millions? What do his battles with and victories over temptation have to say to those caught in the poverty trap because of unemployment, those who have no hope of ever getting a job, those born HIV Positive or with AIDS, those deformed by radiation, the woman who is reluctantly single and aching for a husband, home and family, the elderly housebound person confined to a wheelchair and riddled with arthritis?

After all, Jesus never held any position of worldly power and responsibility, only ever travelled within a limited geographical region and chiefly on foot. He was not a woman in a male-dominated society, nor did he suffer the slow, drawn-out diminishments of old age. He did not suffer the haunting terror of child abuse, nor the shattering of self-esteem brought about by divorce.

Can the claim that Jesus was tempted in 'every' respect as we are, be of any consolation to those afflicted in any of these ways? Can they ever be convinced that he was tempted quite as hideously as they are?

Temptation comes to us in a myriad guises, always subtly suited to our particular personality and condition. But, basically, it has one objective – *to turn us from the truth*, about ourselves, about God and about our world. It seeks to win our allegiance so that we deviate from the path leading to true humanity and fullness of being. It entices us to enter the twilight world of falsity and masquerade. As Thomas Merton has said, 'Sin is . . . an orientation to falsity, a basic lie concerning our own deepest reality . . . The false self is a whole syndrome of lies and illusions that spring from a radical rejection of God in whom alone we find our own truth and ultimate identity.'[1]

Temptations to violence and corruption are usually readily identifiable. But how often are we coaxed gently but insidiously into traps along paths which seem to lead to desirable goals but by very questionable means that pander to our pride, self-interest or lust for power? It is often too late when we recognise the temptation for what it was and see how we were deluded. Jesus certainly faced such temptations – in the wilderness and beyond – and had the clear-sightedness to perceive the hidden suggestion in them, and spurn them resolutely.

He was able to claim, 'I am the Way, the Truth . . .' (John 14:6). His ability to weave his way through all the guileful attractions of illusion and falsity sprang from his intimate relationship with his Father, and his total obedience to him, which enabled him to see things from God's perspective. It was this relationship and his own purity that opened his eyes to the deceptions of the Tempter and gave him the wisdom to recognise when he was being persuaded to pursue right ends by wrong means.

The basic weaknesses in human nature to which the Tempter appeals have not changed over the generations and in different cultures. Sin manifests itself on the surface in an endless variety of ways of course, but, nevertheless, it stems from the age-old roots of pride, jealousy, anger, lust, greed, and so on – roots which are common to all of humanity.

It is therefore immensely helpful to look at these roots as they affected the life of Jesus – the way in which he owned them, wrestled with them, transformed them and harnessed them in the service of love.

Since Christian doctrine and faith firmly hold that Jesus was *fully* human, not half a man, as well as *fully* divine, we need to consider how he coped with the kind of basic, human energies, desires, fears and phobias that we experience.

Anger

◆-◆

How, for example, did Jesus cope with anger? That is a fairly straight-forward place from which to start any examination of the temptations that assailed him, for there is clear evidence that he could be very angry. We have already looked at an undeniable example in the previous chapter – his anger at the corrupt practices of the money-changers and those selling animals for sacrifice.

Probably this was a case of cumulative anger. As hinted at earlier, Jesus may well have been angry on many of his previous visits to the Temple – angry at the injustice to the Gentiles of relegating the outer court of the Temple to them, swamping it with all the parapher-nalia of a noisy market, and so depriving them of a place of prayer which was their right; angry that Jews could and would cheat fellow Jews, taking advantage of travellers to Jerusalem not only from outlying regions of Palestine, but from abroad. Perhaps this was the only visit some Jews would be able to make in a lifetime, the fulfilment of a cherished dream, which would have involved them in great expense. These were the people for whom Jesus felt great compassion as he saw them being overcharged and short-changed. It seems that, on this occasion, his compassion ignited his anger, or that an osmosis had taken place, for there is only a very fine dividing line between the two.

There was more to it than simply the corruption of the market-place, however. The Temple had also become the rendezvous for brigands – men who operated in groups encouraging military resis-tance against the Romans. They were a kind of Palestinian 'Maquis' whose objective was not so much to pass prisoners of war down the line and help them escape, as to make life as intolerable and danger-ous as they could for the occupying powers.

Why would Jesus be angry at that, one might wonder? Why did he not applaud and encourage their zeal? We need to remember, of course, that Jesus, who throughout his life and ministry sought the way of non-violence, probably realised very clearly how these men were putting the Temple and all its worshippers at enormous risk by using the precincts as a rallying point for revolutionaries. What if the Romans got wind of it and decided to attack – particularly during one of the Great Festivals when vast crowds of men, women and children would be gathered?

The Romans were fearful of interfering in any matter relating to the Temple, knowing what a sensitive area this was, and that large crowds can easily be whipped into mass hysteria. So they kept a wary lookout on, but discreet distance from, its goings on. But both the Temple and its officials would have been totally discredited in their eyes if any hint had reached them of plots to use it as an operational base from which to try and overthrow Roman rule, or instigate revolution. They would not have hesitated to take drastic and bloody action to quell at inception any such insurgence. These political activists of Judaism were so dedicated to their cause that the lives of innocent children and devout worshippers (who wanted nothing *but* to worship) were of secondary importance to their cause. That certainly would have angered Jesus as it must do now when terrorists deliberately murder innocent people with their strategically placed bombs in order to achieve their political ends. No dedication, to whatever cause, can be right when it barters human lives in order to reach its goals.

Furthermore, apart from the marketeers and the brigands, there was often such insincerity in the Temple worship that it must have grieved Jesus deeply – a grief that probably went back to his earliest visits. The pride and ostentation of the Pharisees, the tensions and hostilities that existed between them and the Sadducees, the extravagance of the Temple regalia when beggars sat at the gates in rags – all these must have left him with an abiding sadness and a fermenting anger that worshippers seemed to see no inconsistency between profession and practice. The great words of Amos would boom forth, 'Let justice roll down like waters and righteousness like an everflowing stream' (Amos 5:24), and yet injustice of many sorts was rife. Somehow the Temple had become the symbol not only of hierarchical status and wealth, but also of economic and social injustice.

Jesus may have been forced to conclude that impassioned speeches had only a limited power. Words had ceased to penetrate the hard-heartedness of those who sought to make political or monetary

profit. In the tradition of the prophets, an acted parable was needed
– a dramatic action which would stir consciences where words had
made no impression, despite all that Jews believed about the power
within a word to fulfil the purpose for which it was spoken. In
rounding up the animals with a whip and overturning the stalls of
tradesmen and money-changers alike, in protesting that they had
turned God's house of prayer into a den of brigands, swindlers and
thieves, he was pointing to the end of the Temple. It was so corrupt,
and far from God's requirements that its destruction was inevitable.

The anger of Jesus on this occasion was part of his prophetic
ministry of criticism. That prophetic role of protest was only one
part of his vocation. By challenging and dismantling the old order,
he combined within himself the roles of prophet, priest and king.

The way of his ultimate criticism was his decisive solidarity with
marginal people and the accompanying vulnerability required by
it. Genuine solidarity meant knowing and experiencing the same
helplessness that they did.

Here in the Temple, his wrathful anger was his entering into the
radical prophetic tradition particularly of the eighth century BC, which
repeatedly warned the people of God that their worship, if it didn't
go hand in hand with social justice and a deep concern for the poor,
the needy, the outcast – indeed, all who were socially, culturally or
religiously marginalised – would not only be worthless and invalid,
but thoroughly obnoxious to God:

> I hate, I despise your feast days. [Forget about your fasts and your
> sacrifices and all the religious trappings. They are meaningless.]

>> Is not this the fast that I choose:
>> to loose the bonds of injustice,
>> to undo the thongs of the yoke,
>> to let the oppressed go free,
>> and to break every yoke?
>> Is it not to share your bread with the hungry,
>> and bring the homeless poor into your house;
>> when you see the naked, to cover them,
>> and not to hide yourself from your own kin?
>> Then your light shall break forth like the dawn . . .
>> Then you shall call, and the Lord will answer;
>> you shall cry for help, and he will say, Here I am.
>>   (Isaiah 58:6–9)

No sacrificial offerings were acceptable to God if at the same time
the devout worshippers were exploiting the poor and increasingly
ostracising the marginalised. If their lives did not reflect the compassion of God himself then no amount of ritual or religious observance would satisfy him.

'May the contrite soul, the humbled spirit be as acceptable to you
as holocausts of rams and bullocks, as thousands of fattened lambs:
such let our sacrifice be to you today, and may it be your will that
we follow you wholeheartedly' (Daniel 3:39–40).

That is the sacrifice well pleasing to God.

Prophetic anger is a God-inspired anger and consciously or not
Jesus acted within the radical prophetic tradition which brought to
expression and embodiment all the hurt, the human pain and grief
that the 'establishment' sought to cover up.

So it was that, again, his anger was kindled when the Pharisees
planted a man with a withered hand in the Synagogue congregation,
deliberately exploiting his physical infirmity in order to see if Jesus
would heal him on the Sabbath – and thereby furnish them with
evidence to support their accusations against him.

Jesus looked round at them all *with anger* (Mark 3:5), grieved at
the hardness of their hearts and their rigidity which made the letter
of the Law of supreme importance, whilst their total lack of compassion showed that they were blind to its spirit.

Jesus was to encounter this hardness of heart throughout his
ministry. His own inner freedom to interpret the Law in terms of
love rather than legalism was a real threat to those pillars and
bastions of the faith who prided themselves on keeping the details
of the Law to near perfection.

What had happened to the Law? Where was the Law that genuinely
delighted the Psalmist's heart?

I will meditate on your precepts and fix my eyes on your ways.
I will delight in your statutes; I will not forget your word.
Open my eyes, so that I may behold wondrous things out of
  your law.
O, how I love your law! It is my meditation all day long.
I hate the double-minded, but I love your law.
My eyes shed streams of tears because your law is not kept.
                          (Psalm 119:15, 16, 18, 97, 113, 136)

As Jesus grew into manhood it must have saddened him deeply

that far from being a delight, the Law had become an intolerable burden – something restrictive and joyless; rules to be obeyed rather than a spirit by which to live.

In his reflections Jesus had come to see that far from it being the delight of people's hearts – an expression of God's justice and freedom – the Law had been turned into a manifesto for bondage.

Truly devout religious people had found their security in scrupulous obedience to all the minutiae of the Mishnah – the detailed 'fleshing out' of the great principles of the Law – instead of in God. Bogged down in a welter of finer points, particulars and trifles, a legalism that penetrated every possible area of their lives, these worthy people had lost sight, or never caught the vision in the first place, of the Law as an expression of love and reverence – for God and one's 'neighbour'.

When Jesus 'broke' the laws concerning the Sabbath, as he was accused of doing when he healed the man with the withered hand on the Sabbath (Luke 6:6ff.), when on the Sabbath he healed the woman who had suffered for 18 years from an illness that left her bent double (Luke 13:11ff.), he was trying to break away from the crippling conventions which had become attached to the Law like barnacles to a ship, covering it so completely that the 'ship' itself had become obscured. He was penetrating to the heart of the Law, for the Law most certainly had one pulsating at its core, a heart of compassion, passionately concerned with justice.

His criticism of the Law was not simply an attack on legalism in any moralistic sense. Rather it was levelled at those who had twisted the Law and allowed it to become the machinery by which certain social values were upheld.

Christ's willingness to eat with outcasts and the 'scum' of society upset and threatened a social structure that had decreed what was: '. . . acceptable and unacceptable, clean and unclean, right and wrong. Crossing over the barrier of right and wrong implied that in the dispensing of mercy the wrong were as entitled as were the right, and therefore all meaningful distinctions were obliterated.'[2]

These actions, together with Jesus' other violations of social convention, were a heavy criticism of the 'righteousness of the Law'. The Law had become in his day a way for the managers of society, religious even more than civil, effectively 'to control not only morality but the political-economic valuing that lay behind the morality, a social convention that protected the current distribution of economic and political power'.[3] Jesus could not let that go unacknowledged, unexposed or unchallenged, and his anger made him fearless in doing all three.

I believe Jesus was angry when the disciples attempted to stop mothers from bringing their children to be blessed. Maybe the disciples were attempting to protect Jesus from over exposure to the crowds and they decided it was their responsibility to 'handle' this intrusion of women and children, but perhaps Jesus recognised that in the male-dominated society of his day, this was a clear case of how women were often marginalised. We don't read of the disciples blocking the path of the scribes and Pharisees who came to Jesus! And yet, they drained him far more than children whom he obviously loved.

He was perhaps thoroughly irritated more than angered by the sheer meanness of the trick questions the scribes and Pharisees put to him, to trip him up – questions not asked with the genuine intention of eliciting information, but to present him with an impossible choice. Whichever answer he gave, in the eyes of the Pharisees he was bound to condemn himself out of his own mouth. But with his rapier-sharp mind capable of piercing through their motives and laying bare their hypocrisy, he handled these situations with consummate skill, subtlety and wit – usually by hoisting them on their own petard and posing equally penetrating questions in return.

When the Pharisees began to argue with him, looking for a sign 'to test him', Mark tells us 'he sighed deeply in his spirit' (Mark 8:11, 12). He was exasperated by their obtuseness and replied somewhat abruptly, 'Why do you seek a sign? I assure you, no sign will be given to this generation.'[4] And immediately he turned from them, giving them no chance to prolong the argument, and stepped into a boat to go to the other side of the lake (Mark 8:11–13).

One can almost hear Jesus groaning with frustration at the foolishness of the disciples – so unbelievably slow were they to understand what he was trying to tell them even though they had been privy to daily instruction over a long period. For they, more than any others, had been able consistently to hear Jesus preach, teach and expound in parables since the beginning of his public ministry. *And* they had been able to ask for explanations when they were unable to grasp the hidden meaning of his sayings. But here was new wine being poured into old wineskins. Until there had been a bursting of their preconceptions, the long sustained expectations of their day, there would be no deep, life-changing understanding.

The story of his cursing of the fig tree is a baffling one (Matthew

21:18, 19; Mark 11:12–14, 20ff.). At one level it seems as though Jesus was behaving petulantly – out of annoyance or disappointment that it had failed to yield fruit. Even if it was the last straw at the end of a tiring journey it seems a churlish thing to do – out of character and in total contrast to his normal reverence for every part of God's creation. The next time they passed by it had withered. If it was a warning or a comment on the outcome of 'non-fruit-bearing' then it was an exceedingly daunting one. God's mercy usually has more patience than Jesus seemed to display in this case. On the surface it seems more in keeping with the kind of power used by a witch doctor, and oddly harsh. But perhaps the meaning of the action, which certainly involved anger, eludes those of us from the West for whom cursing smacks of the occult. Nevertheless, it remains a puzzling incident.

Was it anger or frustration that he felt when the disciples were worried about not having enough bread? They only had one loaf between them. Jesus said, 'Why are you talking about not having enough bread? Do you still not perceive or understand? Are your hearts hardened? Do you have eyes and fail to see? Do you have ears and fail to hear?' (Mark 8:17–18). Then reminding them of previous occasions when, though they had been without food, 5,000 or more people had been fed and satisfied, and on another occasion 4,000, he asked, 'Do you not *yet* understand?' The disciples may have had reason to wonder. If Jesus had ever shared with them the nature of the temptations he faced in the wilderness (which presumably he must have done since they are recorded in the Gospels), they would have remembered that he refused to appease his own hunger by turning stones into bread. Might he not have extended that discipline to include the disciples? In their experience it had only been when he had compassion on the crowds that food had been miraculously provided. On a Sabbath Day when they were hungry they had plucked ears of corn to eat – and had been heavily criticised by the Pharisees for doing so. Jesus had not produced miraculous loaves on that occasion to satisfy their hunger.

Anger in itself is not right or wrong. It is actually neat energy and therefore neutral. 'Be angry but do not sin', Paul wrote (Ephesians 4:26). It appears that he is not only giving permission to be angry – it is an imperative! Not to be angry in certain circumstances would quite definitely be sinful. For anger is the flip-side of compassion and the lack of one would indicate a lack of the other. At times the strength of our compassion is in direct relation to the extent of our anger. The 'sap' rises equally to become one energy.

In those examples of Christ's anger that are recorded for us, the prophetic indignation, the righteous anger which brimmed over, were wholly justifiable. Far from being sin, they were the right response to injustice in any form. But just as compassion can boil over into anger, so I believe anger can be harnessed in such a way that it is transmuted into compassion.

In our present time, many of the charities and projects launched to help the homeless, the starving, the oppressed, are fuelled by people in whom that neat energy of anger has been transformed into compassion – a divine compassion, even without their realising it.

Perhaps that provides insights for us. We are right to be angry about a great deal of things in contemporary society, and part of the problem that confronts us is that too often we feel we have nowhere to place that anger. It is a well-established fact that repressed anger will either erupt into violence or plunge us into depression.

One of the reasons, perhaps, why we get very few explicit refer-ences to the anger of Jesus is simply because he knew how to direct and channel it into positivity. In his solidarity with the marginalised it became compassion. We need to allow him to reveal himself to us as a truly passionate and impassioned person – so in touch with the roots of his passions that he has no need to fear them or attempt to hide them. He is always in full control of them – never at their mercy – which is why he could be intensely angry without sinning. Does not this ability touch very directly on certain areas of our lives (personal, national and global), where we are guilty of sin because we are not angry? The anger that has no sin in it is that which springs from right causes, which can be expressed at the right time in an appropriate way, and channels its energy positively.

What, however, if we cannot find ways to articulate our anger or to convert it into compassion? We see so much suffering nowadays, so much pain, deprivation, homelessness, hunger and the aftermath of natural disasters on our TV screens, we feel we reach 'overload' and something inside seems to switch off. A psychic numbness sets in. Beyond that point, we may go on seeing pictures of starving babies, dying soldiers, burning houses, flooded villages and wrecked cars and feel very little. The news often seems to be a ceaseless litany of horror stories and human suffering. The question is, do these highly sophisticated forms of communication and the

increasing amount of information available to us actually deepen
our solidarity? Do they call forth greater compassion?

'We might ask', says Henri Nouwen, 'whether mass communication
directed to millions of people who experience themselves as small,
insignificant, powerless individuals does not in fact do more harm
than good? When there is no channel or community that can mediate
between world needs and personal responses, the burden of the
world can only be a crushing burden. Massive exposure to human
misery leads to psychic numbness.'[5]

The proliferation of charitable societies and projects is the response
to this very need. So, numerous young people offer themselves for
periods of voluntary service in deprived areas or help in fund raising.
Those with money can channel their compassion through gifts to
sundry causes. But what if we have neither youth nor money on
our side?

Then, I think, we stand where Jesus stood – weeping. Weeping
over the city because 'it did not know the things that belonged to
its peace', and knowing he was powerless to head off the disaster
that would befall it. He suffered the prophetic anguish of being a
true 'seer'.

He was *moved with compassion*. The bowels were considered the
seat of compassion, and isn't it true that when we are moved
intensely we do indeed experience an inward churning? But the
compassion of Jesus was not only a personal, emotional reaction. It
was a radical form of criticism. It claimed that 'the hurt had to be
taken seriously, that the hurt was not to be accepted as normal and
natural but was an abnormal and unacceptable condition for
humanness.'[6]

The state (as opposed to the Church) is neither built nor maintained on the basis of compassion. Questions of economic viability
largely come before human need. In their election speeches, prospec-
tive candidates speak most convincingly of how they are going to
address the social problems – of unemployment, the National Health
Service, lack of educational facilities, homelessness, the arms trade
etc. But promises get swallowed up in the pursuit of what makes
economic sense. An emotional lethargy seems to descend over the
House of Commons and MPs engage in what often appears to be
their favourite pastime of scoring points off one another in party
wrangling. Meanwhile, paralysis and hopelessness creep upon the
nation as a whole because of its sense of powerlessness. Then,

through sheer spiritual weakness we allow the huge economic gaps between the 'haves' and the 'have nots' to be perpetuated.

Against that injustice, compassion may seem a rather passive channel for anger, but compassion is not powerless resignation. It is not a somewhat feeble attempt to focus our goodwill onto some of the areas of need in today's world. It is the fruit of harnessed rage at the manifest evils of society and the sheer weight of human misery. Instead of allowing that rage to be trapped in us, leading to despondency and ultimately depression, we welcome it, give it permission to surface and express itself actively – but not in violence. Some people have picked up their pens and used them as swords to pierce the density of indifference around us. Others have deflected their rage into protest songs and black comedy. Some have quite literally 'laid down their lives' by practical identification with the oppressed. Others have entered politics, social work or the ministry of the Church. And a very few, responding to a strange and particular call to be the shock troops of the Church, become solitaries spending their lives in prayer and intercession as reparation for the evil that has brought such horrific suffering into the world.

Compassion then has its powerfully active side. Jesus penetrated the numbness of his day by his compassion, his oftentimes shocking compassion, which was a radical form of protest. It highlighted the wrongs. It expressed his criticism of the system, the establishment and current ideologies. Finally, he absorbed the hurt into himself, internalising it, working with it as the raw material of his prayer. This internalisation of hurt on behalf of the marginalised ones is a true reflection of the prophetic anguish that we also meet in Hosea and Jeremiah.

'My heart recoils within me, my compassion grows warm and tender' (Hosea 11:8–9). The intensity of anger is not reduced by its boiling over into compassion. Compassion isn't a cooling tower. It is the harnessing of all that immense energy of anger so that it penetrates and replaces the numbness. It brings to an end cynical indifference and announces the beginning of a social revolution.[7]

The very fact of our coinherence within humanity enables that flow of compassion to travel hiddenly and mysteriously wherever and to whomever God wills. Thomas Merton was one of those solitaries I have mentioned. Within and through his solitude, he was passionately concerned about issues of peace, justice and social order – and exceedingly well informed on the global front as well as on local matters. He spoke of his solitude and silence as a desert.

What is my new desert?' he asked, shortly after entering his hermitage. '. . . *compassion*. There is no wilderness so terrible, so beautiful, so arid and so fruitful as the wilderness of compassion . . . It is in the desert of compassion that the thirsty land turns into springs of water, that the poor possess all things. There are no bounds to contain the inhabitants of this solitude in which I live alone, as isolated as the Host on the altar, the food of all men, belonging to all and belonging to none for God is with me and he sits in the ruins of my heart, preaching his Gospel to the poor.[8]

Was it, I wonder, on the slopes of the Galilean hills, in the solitude and silence of his long night vigils in prayer that Jesus entered into this same 'desert' of which Merton speaks, and there, learned to convert anger into compassion, till he could say, as Merton centuries later did, 'I die of love for you, Compassion. . . . I marry you, the Mother of the poor.'[9]

Very few have the courage to believe that. Fewer still dare stake their entire lives on it. But in that day, when all that is at present hidden from us is made manifest, we shall see just how powerful has been the contribution of those who have embraced the solitary life and those whose prayer has become a hidden channel of compassion bringing healing to humanity.

This is no soft option. It demands courage and sanity to stay with the pain and weep with Jesus. For him there were two aspects of compassion. On the one hand it was a frontal attack upon the society and authorities that effectively controlled not only the morality of the people, but also the social values, politics, economics and even religion. It was a direct challenge to and exposure of the callousness of heart behind the power struggles and the desire to dominate which so sought personal preferment and satisfaction before the well-being of others that it could crush and oppress without any conscience, even doing so in the name of God.

On the other, in his criticism and solidarity, he knew there was power to transform. Feelings of impotence and helplessness can give way to hope, for through the energy of compassion can come the possibility of an alternative society, a new beginning.

Weeping with Jesus can be a way of unblocking pain in ourselves – pain in the face of so *much* heartbreaking human (and indeed, animal) suffering. It can be a prayer rising from the heart that cries, 'Grant us yet more that gift unpriced – a share in your compassion

Christ.'[10] Tears can thus become the very channel through which
Christ's compassion is mediated to those whom he would touch with
divine grace.

Weeping then is an act both of passion and power, and there can
be a great and effective release of energy as the flow of tears journeys
into the crevices of our human pain.

Lust

◇◇

Since Jesus was tempted in *every* respect as we are, we cannot make exceptions and say, for example, 'But not, of course, by lust'. Surely it is not irreverent to acknowledge that Jesus had to face this particular temptation.

He reminded his listeners, 'You have heard that it was said, "You shall not commit adultery". But I say to you that everyone who looks at a woman lustfully has already committed adultery with her in his heart' (Matthew 5:27–8). Obviously he must have known the possibility, perhaps even the full force of such a temptation, although he resisted it. His integrity would not have permitted him to demand of others a standard that he failed to keep himself. Nor, I believe, would he have made so tough a pronouncement if he himself had never experienced any struggle in this area.

At the same time, I have to say that I cannot think it was a major problem for him. I doubt if he was sorely tempted, simply because the very nature of lust would have been so abhorrent to him. We have already seen how intensely angry he could be at any form of exploitation and how intensely compassionate he was towards the exploited. Lust is always highly exploitative. If acted out, it seeks to dominate, control and manipulate – to use another person for personal pleasure and sexual gratification without any regard for his or her ultimate well-being, without any guaranteed commitment or security, or any desire for true relationship. It dehumanises people, reducing them to the level of sex objects, taking all and giving nothing – except an aftermath of sourness.

Lust is dishonouring to the one who is its object – utterly contrary to the deep reverence Jesus always showed towards others. Reverence is an essential part of loving. We all honour, reverence and cherish the people, things and places we genuinely love. And that brings to love a particular quality of purity, for we are not only reverencing the very being of others in all their uniqueness, but also that which is of God in them.

'Love is strong as death' (Song of Songs 8:6), but it also makes us exceedingly fragile and vulnerable. In all his contacts with other people – especially the broken, the outcast, the failed – we see how delicately Jesus approached them, how sensitive he was to their hurts, how lovingly he penetrated to the real person hidden beneath the external veneer but crying out to be accepted. Never did he take advantage of weakness, never did he abuse trust or heap further condemnation on those already so judged by society that all self-esteem was lost. Never did he simply brush people aside.

Lust for *power* can express itself very subtly and persuasively in a need to be needed. It sometimes appears in the seemingly harmless guise of the comforter, the shoulder to lean on, the helper; but behind the kindly outward front is that need to control, possess and enslave. Lust is not always the lecherous glance in the direction of someone else's spouse. It can be the domination of a mother in the cloak of concern and care, keeping a vice-like grip on her child who is ready and yearning to fly the nest and exercise a growing independence. It can be the priest or minister who, in the name of orthodoxy, tightens his control on his congregation by manipulative preaching, in the face of their desire to expand their horizons. Or indeed, it can be a congregation or PCC claiming fidelity to age-long traditions clamping down on the clergy's efforts to introduce changes that would quite manifestly promote growth.

Whatever form it takes – lust for power, lust for someone else's body, or lust for money – it leaves others unfree. Yet in direct contrast to that, throughout his ministry, Jesus loved people into a new freedom. He discouraged any dependence upon him that could lead to a wrong attachment. Legion was persuaded to return to his own village, Jesus moved on from those he healed, sent the forgiven adulteress away free from any obligations, gently instructed Mary Magdalen not to cling to him. He was never driven by a need to be needed or a need to succeed. His own security in being loved left him free from compulsive behaviour and at ease in his self-hood. So he sought neither power over people, nor gratification from them in any form.

The specific lust which Jesus condemns in Matthew 5:28 is, of course, the lust of the eyes. Undoubtedly he had seen it in the wandering gaze of men, and maybe of women too. He himself would surely have appreciated beauty in a woman. Indeed, he may have marvelled at it and gazed upon it with wonder. But because his love had such a quality of purity in it, he would not and could not have dishonoured a woman by undressing her with his eyes. There would have been no lustful desire to possess her. As a sexual being, women may well have been deeply attractive to him, but to behold and recognise beauty (including physical beauty) in another is not necessarily to lust, but to acknowledge, to bow in wonder at, and enjoy the mystery and fruit of God's creativity. And because he saw people 'whole', his eyes would have discerned and reverenced the kinds of beauty that would have totally escaped the merely lustful eye. He could have looked with wonder at the kind of face where an impure gaze would have glanced, but not bothered to linger. Similarly, the nature of his love, in which there was no self-seeking, would vigorously have shunned dishonouring thoughts that invaded the privacy of another.

To look upon another with lust is not to see him/her as of infinite worth and precious in the eyes of God. It is to regard the other as a 'thing' to be acquired, used and then discarded once possessed – once 'it' ceases to be a mystery and a delight. Then the lustful eye will start roving elsewhere in search of new conquests.

Jesus was the embodiment of truth – whereas lust gives birth to lies. It promises what it can never give. It cannot give love. It cannot give joy. It never leads to respect, nor to true relationships. It ultimately burns itself out leaving only bitterness and disgust. Those who are slaves to lust often discover over time that it is one big cheat.

To say that lust could not gain a foothold in Jesus does not in any way diminish the reality of the temptation. His perfect love, his reverence for God in others, his integrity and truth did not protect him from the *temptation* to lust. Indeed, he may have been an even more vulnerable target because of them. The purer a person is, the more likely the Evil One is to redouble the attack, for victory on such a front is worth many fairly easy successes. They did, however, save him from any enticement to yield to the temptation. It was as though it fell on rock where it could find no weak spots in which to take root and flourish into sin.

That provides clues for us, surely? The overcoming of temptation to lust, in whatever form, has to do with the nature of our loving. Lust creates bondage – and at its most extreme can even act out actual bondage scenarios. But the love of Jesus flowing in and through us will leave others truly free. We best combat lust, then, by opening ourselves more and more fully to that divine love which honours, reverences and respects; that cherishes and protects; that beholds the beauty of the Lord in others (which may have nothing to do with the colour of their eyes or their vital statistics!); that walks away in order that others may be free to mature into self-hood.

Something of Jesus' attitude to lust is revealed in his handling of the incident when the scribes and Pharisees came to him dragging a woman caught in the act of adultery. She must have been a very frightened woman, because the penalty for adultery was death by stoning, and a very humiliated woman, for somehow the exposure of sexual sin always seems so much worse than other, possibly far more pernicious, forms of sin. They did this to test him – of course!

Possibly to save the woman from the further embarrassment of yet another pair of male eyes fixed upon her, he bent down and wrote something, or maybe just doodled, in the sand. Perhaps he needed to do this whilst he got his anger under control – anger at their callous exposure of her and at the injustice of the situation. If she was an adulteress, where was the adulterer? She wasn't alone in this act. Why wasn't the man dragged along too, to face the shame, the public humiliation and the execution?

This is one occasion where we see the anger and compassion of Jesus operating together – anger at the delight these men were obviously taking in denouncing the woman from their great height of moral rectitude; anger at the sheer, though perhaps unconscious, projection on the part of the accusers. Quite possibly lust was a problem for *them*, and maybe there was even an element of envy. They were too full of self-righteousness as they denounced this evil, too heated in their condemnation, to see the truth about themselves.

Jesus, however, the great perceiver of thoughts, the one who could always see through sham instantly, wasn't fooled. He recognised that her fault made them feel better about themselves and that their condemnation of her gave them a certain satisfaction.

St Seraphim of Zarov once wrote, 'All condemnation is of the devil. Never condemn each other. Not even those whom you catch at the evil deed. We condemn others only because we shun knowing ourselves. When we gaze at our own failings, we see such a morass of filth that nothing in another can equal it. That is why we turn away and make much of the faults of others.'[11]

Jesus' response to the men was, 'Let him who is without sin among you, be the first to throw a stone at her' (John 8:7). One by one they slunk away, even in their self-righteousness they couldn't pretend that they were totally without sin. He didn't blame them – neither the man, the woman nor her accusers. He didn't need to. He had said all that needed to be said. And, of course, he didn't throw the first stone.

Here, the Jesus who enjoined his followers not to judge others was practising what he himself preached.

As Nicholas Harvey has written:

> The negative judgement I make on another's behaviour or attitude is recognised for what it is, a severe condemnation of myself. It is not that if I continue to condemn others I shall at some future date find myself condemned by others or by God. There is no need for such a condemnation even if it were appropriate, for I have already condemned myself. The saying is a brilliantly incisive way of saying that the habit of negative criticism, whatever it may or may not do to those criticised, points the critic into a corner or confirms him or her in an anti-life posture. It is my distorted perception, not any divine decree, that judges thus. So I am encouraged by the saying to stop this destructive thing to myself.[12]

If it is true that we condemn in others our own sin that we see mirrored in them, then it provides the reason why Jesus had no need and no desire to condemn. That fact that he had never yielded to the sin of lust meant that he saw nothing of his own sin reflected back to him thereby inducing self-righteousness.

After a while, when everything had gone very quiet, he looked up and said, 'Woman, where are they? Has no one condemned you?' She said, 'No one Lord.' And Jesus said, 'Neither do I condemn you, go, and do not sin again.'

His non-condemnation of the adulteress does not show an absence of moral standards. It simply reveals a true compassion as though he absorbed the woman's hurt and guilt feelings into himself. His 'Go and sin no more' left her lighthearted and free of a great burden. He who had taught his followers that it is blessed to be merciful was a living example of that blessedness and a perfect reflection of the God 'who is rich in mercy' (Ephesians 2:4).

Envy

When and how might Jesus have been tempted to sin by a tug of war with envy? Tempted like us in every respect as he was, there must have been those areas in his life where he too faced an inner struggle and had quite consciously and deliberately to turn away from longing for what was not, and could not, be his. How did he prevent envy from robbing him of his inner freedom to be who and what he was, rather than trying to live out a projection of his wishful thinking and fantasies?

Might he, for example, have had to wrestle with envy after his first visit to the Temple as a 12-year-old? Envy of boys who lived in Jerusalem and could therefore study the Talmud and Torah under the most learned teachers within Judaism? Perhaps that time of sitting talking with the Doctors of the Law and questioning them had whetted his appetite for more demanding teaching than he could ever get in Nazareth. Mary may have been bewildered at first by the seeming thoughtlessness of Jesus in causing Joseph and herself such acute anxiety – a 'thoughtlessness' that stemmed from the intensity of his thirst for more knowledge. Was it that much of his inner quest had been blurred and rather diffuse, but at the Temple some of the rather inarticulate, nebulous stirrings within were given a sudden clarity – coming as it were into sharp definition and focus as transparencies sometimes do when projected onto a screen? Naturally he would have felt a strong reluctance to be dragged away from those who were able to help him understand the inner meaning of the tradition and faith in which he was growing up. Perhaps in his discussions with them, a dimly apprehended vocation began to take on some kind of substance and shape. But before he could fully grasp hold of it, Mary and Joseph appeared.

Even if Mary realised from his words that he had begun to have some new and radical self-understanding, she may not have had any inkling of just *how* hard he found it to turn away from what must have been like wellsprings in the desert to his enquiring mind. She may not have understood the sheer cost for him of returning to Nazareth and submitting to parental authority. We must remember too that at this age most children begin to get restive and struggle towards a separateness of identity from their parents. There is a normal, to-be-expected ambivalence in them as they try to do a balancing act between their need for a right dependence and a proper independence.

Did Jesus at any moment feel a pang that could have been the seed of envy that other boys could go on to do a full rabbinic training, whereas it had been assumed that he would either go into, or even take over, the family carpentry business? That does not imply that he was ambitious for personal preferment and prestige, only that he had an insatiable thirst to know more and more of God. And the more he learned of God, the more he realised he was beginning to know himself.

Did he, perhaps, at the start of John the Baptist's ministry have to battle with envy of him – his freedom to 'forsake all', leave home and kindred and friends, go off into the desert, travel light for the sake of the Kingdom of God and begin his ministry, whilst his own duty seemed to be to remain at home in Nazareth as the 'breadwin-ner'? Or could he rejoice unfeignedly, seeing John's ministry as the longed-for 'dawn from on high' breaking upon them? Was it because he was free of envy that in time he could recognise it as a sign that *his* hour had come to begin his own ministry – a genuine call rather than an emulation of John's?

John the Baptist himself was astonishingly free from envy. How else could he have said, '. . . my joy has been fulfilled. He must increase, but I must decrease' (John 3:29–30)? Neither man, it would seem, was threatened by the other; so passionate was their concern for the Kingdom that envy and petty jealousy found no foothold in either.

At the wedding in Cana of Galilee when his mother pointed out that they had run out of wine, his reply sounds strangely jarring (even allowing for the inadequacies of translation): 'Woman, what concern is that to you and me? My hour has not yet come' (John 2: 1–5). It appears almost like a put down, which Mary takes without argument. She turns quietly to the servants and tells them, 'Do whatever he tells you.'

Was Jesus' response a resistance to having pressure put on him to do a miracle prematurely? Was he trying to establish that he needed to discern very carefully the right moment at which to 'go public' in his ministry? Or was there a darker, more subtle reason?

Was he struggling momentarily with envy of the lucky bridegroom? Was it perhaps one among many moments when he had to feel the pain of renunciation – of marriage and of a normal home life with a wife like a 'fruitful vine' and his children 'like olive shoots around his table' (Psalm 128:3)? His 'fear of the Lord' was not going to bring him that blessing. The fact that one makes a renunciation voluntarily – even 'for the sake of the Kingdom' – does not, ipso facto, eliminate the pain and the cost of it. A man who related so well to women and who clearly had a love of children and they of him, a passionate man as Jesus obviously was, must have had to contend with very strong, natural longings for all the blessings and intimacy of marriage – not just once, but many times. And there is nothing improper in that. On the contrary, it is an affirmation of the goodness and right-ness of marriage. But the natural yearnings have somehow to be contained, accepted, indeed honoured and then channelled into loving relationships that are not exclusive with all the particular privileges and commitments of family life. All that is an ongoing learning process, with its pains as well as its joys.

Jesus was a full-blooded, virile young man – not the wan, ethereal figure of so many paintings and stained-glass windows. (Few artists seem to depict him with the hands or muscles of a carpenter!) Would it not have been very understandable if his joy with and for the bridegroom at Cana was also tinged with a little sorrow as he recog-nised that this good and holy 'institution ordained by God' was not to be for him? And if, added to the sorrow, there was an inner struggle with envy going on, it may not be surprising that his reply to Mary seems a little splenetic.

If, however, that is true and envy reared its head even momentarily at the wedding causing Jesus a struggle, I feel sure it would have been as quickly banished. He would not have wanted even the slightest hint of 'sour grapes' to overshadow the joy of the occasion. His generosity of spirit would have overcome the temptation, for he would surely have wanted it to be such a time of rejoicing and celebration as would make this a never-to-be-forgotten day for the happy couple. It would have saddened him had the least cloud of anxiety, embarrassment or shame spoilt their wedding – and to have run out of food or wine at such a time would certainly have done so.

Perhaps, when his mother alerted him to the dilemma of the

rapidly diminishing wine, Jesus saw the wedding feast as a foretaste of the kind of Kingdom celebration that would one day be. Summoning his spiritual energies to do the miraculous, he looked at the large stone jars standing filled with water and quietly and unobtrusively turned them into wine – both in solemnity but also, I can't help thinking, with a sense of real delight. Must he not have enjoyed the fun of seeing the looks of astonishment and hearing the exclamations of approval, as people took their first sips, paused and then began commending their host for reversing the usual order of things. Normally the best wine was served first and afterwards, when people had drunk sufficient for their palates to be less discriminatory, a more inferior wine. Here at Cana, however, the most delectable wine was being served at the end of the feast. Would not Jesus have smiled with deep satisfaction to watch the pleasure it gave the guests and the surprise and relief it brought to their host that the crisis was averted?

From his parables, we know how much Jesus saw weddings as a cause for celebration for he surely knew how 'marriages can be made in heaven' (even when arranged by a matchmaker!) and how much it rejoices the heart of God when two people come to celebrate their love, which originates from him whether or not they recognise it, and express their desire to be united for life. Always he smiles in divine pleasure where his love has taken root in human hearts.

In his poem written for a contemporary wedding couple, Stewart Henderson picks up the sense of laughter, fun and celebration which God shares as the unseen guest at any marriage. Since Jesus would have entered into the joy of God as well as that of his friends, what room could there have been for any lasting envy?

> God gives you this day
> This giggling day
> As the clouds hokey-cokey
> And the bride shines as new
> And the angels remember
> The wine that was water
>
> God gives you this day
> This glowfully day
> Gift-wrapped in paradise
> As the church whoops and chuckles
> At the priest's proclamation

That one joined to one
In Christ, equals one.

God gives you this day
This sanctified day
As He Who flicked stars
Fizzed this
Dressed, blessed,
Entirely-for-you-day
God gives you this day.[13]

Covetousness

Closely aligned to envy is covetousness. Here, whatever battles Jesus had, he must have won them supremely well. Not wanting possessions, he didn't need to covet what others had.

His was the poverty not of misery but of one who never sought anything for himself. Yet he never seemed to want for anything. Out of his own lived experience he could say, 'Do not be anxious about your life. What you shall eat, or what you shall drink, nor about your body, what you shall wear' (Matthew 6:25).

One writer has pointed out that Jesus did not need to make 'an option for the poor' as the Church today is called to do. He did not need to show solidarity with the poor. He *was* poor.

> It is extraordinary how powerful is the appeal and the moral authority of one who strips himself of all worldly pretensions, of all trappings of power, prestige, self-esteem, who deprives himself of the comforts, the conveniences, the facilities that make life easy. Such poverty, cheerfully and willingly undertaken, is an unchallengeable testimony to the Gospel. There is something about it that is the acid test of commitment, something that carries conviction when all else fails.[14]

He certainly didn't covet the acclaim of the crowds, or public recognition or even fame. After healing people he charged them not to tell anyone. He closely guarded the 'Messianic Secret'. When he found himself becoming too popular, he went on to the next town. When the people tried to make him king, he sent the crowd away and disappeared.

As an adult then, he seems not to have had to combat covetousness over possessions, position or honour. He was content to 'travel light' in every respect. Only by doing so could he have made such radical demands as, 'Go and sell all that you have and give the money to the poor'. He could only invite others to experience a joy he had proved for himself.

The rulers – both state and religious – coveted power. Jesus had seen covetousness turn Herod the Great into a monster who so clung to his so-called power and guarded it with such jealousy, he could even have one of his wives and two of his sons assassinated – merely because they seemed to pose a threat to that power.

The real nature of power, however, was so clear to Jesus, he did not need to covet it. He knew the temporal power of the Romans on the one hand, and the ecclesiastical power of the Temple officials and rulers of the Synagogue on the other, were not the sources of true power.

Where did Jesus' understanding of the nature of power begin? Did it have something to do with being born poor – so that he was never in a position to put his reliance in the vast wealth and prestige that gave some people a feeling of power?

By the very fact that he had been torn away (somewhat reluctantly?) from the Temple after his first visit and had accepted his humble life in Nazareth, does it point to his having grasped that real power does not lie in knowledge? Even from his schooldays he may have learned that authority doesn't depend on being part of a power group. If he ever found himself disagreeing with his peer group, did he find it hard to stand on his own and be different, in order to remain true to his own convictions? Did he begin, even at an early stage, to experience the power in weakness – in terms of being outnumbered – but at the same time the power of standing in one's own truth?

Did he taste for himself the power of the peacemaker when he defused the squabbles of other boys and later of his disciples and Mary and Martha? His mother would have been influential in teaching Jesus about the true nature of power. Her own understanding of God's inversions comes out very starkly in the words of the Magnificat: 'He has shown strength with his arm: he has scattered the proud in the thoughts of their hearts. He has brought down the powerful from their thrones, and lifted up the lowly; he has filled the hungry with good things, and sent the rich away empty' (Luke 1: 51–3). She would have made it clear to him too, that her 'fiat' didn't in any way leave her power-*less*. God doesn't coerce or force us to change our behaviour but confronts us with the choice of changing. Being redeemed, then, has to do with choices, and choices give us a right autonomy, the power to give or withhold, and a proper sense of responsibility.

Mary never needed affirmation in herself from Jesus. So many people grow up feeling love is manipulative. It can become an actual curtailment of freedom, whereas true love is always a freeing thing, letting the other person be him or her self. But Mary's security was such that she did not have to exert power over Jesus – her greatest power was her selfless love which gave him personal autonomy. Love is the greatest of all powers. We do not love in order to be powerful. We are powerful because we love.

Sensing the love that flowed between Jesus and his mother, we can begin to comprehend the enormous power they had over one another – a power which neither found cramping, only gloriously liberating.

With that deep, intuitive understanding of where real power lies, it is not surprising that Jesus' entire ministry was an invitation to others to discover it for themselves and to enter into that freedom. No wonder he had no need to covet the pseudo-power and fear-filled tenuous hold on it of 'the Kings of the earth and the rulers thereof'.

With that kind of inner freedom, he didn't need all the emotional props and stays with which we surround ourselves in our insecurity. And because he didn't have that deeply-felt need, I judge his conflicts with covetousness to have been probably more like gentle, sparring matches than full-blown battles. Therein lies the clue for us. Security doesn't of course come by thinking about it, but perhaps by reflecting on the ways we try to cope with our insecurity – ways which hide rather than heal – we can begin to see new possibilities in loving and living, free from covetous desires.

Gluttony

❖❖❖❖❖❖❖❖❖❖❖❖❖❖❖❖❖❖❖❖❖❖❖❖❖❖❖❖❖❖❖❖❖❖❖❖❖❖

This was one sin of which we know Jesus was actually accused in his own lifetime. He was labelled 'a glutton and a drunkard' because he attended parties and was often found to be at what sounds like a good table – eating, drinking and talking, enjoying himself enormously. He seems to have been a popular guest and very welcome in a number of homes.

This accusation, which Jesus knew was being levelled at him, is recorded in the context of a discourse about the contrariness of human nature. 'John the Baptist has come eating no bread and drinking no wine; and you say, "He has a demon". The Son of Man has come eating and drinking; and you say, "Look, a glutton and a drunkard, a friend of tax collectors and sinners!" ' (Luke 7:33–4).

In Luke's Gospel this is immediately followed by an invitation from Simon, the Pharisee, to eat with him in his house – an invitation which was accepted. It was at this meal, of course, that 'a woman of the city, a sinner' crept daringly into a wholly male domain and broke her alabaster flask of ointment anointing Jesus and bathing his feet with her tears.

So, clearly there were some people, even amongst the Pharisees, who were prepared to open their homes to him and share table fellowship – with no hidden tricks or traps to try and make him condemn himself by word or deed.

Jesus enjoyed people and he enjoyed parties. He could enter happily into feasting because he knew the other side of the coin – fasting. Was gluttony a severe temptation to him? If it was, he certainly won some resounding victories!

A man who could endure long bouts of fasting as Jesus did in the wilderness hardly leaves the impression of gluttony. A man who when desperately hungry could refuse to use his divine power to turn stones into bread has certainly resisted that temptation. A man who went off for a day with his disciples for rest and refreshment, without any provisions doesn't sound like someone obsessively concerned about food. When crowds followed him, there was nothing with which to feed them till a small boy offered up his lunch and enabled a miracle to happen (John 6:9).

A man who sat by a well whilst his disciples went to buy food, but declined it when they returned with supplies bought in a nearby village, could not be called a glutton. His reply seems to refer back to his encounter with the Samaritan woman: 'I have food to eat of which you do not know'. And when the disciples questioned if someone else had brought him food, he replied, 'My food is to do the will of him who sent me and to accomplish his work' (John 4: 8, 31–2, 34).

We speak colloquially of some kinds of pleasures, such as listening to music or engaging in lively discussion, as being 'meat and drink' to people when it gives them obvious satisfaction. Here Jesus implies that doing his Father's will gave him such inner satisfaction that even his natural hunger was appeased. That's hardly succumbing to gluttony!

One of the accusations made about him by the Pharisees was that he allowed his disciples to pluck ears of corn on the Sabbath as they passed through a field. They were hungry and ate, even though the rubbing of the corn in their hands to separate out the chaff was considered work. In the Mishna it came under the heading of 'threshing and winnowing' which was forbidden on the Sabbath. The disciples had no other food, and these were hungry young men with healthy appetites. It wasn't even a satisfying meal!

Against this kind of precarious existence, Jesus seemed perfectly free to eat a good meal when invited out; to enjoy both the food and the wine. I imagine him being 'the life and soul of the party' with jokes, fun, teasing and much laughter. Were it not so, I doubt that he would have been so sought-after as a guest. Hosts would hardly invite someone who was going to be a damp squib at the proceedings, or leave them all feeling guilty about enjoying food to the full.

Jesus probably had too much respect for his body as God's creation to give way to the temptation of gluttony. He had too much compassion for the poor to eat enormously and extravagantly all the time. But nor did he deny himself totally the good gift that celebrations with food and drink are! Even had he wanted to, there wouldn't have been enough money for a hedonistic lifestyle. He was not under any compulsion to eat in order to compensate for some emotional deprivation or poor self-image.

At the home of Martha and Mary, it was Mary's quiet presence, sitting, allowing him just 'to be' that ministered to him. Martha's insistence on cooking a large meal (because to her way of thinking that was what a healthy young man needed) was actually a distraction (Luke 10:38–42).

Maybe when they had been for a long time without food and the pangs of hunger gnawed away at him inside, Jesus might possibly have fantasised about a good, hot meal. But the standard of living in the home at Nazareth would certainly have been simple, and his expectations would have been correspondingly so.

As with anger and lust, Jesus appears to have had all his passions and appetites under control, perfectly integrated, leaving him free to enjoy a riotously 'fun' occasion without feeling guilty.

The uncertainty of knowing if or when he would have food to eat, must at times have brought a natural desire for food. But the evidence points to someone who was neither a glutton nor a killjoy and for whom eating was a sacrament of friendship, generosity and trust.

Surely Paul's exhortation to 'moderation' (Philippians 4:5 AV) was exemplified in Jesus as it was in his own experience as a missionary: '. . . I have learned the secret of facing plenty and hunger, abundance and want' (Philippians 4:12).

Pride

◆-◇-◆-◇-◆-◇-◆-◇-◆-◇-◆-◇-◆-◇-◆-◇-◆-◇-◆-◇-◆-◇-◆-◇-◆-◇-◆

Of all the targets the insidious, many-headed monster of pride could have sought to attack, Jesus must have been among the most vulnerable. We have only to consider the innumerable entrées pride could have turned to its own account.

He who warned his followers, 'Woe to you when all speak well of you . . .' (Luke 6:26), knew the dangers of 'increasing in divine and human favour' even in his youthful years (Luke 2:52) and the temptation, whilst giving the glory to God, to scoop up a little on the side for himself.

He must have known as a 12-year-old that the scholars at the Temple were impressed by his questions and ability to discuss with them. He could easily and understandably have taken pride in the fact that they were 'amazed at his understanding and his answers' (Luke 2:47). He could have fallen into sinful pride, as opposed to a healthy delight, in his growing wisdom and physical strength (Luke 2:40) taking personal credit for both. In his adult years, his head could easily have been 'turned' when people flocked to him 'listening to him with delight' (Mark 12:37); when from being an apparent nonentity, he suddenly became a well-known public figure. He must have been aware that he was given an authority in his teaching which their scribes lacked (Matthew 7:29), that his reputation as a healer was spreading rapidly, for was he not constantly besieged by the sick and disabled whose hopes were raised by news of his miraculous cures. Rather like Canute, he desperately tried to hold back the growing tide of popularity triggered by his teaching and healing. He charged those whom he had healed, not to tell others – a somewhat unrealistic instruction one would think, since the healings would be self-evident (cf. Mark 5:43). When in a sudden surge of Messianic hope people tried to make him king – he slipped away to foil their attempts (cf. John 6:15).

He was in demand, much sought after, his name on many lips, his parables widely relayed. Many people, at that early stage, were certainly 'speaking well' of him – and he must have had to meet the full force of the temptation of pride when literally thousands gathered to see and hear him.

How then did he pick his way through the veritable minefield that pride so often is? For, in avoiding one 'mine' we find ourselves stepping on another. Even the very best things we do for the best possible motives – selfless and altruistic though they may be – are actually triggered by a little pride. True purity is very rare.

First, Jesus didn't entertain grandiose ideas about himself. He exhorted his disciples to travel light as they went out on their 'missions' – not to carry any excess baggage. It was a precept he undoubtedly practised himself. He seemed not to need things to give him security; he didn't need mementos such as the gold, frankincense and myrrh of his babyhood, to assure him that he was special. He didn't hang on to the equivalent of certificates or photos of moments of past glory to bolster up his ego.

With the strong sense of self-worth one imagines he had, he was able to choose the way of humility, poverty and weakness. He freely accepted shame and dishonour – and there can be no more certain a defeat to pride than that! He grew steadily in perception where his identity and vocation were concerned, but it would appear that only his Father's affirmation at Baptism and Transfiguration truly gave him his real status and the courage to pursue the near-suicidal course he had to take in order to establish the 'Kingdom'.

His desire to know what people were saying of him was not to boost his self-esteem but to discover whether or not they were on to the right track in their understanding of him. Perhaps more especially, he wanted to give the disciples an opportunity to articulate what might for them have been only semi-formed beliefs and so to take an important stride of faith – an invitation which only Peter took up at that point.

Truly humble as he was, he never sought to take credit for the healings he performed. 'It was not my power that wrought these miracles but my Father's', he said (cf. John 5:19).

It was his Father's will, his Father's voice, his Father's power and purpose that motivated him and increasingly became his whole *raison d'être*. He seemed indifferent to personal acclaim and, if it came his way, he attributed all the glory to the Father. He never took to himself the pedestal people tried to put him on, and roundly rebuked the disciples if they wanted to use their contact with him for self-promotion (Mark 10:35ff.). If they ever basked in reflected glory it would not have been with his approval.

Had Jesus not met some of those subtle temptations of pride head on, and resisted them, his followers would have been able easily to detect chinks in his armour and it would have given a hollow ring to some of his teachings on humility – for example, when he took a child on his knee and talked of the need for childlike simplicity. 'A person who encourages a radically immature humanity to grow up by becoming like little children is not in the least comforting, reassuring or worthy of admiration to those wedded to their immaturity.'[15] Pride would never take that kind of risk. It avoids speaking the unpopular truth or presenting the unwelcome challenge. But then, Jesus never sought to curry favour. Indeed there were times when he was downright provocative, opening himself wide to criticism and even the wrath of others, by – for example – calling Herod 'that fox', and by his infuriatingly silent stance before Pilate.

Pride baulks at the lowliest role and the most menial task. Yet Jesus was prepared to take a towel and a bowl and undertake the servant's task of washing feet (John 13:1ff.). Certainly this final and most memorable act of humility would not have left such an indelible impression had it not been consistent with his whole life in which as a norm 'true lowliness of heart' was prepared to 'take the humbler part'.[16]

Part of his power to resist pride must have stemmed from that inner security of his. When others, albeit unwittingly, touch on raw areas within us and thereby hurt us, when our security is threatened, when our self-image, our sense of worth and self-esteem are damaged by their criticisms, we often react with all our defence mechanisms on 'red alert', or, alternatively, we go into a broody withdrawal. Either way it is the result of wounded pride. Our insecurities make us too fragile to be able to brook adverse criticism or even a seeming slight. We rush to justify ourselves and adjust our slipping mask. But, although insecurity provides a clue to the reasons for a failure in pride, nevertheless pride itself is the bottom line – not insecurity. It is at the root of all touchiness and proneness to take offence. Jesus' words, 'Those who try to make their life secure will lose it, but those who lose their life will keep it' (Luke 17:33), may have been spoken in the context of material gain or loss, but they apply more deeply still to ambition and our desperate attempts to preserve the persona we have created, the self-images we have projected – to impress

e genocide can be the fruit of it. Such jealousy can quite
be described as insane – indeed diabolical.

sy will kill, not simply to protect what it has by right, but
doesn't have and wants. Our newspapers and TV screens
 and plentiful witness to its work in society at every level.
xtreme form it is behind much murder, divorce, burglary,
 devious and manipulative tactics to gain preferment, the
intrigue that lead to the downfall of those in positions of a
oveted by others. The litany of crime – petty or otherwise –
rom jealousy, which often combines with ambition, is as
as it is sickening.

global scale, we see fierce clinging to territorial rights escalat-
 full-scale wars. The carving up of the USSR and Yugoslavia
e downfall of a Communist regime reveals much of the
e instinct of safeguarding territory, but along with it goes
d 'tribal' memories, sinister aspects of jealousy and greed
er.

tering the bloodstream of humanity, Jesus inherited inescap-
s primitive, common instinctual legacy. Of what kind, and
might jealousy have been a temptation that touched down in

now nothing of the possessions and space he had either as
 or as an adult, but there is little to suggest that he was
ed to guard what he had jealously. We do know that he
rded his solitude and personal space in those night vigils of
on the hills of Galilee. That had probably been an established
 long before he began his public ministry – for where else
e ever have achieved physical alone-ness with God? By the
e was an adult possessions certainly had no hold on him.
the only possession of his ever mentioned was the seamless
e neither needed nor coveted things. What he did earnestly
 was freedom – the freedom not simply to be but to become;
edom to become all that it means to be fully human. He saw
clearly how possessions can easily be a barrier to that freedom
e hankering after them a provocation for jealousy and rest-
s.

green-eyed monster that stalks the corridors of power, that
wedges into marriages, that 'eats' into the very fabric of the
heart and turns people into murderers, is one of the most
ve of all evils. Its potential for creating tragedy and sheer
misery is untold.

ourselves as much as anyone else. Only by daring to let them go can
we be real.

Jesus' greatest safety lay in his passion that his Father alone should
be glorified. He never sought honour for himself – his sights were
set in one direction only. Perhaps our own human experiences of
being in love and genuinely longing and rejoicing to see the loved
one honoured and appreciated without any tinge of self-regard, any
jealousy, any desire to divert some of the glory to oneself, is perhaps
the nearest human equivalent we have to this passionate longing of
Jesus, a longing which ultimately led him to the cross: 'Father, the
hour has come; glorify your Son so that the Son may glorify you . . .'
(John 17:1). And because he saw it as a means whereby the Father
would be glorified it was 'for the *joy* that was set before him' that
he endured the Cross (Hebrews 12:2). There was no joy as such in
the physical agony and humiliation of the cross – only the knowledge
that in and through his utter obedience, his Father would be glorified.
Nicholas Peter Harvey writes that for Jesus:

> the question of honour and dishonour – his own or anyone
> else's – is turned upside down, or transcended, or seen to have
> no abiding reality. He had kept very disreputable company at
> times, and the choice (in going up to Jerusalem) was in line with
> the logic of his company-keeping. His plunge into dishonour,
> his willed immersion, remains terrifying. In the New Testament,
> he is presented as having come at this choice from a place in
> himself which was as yet totally inaccessible to his followers
> *in themselves.* 'He was beset', writes Peter Pritchard, 'with those
> wild, bedraggled desires to be with the lonely and the power-
> less'. Such desires left him free of the ethics of honour and so
> gloriously unbound by the compulsion to take offence.[17]

'Why do you call me good?' he asked the rich young ruler (Mark 10:
17). Was he startled to be addressed as 'Good Master'? Was he
concerned at any possible intended flattery or at a mistaken
impression? Or was this another instance of the way in which he
resisted pride – always firmly removing the spotlight from himself
to the Father so that he alone might receive the honour and glory?
For, like a poisonous gas, pride can seep into anything – its presence
barely perceptible until it is too late and it has done its odious work.
It would have been so easy for Jesus to accept the compliment as
sincerely given, and enjoy it, albeit only momentarily.

True goodness, as Jesus knew, belonged to God. Human goodness is only God's goodness channelled. In his incarnation Jesus never tried to grasp at equality with God (cf. Philippians 2:6), never wanted to steal – even in so innocent a compliment – what belonged to his Father.

His resistance to pride had more far-reaching consequences than is perhaps usually suspected. For his was not simply a passive resistance, nor even that he chose dishonour. Indeed, the active resistance was that he chose to *be* dishonour, to embody it and live it out to its searingly anguished end.

'Desire is at the core of this mystery: the unveiled desire of Jesus' whole being to be the epitome of loneliness and powerlessness, and therefore to be free of any shred of the dialectic of honour and dishonour that might prevent this.'[18] He exposed the unreality of shame by plunging into it. The paradox of the crucifixion lies in the fact that 'the tree of shame became the tree of glory'. All worldly standards of power, honour, status and pride were overturned.

> All roles were put on the wobble, all hierarchies at risk from that time onwards. 'Honour and dishonour, praise and blame, what odds?' cries the exhilarated Paul (cf. 2 Corinthians 6:8). For us, the burden of having to stand in and guard the tight network of honour, or of supporting it by colluding with our own exclusion from it, has been lifted. We are to make up in our bodies what is lacking in the suffering of Christ (cf. Colossians 1:24). We too are to be that dishonour, that refuse, that thing of no account which Jesus became. We can be sufficiently awakened to our own humanity to be free to live in his spirit, beyond a distorted sense of honour. Jesus' ordeal (and victory) is the empowering of us to live this way.[19]

Jesus

Jealousy is such a destructive, soul-destro[...] believe Jesus ever encountered it, except [...] cannot be wholly true. For jealousy emerg[...] primitive but still very powerful instincts w[...] preservation and survival – including the [...] young, safeguarding territorial rights, the s[...] a leader, etc. No human being can disen[...] completely from the basic stuff of which w[...]

As we watch these instincts at work in t[...] that they are necessary in the face of the t[...] is evidence of a primitive jealousy among [...] rivalry which is necessarily self-centred sin[...] on it. In the parent animals the protectiv[...] have an extraordinary quality of selflessnes[...] will fight, often even to the death, befor[...] displaced by a rival.

These instincts are part of our common [...] creatures and, in their primitive human an[...] said to be morally neutral. Even to use wo[...] selfless is to give instinctual behaviour a rat[...] which doesn't belong to it. All babies gradu[...] horizons to take in a world beyond themselv[...] revolves around themselves. But we do n[...] centred in a pejorative sense.

The sin of jealousy with its hugely destruc[...] the sophisticated development of these nat[...] supremacy of the tribe becomes horrendou[...] will countenance no rival. Intrigue, treacher[...] its wake. Ruthless extermination of all wh[...]

It is no wonder that we are reluctant to own our jealousy. We try to soften its ugliness by resorting to euphemisms. Nowadays we often talk of being 'threatened'. But it is basically jealousy with a more acceptable label. Rooting around in childhood memories may give us clues as to why certain people threaten us. It may help to unravel some of the causes, but it doesn't remove the deep unhappiness of having something gnawing away inside like a canker. Only profound inner healing will do that. If we try to analyse the reasons for feeling threatened, we usually discover that the successes of others, their greater opportunities for preferment, their power, their charm, popularity, or possibly something quite indefinable about them, all reverberate with our past deprivation. Parental favouritism leaves a vulnerability that has repercussions well into adulthood with the replay of sibling rivalry under certain circumstances. A poor self-image will give birth to jealousy – of, for example, another's reputation. There may be a strong urge on the one hand to tarnish or destroy it by snide insinuations and cruel, unnecessary resurrection of the other's past failures. Or, on the other, it may give impetus to a highly competitive spirit that attempts to outshine everyone else.

People who constantly run others down by recounting stories of their misspent youth, failures in exams or jobs, prodigal wanderings and adult inadequacies, are actually saying far more about themselves than their victims. Despite spilling out all they know under the pretence of humour, the acid eating away underneath is rarely disguised successfully.

Jealousy of this sort, I am convinced, found no chink in Christ's armour. He was singularly unthreatened and, could gladly rejoice in others' gifts. He was neither jealous of another's reputation nor had he any desire to tarnish or destroy it. He did not have any inner compulsion to dig up others' past failings as a means of humiliating and hurting them.

His whole understanding of power meant that he had no fear of being displaced by any rival. How could he be displaced? He had an unshakeable sense of his identity in God (at least by the time he was an adult) – a unique relationship which no one could usurp. He was not therefore dogged by fear and suspicion. But at the same time, he accorded each person a unique place in God, too – a place that was equally unassailable. Rivalry didn't enter into it.

Far from being threatened by the power of others, people were threatened by Jesus' own. Yet in worldly terms he sought to align himself with the powerless, and religious and secular rulers of his day desperately hoped to prove his guilt in supporting one of the subversive groups plotting their overthrow. In his brilliant book *The Shadow of the Galilean*, Gerd Theissen[20] portrays a released prisoner being commissioned to carry out thorough investigations, in an attempt to bring evidence against Jesus that would incriminate him. The authorities needed proof that he was a security risk, an insurrectionist, a dangerous dreamer, a political hazard or a fanatical religious blasphemer. Above all, they wanted confirmation that he was implicated in some specific, planned rebellion. But, of course, there *was* no evidence to suggest that Jesus sought to overthrow the regime of his time. He had no intention of replacing one form of oppression for another, when there was no guarantee of long term stability and security. 'His refusal to be defined by any of these regimes, his claim to an origin, a call and a destiny beyond their control, was the most threatening thing about him.'[21]

By consistently taking the initiative in his encounters with political and religious leaders, it was Jesus who remained in control – not they. Throughout the Passion he was master of the situation. No one was taking his life from him – he was laying it down of his own free will and choice. So, in the Gospel narratives, 'It is the one who surrenders who remains powerful, while the limit to the power of the supposedly powerful is embarrassingly exposed as they exhaust their power in the process of having him crucified.'[22]

Jesus never sought public acclaim – indeed, at times, he shunned his growing popularity. People followed him and 'heard him gladly' because his teaching had the freshness and vitality of personal authority, not because he set out to be a charismatic leader. He 'stayed with' the crowds not to enjoy their adulation, but because he was moved to compassion by their 'lostness' for they were like sheep without a shepherd.

His confrontations with the authorities gave him no feeling of VIP status – the village carpenter turned popular preacher and miracle worker now arguing with the mightiest in the land.

Recognising that he could not take on the whole world in his earthly life he tried to set territorial limitations on his ministry. 'I have not come but to the lost house of Israel' (Matthew 15:24).

What he never sought, therefore, he did not fear losing. He lived untrammelled by any need to establish his status, reputation or work and thus was gloriously free of the weight and red-hot pain of jealousy. Such freedom was highly disturbing and even frightening to others, especially when it cut right across the grain of even those instinctual forms of jealousy that are the basis of self-preservation. On the contrary, in many respects, he seemed bent on a course of self-destruction through his wild surrender.

His suffering was not something simply imposed on him by his enemies but a willed self-offering, a plunging into loss in order to find life – a lostness which he calls *us* to share.

> ... inviting the ending of reliance on carefully constructed ego-survival techniques, often compulsively sustained. ... In a human situation of self-rejection and universal captivity to the consequent mutually destructive behaviour, there appears the one in whom this age-old dynamic is reversed. The one who knows himself loved without limit or condition, and who therefore can be nothing but love, seeks to ... awaken us, his brothers and sisters, to the place in ourselves which is open to the living God, with all the surprise and unlearning that awakening entails.[23]

3

'MADE PERFECT IN
WEAKNESS'

A Sense of Humour

It might, on the surface of things, seem extraordinary that not once in the Gospels is there any reference to Jesus laughing. Weeping over Jerusalem, grieving at the tomb of Lazarus, sorrowful, agonising with loud crying, groaning, deeply saddened by the hardness of heart he met in some, and the lack of commitment in others – we do indeed get a picture of a 'man of sorrows and acquainted with grief'.

Obviously the Gospel writers had to be selective in what they included in their accounts of the life and ministry of Jesus, and New Testament scholars have helped to identify the aim, purpose and particular readership for which each of them was written. Clearly an accurate pen-portrait was not their purpose. Why else are there so many details that get no mention – details which in the writers' view would not have had any particular converting power?

Nevertheless, what *is* given us begins to build up a picture of a warm, attractive, lively personality who, in my judgement, must have had a very strong sense of humour. Partly I would make that claim on the grounds that people were delighted to entertain him in their homes. We know he enjoyed parties; enjoyed eating and drinking and talking. But I doubt that it was all deeply serious talk. Overly serious people can be awfully heavy going – humourless ones even more so. Hosts and hostesses usually anticipate that those they ask to a party will enjoy the fun of it and bring fun with them.

Jesus obviously had a quick mind and enjoyed repartee. He was a brilliant storyteller. But surely that art wasn't confined solely to the telling of parables? For someone who was acutely aware of what went on around him, little incidents would all be grist to the mill for his fund of stories. I can imagine him recounting them with all the verve of a good raconteur, adding perceptive touches of kindly humour to make what might have seemed insignificant memorable, and even more enjoyable in retrospect.

He was young and energetic and probably revelled in the custom-ary Israeli dancing that was all part of the merrymaking at parties. A man in his early thirties living in close company with other young men would doubtless have done his fair share of leg-pulling – and welcomed it in return. I imagine their long journeys would have been spiced with lighthearted banter and a lot of laughter.

One of the probable reasons why Jesus was so appalled at the way the scribes and Pharisees piled more and more minutiae on to the Law in terms of petty regulations – rules they had adopted them-selves and sought to impose on the 'laity' – was because they had made religion so impossibly grim and grimly impossible. It grieved Jesus to see how joyless the Law had become to many ordinary folk, quenching all spontaneity in their attempts to live their faith.

He spoke of the Kingdom of God being like a party, or a marriage feast, which would be celebrated with joy by all the guests (Matthew 22:2ff.; Mark 2:18ff.; Luke 14:14, 15, 15:23–8). When Levi spread a banquet for Jesus (Luke 5:29ff.) the scribes and Pharisees felt they had to investigate what was going on – of course! They said to him, 'John's disciples, like the disciples of the Pharisees, frequently fast and pray, but your disciples eat and drink.' Jesus replied, light-heartedly, airily and with something of a twinkle in the eye, one could imagine, 'You cannot make wedding guests fast while the bridegroom is with them, can you? The days will come when the bridegroom will be taken away from them, and then they will fast, in those days' (Luke 5:33–5).

Jesus seems almost irrepressible. He refuses to let the killjoy attitude of the Pharisees spoil the fun of the parties, or stop him from going to them and enjoying them with a clear conscience.

One important clue as to whether or not Jesus had a sense of humour is given us in the way children were attracted to him. Children are never naturally drawn to humourless people. They find them far too forbidding. He obviously enjoyed them and was defi-nitely very annoyed when the disciples tried to turn them away. 'Let the little children come to me and do not stop them; for it is to such as these that the Kingdom of Heaven belongs' (Luke 18:16).

Michel Quoist captures Jesus' thought beautifully in one of his *Prayers of Life:*

God says: I like youngsters. I want people to be like them.
I don't like old people unless they are still children.

I want only children in my Kingdom; this has been decreed
    from the beginning of time . . .
But above all, I like youngsters because of the look in their eyes.
In their eyes I can read their age.
In my heaven there will be only five-year-old eyes, for I
    know nothing more beautiful than the pure eyes of a child.
It is not surprising, for I live in children, and it is I
    who look out through their eyes.[1]

Probably there were many occasions when he watched the children
playing their games in the marketplace – listened with amusement
to the usual bickering that goes on. Perhaps he picked up a little one
in tears, put the child onto his lap and gently wiped them away and
whispered something consoling or funny. He had noticed how some
children never seem to know what they want. They are constantly
changing their minds and then whining when the others don't keep
in step and immediately change theirs too in a copy-cat behavioural
pattern.

In commenting on the contrariness of human nature – in this case,
adult behaviour – he used this typical ambivalence in children's play
to illustrate his point.

'But to what shall I liken this generation?' he said. 'It is like children
sitting in the marketplace and calling to one another, "We played at
parties and piped flute music to you, and you did not dance. So we
played at funerals, wailed loudly and realistically, but you didn't
mourn." '[2]

You are just like those children never seeming to know what you
really want!

'John came neither eating nor drinking, and they say, "He has a
demon"; the Son of Man came eating and drinking and they say,
"Look a glutton and a drunkard, a friend of tax collectors and
sinners!" ' (Matthew 11:16–19). It was one of those no-win situations
– amusing in children, but very annoying in adults.

Familiarity with the parables has perhaps robbed them of the
initial impact they made on those who first heard them. Everyone
loves a story – but particularly if it is sparkling and witty.

In order to compose a parable, the storyteller needs to be in touch
with where his listeners are. It calls for a profound empathy with
the human predicament, 'An ability to get on the hearer's wavelength,
and a sense of humour.'

Sarcasm has been said to be the lowest form of wit. Some of Jesus' remarks might seem to smack of sarcasm but we all know what a wrong impression the written word can give. What cannot be recorded and transmitted in writing are the facial expressions that went with the remarks or the tone of voice in which they were said.

True humour is never demeaning. It doesn't laugh at another's expense. Of course there are times when it can misfire and be unintentionally hurtful. More often, if it is genuine, we experience it as gentle and sympathetic. It enables us to keep a sense of balance and stops us becoming unduly serious. It makes us see the funny side of life – even when we are frustrated and disappointed by some reversal of our hopes. It helps us to recognise the inconsistencies in human behaviour and tolerate them with a smile. It allows us to make sense of some of the unpredictable turns life can take, even to revel in the unexpected, the logic of inconsistency.

Humour has a light touch and, I believe, a touch of God – hence it must have been very strongly present in Jesus. Have we not marvelled at its power to defuse anger, tension, and bitterness between individuals or groups? How often does it come to the rescue in committees when the air is practically 'blue'? In her biography of Archbishop Desmond Tutu, Shirley du Boulay draws attention to the way in which on numerous occasions his sense of humour has saved a potentially disastrous situation. It is a great gift and a God-like characteristic, for it is part of the equipment of peacemakers.

Humour can transform our prejudices and jaundiced views of life. But most important of all, it encourages us to laugh at ourselves. And it is always something of a rebuke to be told, 'You take yourself too seriously'. If we are pompous it can gently debunk our ridiculous self-importance. God must see us as very funny people a lot of the time and he gives the gift of holy hilarity so that we can laugh with him.

Some of the images used by Jesus in his parables can only be appreciated if we can imagine the smile that went with them. His use of hyperbole often got a penetrating insight across in such a humorous way that people were able to accept it. Had it been given to them straight they would have stalked off in high dudgeon or rounded on him with angry remonstrations. So he spoke about specks and planks in the eye in order to point out that judging is not our business. He had camels trying to go through the eye of a needle (the Greek there means surgical needle) to warn people of the danger of becoming possessed by possessions. Humour turned 'hard sayings' into teaching that could be absorbed at different levels by a whole spectrum of people. Each would hear as much as he or she could receive at that juncture. But the humour in the story also ensured that people would not forget it. Sometimes at the end of a sermon people thank the preacher for the anecdotes and illustrations which they have much enjoyed. And one is left wondering if that to which the illustration was pointing has been heard and digested. The joy of stories however is that they go on doing their hidden work long after the sermon is over. As people reflect on them and repeat them, more and more of the meaning is grasped.

Sadly, some of the humour in the parables Jesus told has been lost through the attempt to turn them into allegories, or by dissecting them and pulling them out of shape. Their funny side has been overlaid by attempts to analyse them and explain them – and we all know how futile and self-defeating it is to try and explain a joke.

What *is* clearly in the Gospels, and is mentioned quite specifically, is joy. John in particular records Jesus speaking of joy to his disciples on quite a number of occasions. He wanted his joy to be in them, that their joy might be complete (John 15:11). No one, he promised, would be able to take this joy from them (John 16:22). Ask, and you will receive, he assured them, that your joy may be complete (John 16:24). And in the great High Priestly prayer of John (John 17:13) he said, 'But now I am coming to you, and I speak these things in the world so that they may have my joy made complete in themselves.'

Since Jesus seems to have seen his vocation in terms of the Suffering Servant Messiah, he would of course have identified closely with Isaiah's enigmatic figure of the Servant-Israel together with all that he knew of the Old Testament understanding of Messiahship (as opposed to the popular messianic expectations of his day). He would have known that his destiny marked him out to be a 'man of sorrows and acquainted with grief'. But not solely so.

In Galatians, Paul lists joy as a fruit of the Spirit second only to love (Galatians 5:22). If the Spirit gives joy to those who are 'in Christ', how much more must Christ himself have been endowed with this gift. It must have been bubbling in him constantly like an underground stream which every so often broke the surface and came forth like a refreshing spring to water the joylessness of others. Therein lies the secret of his attraction. A truly joyful person *is* an attractive person. What's more, the joy can be infectious.

Joy, as we know, often comes with and through pain. Certainly we see the truth of that in the life of Jesus and from time to time we are able to see an extraordinary joy growing and deepening in the face of acute mental and emotional distress and, ultimately, physical weakness and excruciating pain – 'who for the joy that was set before him endured the cross . . .' (Hebrews 12:2).

Recently it was my privilege to be alongside someone dying of cancer. It had been a long battle, very bravely fought – with never a word of complaint about the discomfort and, more latterly, the pain.

Initially she was told that she had possibly a month to live – nine weeks at the outside. Not surprisingly she was dazed and shattered by the news and the prospect of such an imminent death. But she confounded all the doctors and the medical team involved in her case by living for another three years.

Every person who visited her, and all those who spoke at her funeral, commented on the way she absolutely shone with an inner radiance and joy, which increased visibly as she came into 'the last lap' on earth. As with the face of Moses, it was almost overpowering to look at her at times. But each of us who visited and prayed with her came away knowing we had been the ones to receive a benediction.

At the very end she was able to say that her years of illness had been the happiest of her life. I reckon that, to a large extent, she had already entered into her Master's joy before leaving this world, growing closer and closer to him through her suffering and identifying more fully with him in his. Those of us who were granted a glimpse of the Lord's joyful mystery in her, a preview as it were of what heavenly joy is like, have little doubt that she heard the greeting, 'Well done, good and faithful servant' as early one morning, while still asleep, she quietly slipped over into the life beyond, and now knows the fullness of that joy promised to all the redeemed.

Fear, Doubt and Insecurity

◇◇

It wasn't until I met Big Ears, one of the three dogs belonging to our house in Botswana, that I realised the sheer menace of fearlessness. He was little, compact, did indeed have two very large ears and the heart of a lion. But he seemed unable to appreciate that small dogs don't normally take on four alsatians at once, grab cobras by the tail and yank them out of trees, or attack iguanas the size of small crocodiles.

The vet used to call him 'my hero', but I may say our 'hero' gave us many fear-filled and anxious moments. To be without instinctual fear, or any concept of relative size and strength was by no means an unqualified blessing.

Fear is a necessary and natural provision for self-protection. The adrenalin it pumps round the body sets the fight or flight response in motion. It would therefore have been part of Jesus' make-up, although there were times in the face of potentially life-threatening phenomena when he not only showed no fear but was genuinely surprised that his disciples did. He slept without qualms whilst the waters of Galilee churned around him like a boiling cauldron – the winds merciless and the ship rapidly filling with water. He who had lived most of his life inland, had far less fear in this storm than the men who fished these waters regularly and knew their unpredictability.

Fear for the disciples would have been intensified by the Jewish belief that the 'waters' represented chaos and therefore disintegration. 'Save me, O God, for the waters have come up to my neck . . . I have come into deep waters and the flood sweeps over me', the Psalmist cried (Psalm 69: 1–2). The disciples would have had a double-edged fear of drowning – but apparently Jesus did not share it. In view of this concept of chaos, his amazement at the disciples' fear seems a trifle odd. But possibly it indicates the extent to which he was at one with creation and at home in the natural world. His fearlessness would not seem to be the sort that, unlike our little dog, deliberately courted danger out of delusions of grandeur or a lack of realism about his powers. Perhaps his 'Peace be still!' was as much an invitation to his disciples as a rebuke to the wind and waves – an invitation to be at peace with the environment in which they lived, as he was.

Did he perhaps have little fear of heights either? When the angry synagogue congregation drove him to a precipice on the outskirts of Nazareth for his (in their view) unwarrantable blasphemy, it could have been that he 'passed through the crowd' (that extraordinarily ambiguous statement in Luke 4:30) by taking a very narrow, near vertical track down to the caves of Arbela (known to him in all probability from explorations at a youthful age when boys get up to daring escapades). Resistance fighters had used these caves as a hideout and Herod had been able to find no way of flushing them out, so dangerous was the descent with its sheer drop down into ravines of immense depth. Some Zealots had voluntarily plunged from the caves to their deaths rather than risk capture.

Being so at ease with his environment, one could imagine Jesus identifying with the words of the prophet: 'The Lord God is my strength, and he will make my feet like hinds' feet, and he will make me to walk upon mine high places' (Habbakuk 3:19).

Natural, instinctual fear is therefore merciful and manageable, and only necessary as long as we don't put ourselves deliberately into those situations where it will confront us. For example, we don't go bungee jumping if we are afraid of heights or motor racing if we can't cope with high speeds.

It is difficult to imagine that Jesus had to grapple very much with phobias either. For again, his unflinching trust in God would have neutralised such fear. Fear so often arises from a sense of powerlessness, but his harmony with the natural order and his power to bring order out of disorder, in many ways made him less vulnerable to the fear of being overwhelmed and out of control, which for us are often the ingredients of phobic and irrational fear.

What I feel sure he must have shared with humanity to the full, by virtue of his extreme sensitivity, was the deep-seated fear of being misunderstood and misjudged, fear of exposure, fear of being a failure, fear of having given one's life to a particular work or cause only to discover one was wrong or misled all the time, fear of rejection, fear of abandonment, fear of annihilation itself. What it meant to plunge headlong into the very abyss of all *those* kinds of fear as Jesus must have done in his Passion, is beyond all human comprehension. And, of course, all his worst fears were realised in some measure . . . until that final 'it is accomplished' by which point it would seem fear had been banished.

His dread is clearly seen in his agony in the Garden of Gethsemane – not so much, I believe, the dread of physical pain, though that would have been part of it. For him, it would have been more on the lines of what Kierkegaard called the 'existential dread' – of becoming nothing; of mental, spiritual and physical annihilation.

Perhaps it was a very immediate and physical, indeed instinctual, fear he felt, however, as the detachment of soldiers together with the police from the chief priests and Pharisees stormed him in Gethsemane. The adrenalin must have been pumping rapidly round his body, the heart pounding and the breathing coming much faster than normal. With all the fight or flight instincts moving into action – he did neither. He simply stood his ground taking the line of non-resistance, thereby putting himself into the controlling position.

What it must have cost to continue to desist from fight or flight as he stood accused but silent – before Pilate, the chief priests and scribes, Herod and ultimately the screaming mob – we cannot begin to calculate. It is strangely poignant that he who bade his disciples not to fear what they should say when brought before kings and governors and ruling authorities, assuring them that what they should say would be given them in that hour, remained silent himself in that self-same situation – hearing the accusations brought against him, but not once leaping to his own self-defence (Matthew 10:19). He who told people not to fear what others could do to the body – for they couldn't touch the soul – had also to experience the appalling fear that surges forth in any creature, human or animal, when faced with imminent torture and painful death (Matthew 10: 28).

'Walking on high places' can be metaphorically speaking, a spiritual as well as a physical danger. As he clambered up and down between the wadis and pinnacles in the Judean wilderness during that extended time of fasting and testing, I wonder if he ever compared the possible danger of one false step, of the risk of one slip and the fatal fall it could cause, to the danger of losing his surefootedness in 'walking the heights' of God's will for him as he discerned it. Doing that will was an ascent of faith to the dizziest heights ever undertaken by a human being. It was an ascent he made in light but also in heavy darkness. Subconsciously, we may be tempted to think it was all so much more straightforward for him than it is for us. But always the greater the height the further there is to fall, and in consequence the more acute must be the fear. His fear would have been in part an aspect of that holy fear which is a longing that God's name should be glorified in all things. He also knew what was at stake. He sought to do always those things which pleased his Father (John 8: 29), to offer the whole of his life in total obedience – an unblemished sacrifice.

The knowledge that pride could so easily and insidiously poison that longing and lead him to 'fall from the heights' would have been part of the hinterland of truth and self-awareness which acted as a safeguard.

He was surely aware of the dangers of which St Paul later wrote to the Corinthian Church: 'So if you think you are standing, watch out that you do not fall. No testing has overtaken you that is not common to everyone. God is faithful, and he will not let you be tested beyond your strength, but with the testing he will also provide the way out so that you may be able to endure it' (1 Corinthians 10: 12–13).

His sympathy with others in their fear, is an indication that Jesus knew in himself what it was like to wrestle with it and feel crippled or indeed paralysed by it. The sonorous toll of his 'Do not be afraid' rings through the Gospel far more often and more clearly than his injunction, 'Do not sin'.

Sensitivity

One of the moments in *Godspell*[3] that stood out for me when I first saw it and which has remained with me ever since, was of the young Christ receiving a verbal hammer blow from one of the disciples. Almost simultaneously he opened his arms wide and for a moment there was total silence as he 'received' the blow. He seemed so young, defenceless and vulnerable; to open one's arms is a gesture that leaves us wide open to the risk of being wounded. If in our own experience we know that the greater our capacity to love, the more vulnerable we are, how much more must that have been true of so intensely sensitive and loving a person as Jesus?

When, therefore, he was deeply hurt, as clearly he was, where did he place that hurt, and how did he handle it? By what process were his wounds healed?

One way of coping is often to descend into varying moods of anger, a desire for retaliation, brooding resentment, self-pity, endless mental reconstructions of hurtful events and relentless licking of wounds. But did Jesus have to pass through any or all of these stages before he could finally 'let go' of pain and forgive? Or was the nature of his love such that it allowed no entrée to negative feelings in the first place?

Sensitivity is a double-edged component of love, with both its positive and negative aspects. Great sensitivity towards others, on its flip side, means an equally acute capacity to be hurt oneself.

They cannot be separated out, it would seem. The blessing and the curse go together. Would that have been different for Jesus? If not, then his ability to be hurt, by virtue of the lengths to which his love would go, must have been staggering and gives an even sharper cutting edge to the question, 'How did he deal with hurts?'

One possible clue to his power to bear wounds and yet neither return the pain nor repress it, lies in his own, proper sense of self-love. His rock-like security which came from knowing himself to be loved deeply and uniquely by God, accepted and (from his baptism onwards) approved by him, meant that while he was desperately and undeniably wounded by cruelty and treachery in others, by criticisms, taunts, whisperings and innuendoes, he was not threatened at the very deepest level of his being. The wounds didn't touch his sense of self-worth or identity. Since he wasn't looking for or needing approval other than from God, the disapproval of others didn't raise in him the kind of self-doubt and feelings of rejection that frequently haunt those of us who are less secure. His pain would not have been that of a diminishing self image so much as the pain of being despised and rejected when 'love was his meaning' – his only meaning.

Even in Jesus love didn't arrive fully-fledged and ready made. He had to *learn* obedience (another component of love) through the things which he suffered. 'It was fitting that God, for whom and through whom all things exist, in bringing many children to glory, should make the pioneer of their salvation perfect through sufferings' (Hebrews 2:10). That word pioneer is very striking. A leader may guide people along a charted path with maps and the advice of those who have already explored and travelled that way. A pioneer, however, is breaking completely new ground – venturing where no one has gone before. A pioneer changes the possibilities. So with Jesus. He came to pioneer a new way of becoming. In him, whole new dimensions of life, love and moral consciousness can be explored. As Andrew Elphinstone wrote, 'If that meeting of suffering with love which denotes forgiveness was the experience in which Christ was "made perfect in suffering", then that must also be the way of our own perfection and the means of our first touches of participation in divine nature.'[4]

Part of the stratagem of evil is to take pain (which in itself is neutral) and commandeer it as one of the chief weapons in its armoury. We need to grasp that pain is a battlefield – not the battle itself. Only in that way can we see how on that battleground (i.e. the experience of pain), it is possible for evil to be put down and for love, in the same experience, to be brought to its most authentic expression.

We need, of course, to be clear that for Jesus, pain, suffering, wounds to his sensitive spirit, were absolutely real. They did not bounce off him because his divine skin was somehow considerably thicker than ours. He had neither learned to cover himself with layers of protective, pain-resistant armour, nor had he any practice in retaliation. Innocence, integrity and love (including self-love and self-respect) were his only guards – and the gift of a quick mind that could detect the subtleties of temptations. The final conflict between evil and love fought out on the cross, that supreme battlefield of pain, could never have been won, had Jesus not been preparing for it throughout his life, rehearsing that victory in lesser ways as he faced and absorbed suffering.

His injunctions to his followers to 'love your enemies and pray for those who persecute you', and 'if anyone strikes you on the right cheek, turn the other also' (Matthew 5:39, 44) were not idealistic, pie-in-the-sky precepts. They had been hammered out on the anvil of his own experience and forged in the furnace of his ever-deepening love. His handling of hurts was no sinecure. He was 'in training' all through his life, learning to take hold of suffering, of whatever sort, and to achieve a supremacy of love over it. 'The thing in which love becomes most powerful and most clearly intertwined with pain is forgiveness, where love triumphs completely over the provocations offered by pain.'[5]

Most of us probably fear pain of the body less than pain of the mind and heart. We know little of Jesus' experience of bodily pain before his agonising death but there is plenty of evidence of the hurt his spirit sustained.

To be rejected by his own people – the townsfolk who had watched him grow up and who had regarded him highly as an adolescent – was a terrible blow to his spirit. He had wanted them to be the first to hear his proclamation (Luke 4:16ff.). No matter how well we are received by strangers, no matter how much they appreciate what we do, it never compensates for the love and affirmation we look for in those we love the most and who know us best.

He must have been wounded when his healings were attributed to Beelzebul – the prince of devils (Luke 11:15). What was demonstrably the power of God at work, was seen as the power of evil. That kind of spiritual blindness was, Jesus saw, the only thing that is unforgiveable. For, in order to be forgiven one must be able to see right from wrong, good from evil and have the moral and spiritual 'eyes' to distinguish between them. But if one looks on Incarnate Love and calls it Incarnate Evil – how blind can one be? Indeed, how hope-less?

Was he not hurt when the ten lepers he had just healed simply left him standing and rushed off in joy to show themselves to the

priests, receive the 'all clear' and a new bill of health, and so resume
a normal life again? As Jesus watched them go – rejoicing for them
in their new freedom – was there also an inward pang that they had
taken what he had to give without any sign or expression of gratitude? Was the wounded feeling reflected in his face which the one
leper, looking back, saw? Jesus had touched them (Mark 1:41) – an
unthinkable, courageous, forbidden thing to do, which would have
rendered him ritually unclean as well as exposing him to the risk of
infection. Instead of becoming contaminated himself however, it
worked the other way round. Jesus' cleanness and wholeness seemingly infected the lepers.[6] Mercifully, whatever it was that prompted
him, one leper came back to say 'Thank you', thus warming the heart
of Jesus.

'How sharper than a serpent's tooth it is to have a thankless child'
said King Lear.[7] Jesus must certainly have known that biting pain
which sheer ingratitude can inflict.

He was obviously irritated, but was surely also wounded, by the
repeated attempts of the Pharisees to find fault in him, to trip him
up with their trick questions and to discredit him before his followers. Though Jesus was shrewd enough to see exactly what the
Pharisees' intentions were, he must have been deeply saddened that
the very people who should have been his allies (for they were sincere
people, sincerely trying to please God) had become his enemies.

Must he not have felt hurt when, despite all his teaching and
example, the disciples still had not grasped the true nature of greatness? 'The kings of the Gentiles lord it over them', he said, 'and those
in authority over them are called benefactors. But not so with you,
rather the greatest among you must become like the youngest, and
the leader like one who serves ... I am among you as one who
serves' (Luke 22:25–7).

With that he demonstrated the meaning of servanthood by washing their feet. If actions speak louder than words, then clearly this
was a compelling message delivered with a most powerful and memorable visual aid. For here were the disciples, on the very eve of
Jesus' crucifixion, prior to his one remaining night and very last meal
with them, jockeying for positions of importance, trying to establish
who was greatest and who the least. How eagerly he had looked
forward to sharing this Passover meal with them, he told them, yet
it very nearly foundered on the rocks of their pride before it even
got started. No one was willing to be identified as that least important
person whose job it was to wash the feet of others.

It must have been a bitter disappointment to Jesus that his disciples seemed to have grasped so little of the true meaning of humility despite all they had heard him teach and seen him practise. There was so little time to drive this essential message home. But no one would be able to forget that incarnation of humility at the Last Supper.

The deepest and most unspeakable wounds to his sensitive soul were still to come – the betrayal, the denial, the desertion by every disciple (as he had predicted) except Peter and John (Luke 22:54 and John 18:15) who followed him at a distance, and ultimately the seeming abandonment of God.

The denial must have been a searing pain to the heart of Jesus, but he had foreseen that dear, blustery, impetuous Peter would be tripped up if challenged; he knew that fear would bring out the coward in him, make him panic, lose his head and blurt out the first thing that came to mind by way of self-defence.

When Jesus turned and looked on him (Luke 22:61), it would have been a gaze without any trace of condemnation in it, only compassion. He knew how Peter would quickly break his heart over his failure – at being caught off guard and thus disowning the Master he loved more dearly than anyone else and for whom he had promised to lay down his life. Mingled with the compassion, there would certainly have been a look of gratitude too. For, after all, Peter's loyalty would not have been put to the test, the denial would never have happened if, like all the other disciples except John, he had forsaken Jesus utterly and fled to safety. He, at least, had been courageous enough to follow Jesus from afar – which eventually led him right into the courtyard of the high priest. It was a daring thing to stand round the fire (a complete stranger) warming himself along with the servants and guards. At least there were two disciples, as near at hand as was permitted them, trying to support Jesus. If the outcome of Peter's attempt was denial, was it any worse or more wounding to Jesus than the passive denial of the others in their desertion?

Jesus, in his love, wasn't into keeping a score of wrongs – even with such appalling wounds to his heart as the disciples' infidelity had inflicted on him. Hadn't he told Peter to forget about scores when it came to forgiveness? 'How many times do I have to forgive?' said Peter. 'Seven times?' 'No, 490 times', said Jesus, 'but stop trying to count.' (My paraphrase.)

Christ's look in that courtyard, and later in his very personal exchange with Peter over a breakfast of freshly baked fish, was unquestionably rich in mercy. He gave Peter the chance to own his love publicly, to assure Jesus of it face to face, a heart-rending but redeeming three times. It must have been a breaking open for Peter of his still throbbing wound in order to give him inner healing and a reversal of despair. John was later to write, 'Whenever our hearts condemn us . . . God is greater than our hearts, and he knows every-thing' (1 John 3:20). Peter experienced the truth of those words in that life-changing gift of forgiveness he received from his wounded Lord.

It is hard to imagine how Jesus must have felt when he heard the crowd cry to Pilate, 'We have no King but Caesar' – they who regularly sang 'The Lord is King, let the earth tremble', and knew the familiar and oft-repeated words of Isaiah's prophecy, 'I am the Lord, there is none other'. The revolutionary slogan of their own day was, 'No King but God' and the whole thrust of Jesus' message had been to announce that God was now at last becoming King, his Kingdom was being established. His piercing sorrow was not simply their denial of him and his prophetic message, but their denial of their own tradition and their own religion. There at the seat of Judgement before Gentiles, they denied their God. No wonder Jesus remained silent. He must have been in the kind of total shock that follows a traumatic experience.

Over and over again in his ministry, Jesus must have had to struggle to meet hurt with love rather than revenge, to offer forgiveness in exchange for pain. But although, the selective Gospel accounts flow smoothly and easily, we mustn't imagine that forgiveness for Jesus was ever effortless. He must often have wrestled and agonised in his nights of prayer. 'In Christ half-seen questions and half-realised principles came to the fore',[8] and always there was that hideous temptation, 'You don't have to suffer!' If your own people reject you, call down fire from heaven to consume them. If people don't thank you, call back the cleansing and return to them their infection.

Have I the power to set my face to a path of self-sacrifice and suffering, to scorn the line of least resistance? Only in Jesus was the answer ever completely 'Yes'. At the touch of provocation, we in our frailty often react more readily by way of self-defence than self-sacrifice – 'anger is a thousand times easier than forgiveness'.

People will rise with enormous courage and generosity to natural disasters or afflictions suffered in wartime. That kind of suffering often brings out the heroic. There are countless real life dramas where people's willingness to lay down their lives to save others has shown something of the divine image they bear. But it is in the innumerable woundings, injustices and enormities which are our day-to-day experiences and which flow back and forth from one person's vulnerability to another's, leaving legacies of anger, hate, resentment, desire for revenge that we feel, as soon as the pain begins to die down, a terrible compulsion to start poking the embers and fanning the flames again. It is in this kind of recycling of the hurts that evil can have a heyday. It will always be a danger zone for many of us, every time someone tramples on (or even simply touches) our sensitive areas. If we have already been deeply wounded many times in the course of life, we are almost certain to have developed all sorts of defence mechanisms to protect ourselves from further hurt – mechanisms that leave little room for heroic love.

It seems as though in some mysterious way, Jesus was able not only to resist retaliation, but to absorb and internalise the pain, to stop an ongoing cycle of retaliation, to prevent the proliferation of evil. In the same way that the water in a washing machine absorbs the dirt from the clothes leaving them fresh and clean, so Jesus did with the taunts, the gibes, the cruel lies by which he was wounded. Unlike a vacuum cleaner which also absorbs dirt which it then stores within itself, the washing machine discharges the water and the dirt together leaving both the clothes and the machine itself clean. So, true forgiveness leaves both the offender and offended free. We can of course be like the vacuum cleaner: 'If you retain the sins of any, they are retained' (John 20:23). But, whoever's sins we remit, they are remitted (literally 'sent away').

True forgiveness then consists of absorbing *and* discharging. We are best able to discharge the pain in prayer – but not always straight away. At first it may be that we can only 'let go' little by little. That does not matter provided we genuinely desire to let go as the wounds gradually heal, until we come at last to release all anger, bitterness and lingering resentment. Somewhere in the process we shall probably recall the parable of the unjust debtor, and will need to look again at the sheer scale of Christ's woundings – and so get our own into proportion.

It will be easier to understand what the inner action of forgiveness really is if we look at it as an encounter with pain in which love gains the supremacy and evil has no opportunity to proliferate. Forgiveness is the exact reversal of rendering evil for evil under the stress of pain. It is the rendering of unbroken and uninterrupted love in return for whatever pain of malice or injustice has been inflicted. But it has to be understood that to give back only love for hurt is extremely far from acting weakly as a doormat on which others may tread with impunity. The moral demand that lies upon the forgiven is as powerful as the moral requirement of the forgiver to forgive. Christ holds the world in his claim upon it to match love with love, and the world can only be at peace with itself (and with him) when this claim has been met.[9]

Where the analogy of the washing machine breaks down is that there is nothing automatic about all this. We cannot simply 'switch on' forgiveness. It is an act which engages our 'unruly wills and passions' as the Collect puts it. We need a limitless supply of that enabling which we call grace. It is not until we have really plumbed the depths of personal forgiveness that we are granted to see the point at which evil is disarmed and the corresponding point at which pain is lifted to creative power.

How did Jesus cope with his hurts? By love, of course. The final answer lay in the quality of his love – love which transmuted pain, taking it from the armoury of evil and turning it into a triumph of grace.

This may sound theologically 'neat'. But forgiveness is so demanding, it is never tidy. There are often unravelled tangles, unfinished business, loose ends – but that is not the important thing.

> Love lets the past die. It moves people to a new beginning without settling the past. Love does not clear up all misunderstandings. In its power, the details of the past become irrelevant; only the new beginning matters. Accounts may go unsettled; differences remain unsolved; ledgers stay unbalanced. Conflicts between people's memories of how things happened are not cleared up; the past stays muddled.[10]

What does matter is the mutual freedom that forgiveness brings. For not to forgive leaves us as much a prisoner as the one guilty of wounding us. Jesus whose passion it was that people should be free – in the sense of knowing a true inner freedom – never seemed to get trapped himself as a prisoner to negativity or destructive power.

One of the secrets of his victory in this respect was, I think, brilliantly captured in that poignant scene from *Godspell*. Jesus stood there, looking bewildered and hurt, as though he had been struck a physical blow. And he stood in silence – perfectly still – for what seemed like a very long time to the totally rapt audience. It was electrifying!

Silence in the face of hurt was his great ally. We can see this in his silence before his accusers, before Pilate and Herod and the crowds, in the deepest of all his experiences of pain. But silence was undoubtedly something he had practised all his life. For on those occasions when people hurt him, as he took the pain down into silence, he would be able to discern where it was really coming from – what wounds and fragility in the other had caused him or her to wreak such damage. Where in their past had they been deeply wounded? What in their present circumstances meant they were hurting so badly that they had to lash out at others? Understanding thus can give rise to compassion. 'To know all is to forgive all', and I believe Jesus learned to keep silent in order to 'hear' what was going on in the depths of the other. Our problem is that often we react instinctively when hurt, lashing back like an animal when attacked. We cannot hear anything but our own screaming hurts. The divine image within, with the capacity to draw the pain down, reflect upon it, see the causes behind it, offer it up for healing and put the whole lot 'through the washing machine', doesn't get a chance to come into play.

What Jesus was able to do by understanding, compassion and forgiveness had far-reaching effects. For,

> . . . our own struggles towards inner peace and harmony are never purely a private concern, although they may seem to be so. In life we are all exposed to destructive forces and we can react to them in different ways. We can absorb them, intensify the destructiveness in our inner heart and send them out with more destructive power than before, or we can absorb the violence as Jesus did, transform it within and return it in the form of forgiveness, blessing and kindness. An inner act of pure love is more effective and creative than any amount of external activity. When the final judgement comes, I am sure we shall all be surprised when we discover who the real heroes and heroines of the world have been, who sustained it and saved it from destruction. They will probably be very obscure, unknown people of healing hearts, who absorbed bitterness, violence and

hearts and generated a spirit of forgiveness, gentleness and hope.[11]

And generating a spirit of forgiveness can have cosmic effects as the life and death of Jesus show. In him, all evil, all negativity, all pain was absorbed and transformed by love: like a divine alchemist he perpetually turned base metal into gold. He calls us to share in this work, but we can only do so when we begin to realise just how rich in mercy he has been towards us, just how much our own negativity and destructiveness have gone through the crucible of his transforming love, how totally he has accepted us and offered us forgiveness and restoration.

In the face of wounds to our sensitivity then, a choice is before us – to absorb them in such a way that they erode all our joy, or to absorb them, discharging the pain and the evil that have latched on to them.

Discharging carries with it a heavy responsibility. It has to be done through appropriate channels. Washing machines are not expected to discharge their dirty water all over the kitchen floor but through the proper waste pipes. And the discharging is a controlled act – it has to wait for its proper place in the whole cycle.

Here again, I think we have come upon one of the secrets of how Jesus handled hurts. He *did* discharge them – in the proper place in the cycle of his daily life. That place was prayer. But also, I like to think that he was then able, having drawn the pain down into his being, listened to it and absorbed what needed to be retained, to discharge some of the memories by sharing with trusted friends. Would he perhaps have allowed Mary of Bethany to enter into some of his woundedness – and correspondingly received comfort from her? His deepest resources were, of course, in God. He would naturally turn to his Father first – in pain, bewilderment, anger, frustration, but also joy. God was his lodestar. But he needed human understanding and comfort too. He wasn't wrongly self-contained. He didn't simply mask his vulnerability and button up his emotions. Nor, however, did he let them spill out in an uncontrolled, damaging way. He was not governed entirely by instinctual behaviour. He may well have had to resist the temptation to react instantly from a place of deep hurt, but that kind of discharging would not have been in the proper place within his cycle of response. He waited, not opening his heart to others, until the pain had done its inner work and he could safely share without perpetuating the memories of the wounds and thus preventing them from being healed.

Discharging has a counterpart. At one time, our Convent kitchen used to boast an enormous and rather antique oven. It stood some six feet high and had two large drawers of about five-and-a-half feet in depth, one under the other, which pulled out rather like the drawers in a mortuary. When, as postulants, we were initiated into the mysteries of this unusual piece of equipment, we were warned against opening it too frequently. Each time one or both drawers were pulled out, the oven lost a great deal of heat. So, we were bidden to be well organised, think ahead and exercise the greatest possible economy in opening it.

As part of our novitiate training too, we were exhorted to practise 'continence' – not a word in general usage. It comes from the Latin verb 'continere', which means to hold or to restrain. The opposite, incontinence, means, of course, to be uncontrolled or unrestrained, but is now associated almost exclusively with one particular form of loss of control.

The Desert Fathers used to teach their disciples the need for continence by reminding them that if one has a jar of aromatic perfume, it is inadvisable to keep removing the lid for, that way, the fragrance of the perfume is given off into the air and weakened through dissipation.

The novitiate teaching was not, of course, simply about ovens or perfumes. It was about the need to practise restraint and continence in the opening of our hearts to others. There is a strength to be found in containing things within, at least until we have reflected, absorbed and integrated them at depth. Equally, it can somehow be a dissipation of energy to 'take the lid off' too readily, to pour our hearts out endlessly and promiscuously to a whole range of people who might be willing (or forced!) to listen. And, of course, one runs the risk of receiving conflicting advice and consequently being thrown into complete confusion.

A priest once told me how he had his first real taste of retreat when he was lent a little chalet part way up a mountain. Having a family of four children, he didn't often have the chance of real solitude. During those days alone on a mountain, one thing came to him very clearly. It was as though God asked him, 'When you are in trouble, when you are hurt or let down or betrayed, to whom do you go first?' This question kept repeating itself in him and he felt very challenged by it. In all honesty he had to admit that his immediate reaction was to pour it all out to someone else. If his wife was at home, she had to lend a sympathetic ear. If he was alone, he would pick up the phone and ring, not just one friend but several, or he would write a lengthy letter articulating his feelings. Only much later, when he felt he had discharged a great deal of his pain or anxiety did he think to turn to God. 'Why not tell me first?' God seemed to be saying to him. Why not indeed! It might well have obviated the need to overflow in all directions (and incidentally would have reduced his phone bill!).

It's not a bad thing to stop occasionally and consider whether or not we are in too great a hurry to rush to others to open our hearts, to share something prematurely before we have had time to reflect and receive from the experience some of the 'treasures of darkness' that it offers and find the real growth points that can transcend the pain.

Always, then, it is important to pause and reflect before offloading our inner turmoil onto someone else and ask ourselves: 'Is this the right moment and the right person to whom to open my heart? And have I sought a human resource before the Divine One who is ever standing at the doors of our hearts patiently knocking to let us know that he is there waiting to make our "yoke easy and our burden light"?'

We can, of course, go to the opposite extreme. When we brood and allow our wounds to fester inwardly (inevitably getting things magnified through an over-restraint which has more to do with repression than continence), Christ longs that his compassion should be mediated to us through friends and other members of his body, the Church. There are those with deep sensitivity and listening skills who are able to incarnate Christ's compassion and healing to us when we are bruised by present wounds or memories of past ones.

He wants our memories to be contained until they have reached the point in the cycle of integration where they can be shared safely and only for purposes of healing – not for a negative rehearsal of the painful events or out of vengeance. The alternative can lead to untold harm.

As I write, we are seeing daily, on the news, the devastating effects of a ship that was unable to 'contain' its cargo when it foundered on rocks off the Shetland Islands. Right now, the *Braer* is spewing out its 85,000 gallons of crude oil doing untold damage to the wildlife for miles around. Added to which, the entire atmosphere is polluted and everything on the islands is covered with a film of oil – the grass on which the sheep should be grazing, the food and drink people are consuming, clothes, hair, furniture . . . everything. The stench of oil is appalling.

It set me thinking about the dark, damaging, wounding things that can issue forth from us at times when we are unable to control, restrain or check our thoughts and our tongues. We are capable of spreading poisonous observations and remarks into the environment around us, polluting it. And perhaps *we* carry an excessive load of potentially damaging 'cargo'. Just as the tanker has no further control over the oil once it has been discharged into the sea to be at the mercy of wind, waves and tides, no more can we exercise any further control over our verbal spillage once it has leaked out.

Sometimes in a burst of temper, people pour out a volley of appallingly wounding things which reduce the other person to a crumpled heap. Often, the offender will come back later in horror and anguish at what they have said and cry, 'I'm sorry. I didn't mean it.' But, the trouble is, we can't help feeling that it was *exactly* what they really thought. What they didn't mean to do was lose control and let it out. What they didn't intend was for the 'storage tanks' to rupture under stress and discharge all the bitterness and resentment they held. Obviously it is better not to be carrying that kind of cargo in the first place, but we all do at times.

The victory of the cross wasn't achieved simply at Gethsemane or Golgotha. It was the result of a lifetime's continence. In all his perplexities, on all the many occasions when he must have been deeply hurt, Jesus would surely have turned first to his Father. Was that part of what he did in those solitary nights on the hills of Judaea and Galilee? If he was tempted in all points as we are, then he would have been tempted to retaliate when hurt, to demolish his opponents, cutting them down to size with a few devastating and scathing criticisms. Yet, when he maintained a dignified silence, it was the fruit of a lifetime's practice of continence. Only in that way could he have held his tongue in the face of false accusations and the religious leaders' deliberate twisting of his words and actions.

He could certainly denounce his opponents if it was a matter of truth or justice at stake, but his words were always under perfect control. I cannot think of one instance where he struck back out of personal hurt – but of *plenty* where he did not.

The words of Andrew Elphinstone well describe Jesus when he writes of a 'positive, redemptive response to pain in which, for love's sake, the hurt is contained by refusal to return it with anger and in which love and goodwill are maintained unbroken towards the offender'.[12]

Thus, instead of being like a stricken oil tanker spewing out its black, polluting, lethal contents, for Jesus 'the original hurt is isolated and so, being contained within the hurt person, is not instrumental in bringing about an increase in the total amount of pain and a consequent proliferation of evil . . . (in fact) the evil is robbed of its power to do further damage'.[13]

When we place that disciplined continence alongside the appalling, unimaginable pain of betrayal – by one of his close, specially chosen friends – we begin to grasp in small measure something of the incredible scope of Christ's forgiveness. For though his forgiveness of Judas would have been unlimited, it did not in any way reduce the extent of the hurt. Jesus' example teaches us that we can freely forgive even though we have been and still feel deeply hurt; it is one of the mysteries of grace.

What the mockery, the mental and physical torture, the taunting challenge to come down from the cross must have done to the sensitive spirit of Jesus is beyond our imagining. Yet, because of his continence, the hurt was contained and not returned. 'When', as Andrew Elphinstone continues, 'the supernatural will to love has become entirely dominant over the natural will to take revenge, the pain is absorbed – redeemed – in the hurt person and healing flows from that person to the original offender.'[14]

We are back to the choice before us – continence or vile leakage. Conformity to Christ's likeness when hurt will have in it all the hardness and self-discipline that he had to exercise. But it also has for us the hope of changed possibilities, of being able to return forgiveness for hurt because 'the blessed and most glorious wounds' of Christ himself make this possible.

A Psychological Evaluation

◇◆◇

It is important in a book of this nature that some consideration should be given to the possibility that Jesus' beliefs were those of a mentally abnormal, even deranged person.

Some of the medical writers of the nineteenth century who embarked upon a 'psychiatric' interpretation of Jesus came to the conclusion that Jesus suffered from some form of paranoia.

The word goes back as far as the Hippocratic writings, though it is used there in a general sense, as meaning simply mental disease. It was introduced into German psychiatry in 1818 but with such a loose definition that at one time up to 80% of the patients in European mental hospitals were diagnosed as suffering from 'paranoia'. Gradually it came to include illnesses characterised by ideas of persecution and grandeur in varying degrees. It was used by patients who exhibited almost entirely a distortion and misinterpretation of actual facts, or some elaboration with fabrication, or who showed such a loss of contact with reality that it was accompanied by hallucinations. And of course it is not at all uncommon for the delusions to have a religious connotation.

Given that in order to make a psychiatric diagnosis one must have a good case history and that 'the perils of diagnosis "à distance" are great',[15] on what grounds did these and subsequent medical writers suppose that Jesus suffered from paranoia?

The suspicion that the mind of Jesus might somehow have morbid characteristics was voiced long before psychiatry became interested in him, but, over the years, writers have claimed some of the following:

- that Jesus lived with the quixotic idea that he was destined to appear in a blaze of supernatural glory, surrounded by angels, on the clouds of heaven, to judge the world as the expected Messiah and to establish the Kingdom which was to emerge.

All of which, it was held, indicated a fanatic – still in possession of his faculties because his expectation had its roots in the popular and historical conceptions of late Judaism – but nevertheless a fanatic.

- that Jesus was a hybrid, tainted from birth by heredity, who even in early youth as a born degenerate attracted attention by an extremely exaggerated self-consciousness combined with high intelligence and a very slightly developed sense of family and sex. His self-consciousness unfolded slowly until it rose to a fixed delusional system, the peculiarities of which were determined by the intensive religious tendencies of the time and by his one-sided preoccupation with the writings of the Old Testament. Ultimately he arrived at the point when he related to himself all the Scriptural promises for the fulfilment of which people looked and longed expectantly.

- that his vision during his baptism was a case of visual and auditory hallucination which often accompanies a greatly excited mind, and that probably he suffered too from voices which seemed to come from within.

- that he was sometimes liable to strange and apparently groundless moods of depression (cf. John 12:27) as for example before his arrest when he was in a very nervous, excitable state. He knew what a risky game he played and was weighed down with fears and ominous misgivings. The completely senseless cursing of a defenceless fig tree (Matthew 21:19) is cited as an illustration of the 'boiling over of severe spiritual excitement'.

- that his public ministry stretching over three years showed a mounting megalomania which formed the focal point around which everything else revolved – as proved by all his sayings, teachings and sermons which culminated in the single word 'I'. William Hirsch[16] even went so far as to assert 'no textbook on mental diseases could provide a more typical description of a gradually but ceaselessly mounting megalomania than that afforded by the life of Jesus'.[17] Jesus, in Hirsch's view, in so far as he believed the predictions of the prophets applied to him, was manifesting a characteristic typical of paranoiacs, who apply to themselves everything that they ever see or read. For example, the claim to be descended from David is consistent with a well-known pattern in youthful paranoiacs, who tend

to substitute their real descent for a highly colourful and fantasised one.

- that the Transfiguration was another hallucinatory experience
  – for while Jesus heard a voice from heaven reiterating his
  divine sonship and coming glorification, the people round
  about heard only a clap of thunder. (Although this is often
  claimed, it is not biblically authenticated.)
- that Jesus showed the notable secretiveness of a paranoiac –
  his Messianic destiny and some of his teachings are shared as
  'secrets' with a select group.

One cannot, of course, study any individual in a vacuum, because
no one lives in one. Each of us is conditioned by our environment –
its religious and social ways and belief. It is important to note,
therefore, that some of the above conclusions are reached without
an understanding of the historical and contemporary setting in which
Jesus lived. It is nonsensical to speak of the 'intensive religious
tendencies of the time' and of the youthful Jesus' 'one sided preoccupation with the Old Testament' when, as discussed in Chapter 1, it
was the only subject taught in synagogue schools – i.e. the Scriptures
and related texts. If Jesus had a lively mind, then its energies would
have been more narrowly focused than those of a contemporary
Western schoolboy whose interests are required to be more diffuse.
His education consisted entirely of a study of the Scriptures – Torah,
Talmud and Mishnah – and the history of his people, the Jews. Such
specialisation was bound to lead to an intensity of interest.

To depict him as having delusions of grandeur about his ancestors
could be wholly unfair and inaccurate. It was considered fairly well
established that the family of Jesus on Joseph's side was descended
from David. Members of the royal family were among those who
returned home from exile in Babylon under Cyrus. The first caravan
was led by Zerubbabel – of the family of David. He also played an
important political role immediately after their return. Blind Bartimaeus addressed Jesus as 'Son of David' and at his triumphal entry
into Jerusalem, the people sang joyfully 'Hosanna to the Son of David'
(Matthew 21:9). This tallies with Paul's understanding (Romans 1:3)
almost three decades after the death of Jesus, that his royal descent
was well-known and generally accepted.

We are told that people murmured against Jesus, whispered about
him, falsely accused him, all of which would normally be guaranteed
to cause acute distress to anyone suffering from paranoia. It was

once said of Albert Schweitzer that he went his chosen way, quite oblivious of the antiphonal choruses of praise and blame which surrounded him. Those who later came to acclaim him, almost as a saint, often forgot that he was the centre of violent controversy at the time, in every sphere where he moved.

Although Jesus might not have been 'oblivious' of the praise and blame which attached itself to him, and indeed may have been deeply hurt by some of the latter, he was not disturbed by it or deflected from his course. In that respect, he could hardly be described as typically paranoid.

The psychopathologists made much of the 'I am' sayings of Jesus in the Fourth Gospel without taking into account the special style, purpose and significance of that Gospel. Similarly most of their references to moods of depression and ideas of persecution are drawn from it. Whereas taking into account the date, purpose and readership of the Fourth Gospel, we can appreciate very different interpretations. There is a distinction to be drawn between depression and deep spiritual and mental anguish. In our own experience we know that obedience to an inner sense of call may cost us great anguish as we go beyond ourselves in self-giving. But it cannot be equated with depression. For Jesus, his passionate desire to do the will of his Father meant it was 'for the *joy* that was set before him' that he endured the cross (Hebrews 12:2).

When the psychopathologists maintained that Jesus had numerous hallucinations during his lengthy stay in the wilderness, which led them to affirm that this was a phase in the development of his psychosis, were they then writing off as inauthentic all mystical experience in terms of paranoia and mental illness? If so, what of so many of the saints whose life-changing experiences cannot be explained in psychological terms?

> To form a judgement about any person on the sole basis of his acts is contrary to all psychiatric practice and has always something suspicious about it. If this is true for the present age, how much more restraint must be exercised when we are dealing with people from a very distant epoch and with imperfect and uncertain traditions! For this reason the constantly recurring instances of historical epilectics, like Mohammed, Julius Caesar and even Napoleon I himself seem very questionable and legendary. Even more uncertain is the ground on which we tread when

we endeavour to investigate, in the light of modern psychiatry, the minds of people from a distant epoch.[18]

Did Jesus then suffer from the same kind of analytical treatment as other historical figures in the attempts of different 'experts' to 'explain' his exceptional powers, his self-understanding, his response to a vocation, his qualities of leadership and his disturbing influence?

Speaking of his impact upon the American peoples, Shirley du Boulay says of Archbishop Desmond Tutu in her biography of him: 'Typically of this small man, whose heart and mind span so vast a spectrum of human characteristics, the effect he had on Americans ranges from awed reverence to accusations of demagoguery.'[19]

Apart from the reference to height, it could be a description of the impact Jesus made on his contemporaries. The trouble is, people try to do the impossible and categorise greatness. But it can't be done. For one thing it is quite often eccentric (in the literal sense of standing outside oneself), for another, when the Holy Spirit is working in and through a person, paranormal powers and exceptional behaviour could result which may appear to show certain similarities to mental illness. But it is very far from *being* mental illness and mustn't be so labelled simply because it is not understood. Many of the saints give ample evidence of this. The world can never fully grasp or give adequate explanation (medical or otherwise) of the varieties of experience in the spiritual realm.

The words of Janet Morley's prayer for Pentecost highlight this and seem extraordinarily applicable both to Archbishop Desmond Tutu's ministry and even more to the heart and mind of Jesus himself.

> Spirit of truth
> Whom the world can never grasp,
> touch our hearts
> with the shock of your coming;
> fill us with desire
> for your disturbing peace;
> and fire us with longing
> to speak your uncontainable word.[20]

4

'LOVING
AND BEING LOVED'

Relationships

Jesus appears in the Gospels to be a man with no shortage of friends. That people liked him and found him attractive is obvious from the way they followed him eagerly. If he went up a mountain, they waited for him to come down; if he sought refuge in the desert, they followed him; if he crossed the lake to get some space to himself or with his disciples, they ran round the shore and were there to welcome him as he stepped out of the boat.

His generosity in healing the sick, giving individual attention to those in trouble, his compassionate touch and his authoritative teaching all made him a besieged man. He was popular in the literal sense.

He was undoubtedly a sociable person and enjoyed people – and that communicated itself, drawing people to him like a magnet. But it made it all the more essential to have those closer friends with whom he could risk greater intimacy, share more deeply, feel himself energised – and know he would be met by understanding and mutuality of love and respect.

As with all of us, relationships went in ever-deeper layers. There were the friends who gave him hospitality with the special bonds created by table fellowship. He had friends in Jerusalem who were ready to lend him a donkey or an upper room simply for the asking. He knew something of the day-to-day life of the city and obviously was sufficiently well acquainted with its inhabitants to point out any unusual personal custom or routine, such as a man carrying a pitcher of water. These were probably among his more casual friends.

At a deeper level still were his disciples with all that they gave him of companionship and support. The fact that 'they all deserted him and fled' (Matthew 26:56; Mark 14:50) in that traumatic moment of his arrest, must not blind us to the real sacrifice those men made in 'leaving fathers, mothers, wives, children', homes and livelihoods to follow Jesus – without security, without financial reward, without the promise of future glory. On the contrary, they were given ample warning that their relationship with him would lead to rejection, suffering and even death. Yet they stuck to him and, though they may have shared Thomas's gloomy prognostication at times, nevertheless did not turn back until the very end when, waking out of sleep to sheer pandemonium, bright lights and hostile faces, they panicked.

They loved him even when they were bewildered by him. He commanded their loyalty, respect and support, even though by responding to his call they found themselves in daily proximity to men who, in the normal course of their life's work, they would never have encountered let alone chosen as companions. He, as the unifying power amongst them, was able to hold together the Zealot and the quisling, the Jew with the Greek, the cautious, quiet introvert with the impetuous, blustering extrovert, the intellectual with the unschooled, the town dweller with the country born.

When a group of people live together, not by choice, but as a result of a common call of Christ, then only his grace powerfully operative among them can turn their togetherness into community. And of course, in Jesus the disciples had a supreme model of how love transcends all social distinctions and cultural barriers. He deliberately chose to call a heterogeneous group in order that 'they might be one' and demonstrate the transcending love made possible in the new Community of the Kingdom.

He himself

> mixed freely and easily with people of all sorts, the rich as well as the poor. He did not romanticise about the poor. He did not blame the rich for being rich, but he did not seek to imitate them. He mixed with sinners and thought nothing of it. He also mixed with good people, the officials of the temple and others. For him it was a matter of indifference who they were or where they stood on the social ladder or in popular esteem. They were all equally children of the one Father, his own brothers and sisters.[1]

The distinctions that are so often considered important by others were quite irrelevant to Jesus. People mattered intensely to him, therefore, sweeping aside conventions, he could engage with a Samaritan and a Syrophoenician woman, with the despised tax collector and the condemned adulteress, with the Sadducees and their age-old enemies the Pharisees, with a Roman centurion and a rich, young ruler. He had come, as he said, to 'the lost house of Israel', but he was by no means rigidly exclusive. He also *wanted* to mingle with the mothers and toddlers and laugh with the village children as they played in the marketplace. He had just the right touch with the earnestly enquiring Nicodemus but also with the enthusiastic would-be follower who had not weighed up the cost of discipleship.

Inevitably therefore, with his available, accessible personality, and the perpetual drain on his emotional energy, he needed to have those special relationships where he could relax in the warmth of total acceptance and understanding, relationships that were nourishing and revitalising. The deepest of these may well have been the gift of women to him.

Mary, His Mother

A N Wilson suggests

> At the beginning of his public life, Jesus appears to have been
> in a state of conflict with his family. His recorded utterances
> about the family as an institution are all hostile to it. Though
> he insisted on the necessity of monogamy, he praised those
> who left their mothers, fathers, brothers, sisters and wives in
> order to be his followers. All this suggests that relationships
> with his own family . . . were, to say the least, tempestuous.[2]

If Mary had been fostering Jesus' vocation from early childhood,
as seems most probable, then it would hardly have surprised her
when the time came for him to leave Nazareth and follow that call.
The sword may have pierced her heart many times in his youth as
she detected a deepening in his understanding of his vocation and
foresaw the day of inevitable separation. In her humility she might
well have been surprised at times when there were sudden evidences
of his growth in wisdom and maturity. Like any good mother, she
would have learned from her son. She must have marvelled at his
insights and, perhaps, as his spiritual life entered new dimensions,
she may have been moved, possibly to tears, as it became apparent
how central to all his thinking and desiring God was becoming.

Of course she would dread the day when his 'hour' would arrive
and take him from her, possibly, indeed probably, never to return
home. That would have been natural enough. But they must have
talked about it and prepared for it. Jesus could scarcely have remained
at home in Nazareth till the age of 30 without some discussion of
the unusual circumstances in which he remained single. Mary and
Joseph must have wondered, when Jesus was still just a teenager,
how they would handle questions about marriage – *his* marriage.
Others of his age would probably be excited at the engagements

being arranged for them, for these could be made whilst a child was still quite young. Engagements often lasted many years, until the penultimate year of betrothal before the wedding. Did Jesus ever ask why Mary and Joseph were neither casting around for a suitable partner for him, nor employing a matchmaker to do so? Was it Mary herself who gently explained that sometimes a special call of God precluded marriage? She herself may have laid the foundation of the saying that A N Wilson claims reveals a negative, even hostile, attitude to family life (e.g. Mark 3:31ff.). Though as Jesus grew and pondered these things in his heart and made them his own, for him the renunciation would surely have been embraced voluntarily 'for the sake of the Kingdom'.

Probably for the last decade before he left home he would have been aware of the speculations of other parents in Nazareth. With few exceptions it was obligatory for all Jewish men to marry and father children. If they failed to do so, they were accused of 'slaying their seed'. As a healthy, wholesome, and, in all probability, very personable young man, there could have been a good many mothers in Nazareth and beyond who coveted him as a son-in-law, and fathers who would have been proud to let their daughter marry him. Knowing how considerate and caring he was towards his mother, they would have had few qualms at such an arrangement. If he *were* sought after in this way, it would have been hard for him to handle the nudges and winks, the innuendoes and unsubtle hints with which he would have been confronted – frequently and doubtless embarrassingly. But, he would probably have coped by using some good-natured blocking devices, courtesy and humour. Or perhaps it was on this front that he first learned how to meet loaded questions, without being caught out by them?

At one level, then, I see Mary as prepared for the time when she would have to let her son go, fully and finally, to fulfil his God-appointed mission. Since she had known its nature from the time of his conception, it would hardly have been likely to cause conflict between them.

If he had brothers and sisters, they might well have found it very difficult to accept that he was leaving home for an unspecified job and a precarious lifestyle. They may have been anxious, too, as to which of them would have to take over the responsibilities of being head of the family. It is not unusual for a vocation, especially a religious one involving celibacy, to meet with resistance from a family – often through incomprehension and fear. If not among his immediate family, Jesus would, and did, have his critics among the people of Nazareth. He had to suffer the sharp pain of being misunderstood, a pain that is clearly echoed in his words, 'A prophet is not without honour except in his own country and amongst his own people' (Matthew 13:57). Having to face such misunderstanding himself, he knew his followers would not be spared it either.

Even so, even with the foreknowledge given her by Gabriel and Simeon, the reality of the break with the past domestic security of having her son beside her – as breadwinner as well as companion – must indeed have been like a sword in Mary's side. Anticipating pain does not in any way diminish it when it comes. It only gives better coping skills. Then, having released him with generosity of heart to follow his great and divine call, what happens? Poor woman! What a jolt his line of action must have been to her.

As Tom Wright points out,[3] Mary must have had to repeat that, 'Son, we have sought you sorrowing', because she could not understand what was happening to him. Here, her beloved son, who had enjoyed a quiet home life, who had been so highly respected in the village, is suddenly taking up with the most disreputable of the rabble in town. He makes friends with people on the wrong side, with people of the wrong sort; he gets on easy terms with quislings, the tax men who are collaborating with the occupying forces. He seems to exercise a strange fascination and attraction for young women of quite the wrong sort. And at the foot of the cross . . . there is a sense of history repeating itself. For three years now, not just three days, she has sought him sorrowing: and now she finds him at last. So this is where it has all led.

> Woman, what have you to do with me?
> My hour has come, now, but not the way you wanted:
> All I can do this time is change the water into
> Blood: your blood, from my veins,
> From the wound
> In your soul and my side.[4]

While, therefore, she had let go at one level, were there others where she had not fully faced the meaning of separation – by which I mean, separation in an everyday sense of the capacity to allow someone to be a person in his or her own right without undue dependence on others? And, too, for that person to achieve an inner separateness from illusions and idealisations that may have persisted because of a wrong dependence. Bonding, as we now know, is essential to the emotional and indeed physical health of a child, and separation is essential to full maturity. Somewhere in between the two, there are the years of tugging and pulling as a young person seeks to find and establish a personal identity and make the final umbilical detachment. But the success of that necessary separateness goes back to the beginning of life:

> . . . when an infant needs to have reflected back to him a sense of his own intrinsic goodness and effectiveness; this is conveyed by his parents' attentiveness to him and delight in him, which affirm him in his being. At the same time the infant is learning to manage the inevitable and necessary frustrations of life, at first by means of the primitive mechanisms of splitting and projection, and fantasies of omnipotence, and later gradually coming to a truer sense of reality in terms of his own separateness, dependence and limitations.[5]

Certainly Mary and Joseph would have given that attentiveness to, and delight in, Jesus that reflected back to him a sense of his own intrinsic goodness, worth and lovableness. He would have grown in security and selfhood as they gazed on him in wonder and love.

Was it because of the rumours she heard of the strange company he kept that Mary and his brothers and sisters went looking for Jesus? She seems not to have wanted to talk with or even confront him before the crowds surging around him. So, waiting outside, they send in a message (Mark 3:31ff.). And that is the point at which Jesus makes one of those utterances seized upon by A N Wilson as evidence of family tension: 'Who is my mother? Who are my brothers and sisters?' Their appearance at that point gave him a didactic opportunity to put before his hearers the supremacy of God's claims – claims that could even seem to be in direct conflict with all the natural ties of home and family.

> He is at odds not with his family as such, but with whatever it is in him which would settle for their definition of him, which would be happy to allow their perfectly proper hopes and fears to dictate his course. The picture is not, however, that of a child seeking to throw off a grown-up tutelage now found oppressive. It is rather that of someone seeking to hold to his chosen course against the pull of everything in himself that would domesticate him, that would douse the fire in his belly. . . . It is possible to

choose a familial identity which dictates the whole shape of your life. The maintenance of family relationships can become an absolute, and as such a destructive, alternative to living your own life.[6]

His words were not, I am convinced, intended to be disrespectful. Had it been so, then there surely would have been a rift between them. Whereas, on the contrary, we know Mary supported Jesus in his mission – at least towards its end – by being amongst the group of women followers from Galilee who ministered to his and the disciples' needs. It seems to indicate that she too had renounced her home life from time to time 'for the sake of the Kingdom'. She may also have felt drawn to stay close to Jesus not as a possessive mother but as a devoted follower.

After he first left home, it is *conceivable* that she may have felt a bit left out. She had been so instrumental in bringing God's plan to fruition (indeed parts of the Church even grace her with the title of Co-Redemptrix) that she may have decided to leave Nazareth and share in the fulfilment of what had been begun in her – not for her own glory, but to see God's word accomplished, not because she wanted to cling on to Jesus but because she was as eager to see the dawning of the Kingdom as he was.

When he seemed to address her harshly, as at Cana of Galilee (John 2:4) in response to her concern at the wine having run out at the wedding feast, could it have been partly his need to establish the fact that he had 'left home' emotionally as well as physically – no more dependence, voluntary or otherwise. Now *he* must be responsible for discerning God's *Kairos*, be totally free to respond to the intuitions of his heart as he tuned in ever more acutely to the Father's will?

We need also to remember that what to Western ears sounds extremely rude, is not so in Aramaic. 'Woman' was a normal form of address (as it still is in, for example, Marathi where the word *Bai* has the same meaning and is used with great respect), and he was probably saying no more than, 'Mother, you must let me be the judge as to what is the right timing and appropriate way to begin my public ministry'. If it *were* a mild rebuke, she took it humbly, and quietly instructed the servants to do whatever he told them to do.

Whatever undercurrent there might have been of a need firmly to establish his independence, the situation was saved and the host spared the disgrace which would have befallen him, under the Eastern laws of hospitality, had he failed to supply sufficient food and wine for his guests.

Maybe there were occasions when there was still a remnant of that primitive masculinity which struggles with the domination of woman. The struggle, as we saw earlier in Chapter 1, begins early in life and intensifies around the time of puberty. The boy resists being drawn into the vortex of regression that would lead back to his original identification with mother. But the struggle often continues well beyond adolescence. In fact there is a sense in which masculinity develops in an endless struggle against mother and against original femininity, with all its traps from outside and inside.

In the *Odyssey*, Homer paints in vivid and unforgettable images, the endless struggle of man against woman and his fear of her engulfing presence. From the moment when Odysseus escapes from the formidable Cyclops, he encounters woman in all her phantasmic power. In Antiphates' wife he meets the man-eater woman. In Circe he encounters the seductress who enjoys trapping and humiliating men; in the Sirens and the Scylla and Charybdis he faces formidable engulfing feminine forces, while Calypso, a more benevolent and gentle goddess, is still dangerous because she seeks to keep Odysseus on her island for ever and prevent him from reaching Ithaca and regaining his kingdom. It is remarkable that all the forces of regression in Odysseus' travels are represented by women or female forces which he will have to defeat, overcome or outwit in order to reach Ithaca the goal of his journey and thus fulfil his masculine identity.[7]

Did Jesus ever feel that, like the gentle goddess Calypso, there was a dark, hidden force in Mary that wanted to keep her son 'on her island for ever' and thus stop him reaching his Kingdom? If, by any chance, there was ever a small element of that tendency in her, it was surely unconscious and by no means dominant. That perfect obedience that had accepted her own vocation with all its attendant suffering continued in her acceptance of his. But she was human, and it would have been impossible for her to avoid some of the very normal mistakes of parenting. No parent is faultless, for none of us has had a perfect parent model. All parents bring into their relationships with their children a legacy of wounding from the imperfect parenting they received themselves. But Mary's obedience and trust, so manifestly evident at the Annunciation, would have deepened with the passing years as she watched the nature of true or perfected humanness—in-the-making and learned to stand back and give her son space to discover himself – in relation to God and in relation to his vocation. Between them, she and Joseph would have done their utmost to make life as normal as possible for this very exceptional child. As one of the *anawim*, her desire to see the Kingdom of God established would have been, as we have seen, almost as intense as that of Jesus himself. Overriding any human frailty, her willingness to yield her son fully to his mission would have been expressed by that very renunciation for the sake of the Kingdom of which he spoke and which would yield a hundredfold.

Nevertheless, her pain and bewilderment must have been unbearable as she stood at the foot of the cross and realised the full impact of Simeon's prediction: 'A sword shall pierce your heart also.' The previous piercings were mere pinpricks and scratchings compared with this final excruciating plunging of the sword into the very centre of her being.

As he gazed down on her in his own agony, did Jesus have any sense of having failed her? Of having excluded her? Yet, how could he have told his followers that those who were not prepared to lose fathers and mothers 'for my sake and the Gospel' would be unworthy of their calling, if he had not been prepared to lose his own?

'He whose family ties are so strong that it is all-important to wait until his father has died and been buried (which being perhaps several years hence could mean an indefinite delay) before leaving home to follow Christ, is not fit for the Kingdom.'[8] So Jesus had said – but he could hardly have done so if he himself were so demonstrably attached to his mother, or she to him, that neither could make that necessary renunciation themselves, for the sake of the Kingdom.

I believe there was such a mutual surrendering of one another, despite any moments of natural weakness and human longing, that Mary was able at the last to comfort her son in his final agony simply by being there, staying with him in silent and adoring love, knowing that he had completed his work in the perfect obedience of total surrender to the Father. His gratitude to her must have been inexpressibly profound. 'We have no need of words, my Son and I', she said (in words put into her mouth by Dorothy Sayers) so great was their bond of understanding. As they came to that moment of final glorification, there must have been a 'rending of the veil' of the mystery with which she had lived and been pierced from the day he was conceived in her womb.

The Household at Bethany

Bethany was only an hour's journey from Jerusalem – near enough to be very convenient when Jesus went up for the feasts, and yet far enough away to offer peace, quiet and freedom from the pressure of being constantly surrounded by crowds.

Little detail is given of the family but there is a clear impression of intimacy with Jesus and established friendship. Martha, a good natured, practical lady is not afraid to speak her mind to him. 'Lord don't you care that my sister has left me to do the chores? Tell Mary to get up and help me', she says (Luke 10:40), and there is, perhaps understandably, an undertone of irritation. Jesus' reply, 'Martha, Martha, you are careful and troubled about many things. But one thing is needful: and Mary has chosen that good part which shall not be taken away', (Luke 10: 36–42) has sometimes been used to argue that the contemplative life is superior to the active one. The 'one thing needful' could refer to the Kingdom of God, or to the restfulness to be found simply by being with Jesus. It could also be a challenge to break with convention. For, if we pause to consider the customs amongst Jewish people of that time, we know that hospitality was a sacred duty, indeed a prized duty when it was a friend who was visiting. With all her conditioning from childhood onwards, Martha was doing what she had been trained to do. It was the practical expression of highest courtesy, and, in the case of Jesus, love too. Was Mary then behaving in a very untypical way for a Jewish woman? To Martha's way of thinking she was displaying the utmost discourtesy. Not unnaturally she was appalled. There may have been an element of jealousy that Mary could sit and listen to Jesus' news, enjoy his humour and receive all sorts of gems of wisdom, whilst she had to work doubly fast. The thought running through her mind may have been that they could both have enjoyed his company equally, if they shared the practicalities of making their much-loved guest comfortable.

Daniel Rops writes:

> It would appear that Jesus stayed in this friendly household during the months of October, November and December of the year '29. It was convenient for him, since he could go to Jerusalem whenever he wished without being obliged to spend the night there. It was off the beaten track and doubtless he felt safe there, but all the same we must admire the courage of this devoted family who were not deterred by the hostility of the powerful from welcoming their friend as a guest.[9]

Might it not have been that Jesus' reply was not so much a rebuke as an appeal to the nature of their friendship? If Daniel Rops is right in thinking Jesus stayed in that Bethany home for three months apart from all his previous visits, could it have been that he was implying, '*Martha*! Don't we know each other well enough for me to be regarded as "one of the family"? You don't need to put yourself out to treat me like any ordinary guest. I'm like a second brother to you. Come and sit down and let's just relax together and enjoy each other's company.'

During my time in Botswana, I travelled in the Kalahari desert to visit isolated people in several villages. Sometimes we would drive over very bumpy tracks, stirring up a cloud of sand, for four hours or more – all in intense heat. When at last we arrived at a village, there would be greetings and much shaking of hands. Then we would be led to some chairs and everyone would gather round to talk. The priests with whom I was travelling (themselves Batswana) would be kept very busy sharing news from Gaborone and other larger towns on the eastern side of Botswana, which the isolated desert dwellers longed to hear. As a westerner, after such a desperately tiring and uncomfortable journey, I longed for rather different things – water to freshen up and a mug of tea. But it was sometimes an hour or even two before a drink was provided. Talking was more important, and even when our hostesses began to think about some tea, it would take quite a while to get the open fire going and for the water to boil. For me it pointed up the difference in our customs. In our way of life, if someone arrived after a long and very tiring journey, almost the first thing we would do would be to show them where the bathroom was and plug in the electric kettle to make tea straight away. Only with a cup in our hands would we then settle down to talk.

Perhaps then, far from being lazy, Mary had got her priorities right. Talking and listening were of the first importance and Martha had not left enough space for that before leaping up to see to the Master's material needs. Mary's stillness and receptivity ministered to him in a far more satisfying way than could any amount of food and drink.

When their brother died, it was Martha who went out to meet Jesus with the admonition, 'If you had been here, our brother would not have died.' Martha it was who went in to Mary and said, 'The Master is coming and is calling for you.' Mary then went out to Jesus and said much the same – as a statement of fact rather than rebuke (John 11:2ff.). Had they not listened to numerous stories of healings Jesus had been able to perform – on complete strangers? Yet, here they were, his special friends, and just when *they* needed his healing power, he was somewhere else and not immediately accessible.

Jesus wept – an empathetic weeping with them. He must have felt rent in his sensitive heart to see the distress of these two women whom he loved so much.

The onlookers thought he was weeping for the loss of Lazarus. But might it not have been that he had foreknowledge of what would happen, and that the greatest of all his miracles would be wrought there in Bethany involving the family that claimed such a special place in his affections? For that miracle to take place, he had been obliged to abandon the sisters to enormous grief. At the same time, he would have felt their pain acutely. One wonders what the disciples thought, knowing as they did that Jesus had deliberately lingered for two days before responding to the sisters' cry for help, 'Lord, he whom you love is ill' (John 11:3). Were they surprised therefore to see Jesus weeping, knowing that, had he chosen to do so, he could have arrived earlier? Though admittedly, if Lazarus had been dead for four days by the time he arrived, he would still have been too late by one day, even had he set out for Bethany at once.

So little is told us of this special family – and least of all about Lazarus. It would seem that he lived with his sisters. They are the ones who are heartbroken at his death. No mention is made of a wife or children. Had Lazarus been married, would they not have featured in the story at least as co-mourners with the sisters? Indeed, their grief would surely have been even greater than that of Mary and Martha. Would it not have been his immediate family, rather than the sisters, who would have sent to Jesus to come to his dying friend?

There is no indication of their ages, of course, but since they were such close and supportive friends of Jesus, one would imagine they were probably his contemporaries.

If so, it was an unusual *ménage à trois*. Why was Lazarus not married – given that marriage was obligatory for Jewish men with few exceptions? Why, too, were Martha and Mary unmarried since normally they would have been engaged, betrothed and married whilst still fairly young? Even if their parents had died, other older members of the family would have stepped in and taken responsibility for their future, in the normal course of things.

Tom Wright says in his introduction to *Who Was Jesus?* that the Church has no vested interest in preventing people from coming up with new ideas about Jesus,[10] so I dare to share a question I have often asked myself (a question based on hunch since there is no way to prove or disprove the theory) and it is this. Was Lazarus perhaps handicapped – physically, mentally, or both? If so, it would help to explain the unusual composition of the household, the unmarried state of (it would seem) all three, and the intense grief of the sisters which was later to be shared by Jesus. A source of quite unique love would have been taken from them, for any of us who have lived amongst handicapped people will know all that is captured in that word 'unique'.

In one sense, all love is unique. But the love and affection of the mentally handicapped can be particularly refreshing because of its simplicity. It is what it is – direct, uncomplicated and often very demonstrative. Of course some people with handicaps can be canny and even manipulative, just the same as those without them. More often than not, however, there is an innocence about them, a certain transparency that rebukes our duplicity.

'Jesus wept', yet as far as we know he didn't weep at John the Baptist's martyrdom, or as he touched the bier of the widow of Nain's only son in compassion for her grief (Luke 7:11ff.). We hear nothing of the death of Joseph or any grief he felt at the loss of a man who had played such an immensely important part in his early formation. Yet, over Lazarus, he wept in such a way that it has been recorded – the only occasion that it is, other than his tears over Jerusalem.

Might it have been because he was aware just how great was the loss of this singular gift to the sisters, and indeed to the whole community? In Lazarus's death they would have lost that wealth of simplicity, vulnerability, purity and love that they had continually received from him, together with a lack of self-consciousness or complex motivation. Not without reason do the Russian Orthodox call people with handicaps 'The Holy Ones'.

Had Jesus recognised in Lazarus a 'holy one'? Did he represent for Jesus almost an alter-ego? Was he as near to the Father's heart as any Jesus had met? Was the great anguish of Martha and Mary partly because, with the loss of Lazarus their brother, they felt it was like losing the presence of Jesus himself from their home? Like many mentally handicapped people, Lazarus may have borne more of the *imago Christi* than do so-called 'normal' people. In their deaths we lose a rich, spiritual vein that runs through society; we lose their particular insights that have the power to go to the very heart of a truth.

When Jesus raised Lazarus, was he still handicapped? I like to think so, and perhaps Jesus realised how much the world at large needs the 'holy ones' to be a purifying agent in the midst of so much corruption, intrigue, greed and struggle for power, in which society as a whole and we as part of it, are ensnared.

If Lazarus were raised as the Lazarus they had always known and dearly loved, then it would account for the rather surprising fact that we hear no more of him. Why, for example, did he not go up to Jerusalem to stand by and support Jesus? Was it that Jesus suspected that this visible evidence of his power would only exacerbate the anger of the religious authorities who had heard accounts of the miracle of Lazarus's resurrection? Very probably, in their desperate attempts to stop rumours spreading, they would have seized Lazarus and put him away. Jesus would not have wanted to expose him to danger and the terror of being separated from his securities. He probably wouldn't let Lazarus go up to Jerusalem and face the incredulous gaping of the crowds ... or the ridicule of those with no understanding of the unique giftedness of the handicapped and of the specially dear place they hold in the heart of God – for there is a permanently child-like quality about them. And had not Jesus said very emphatically that only the child-like would be able to enter the Kingdom of God? In his own vision of the Kingdom, would Jesus not have seen Lazarus as having a place of pre-eminence?

John

<hr />

No clues are given in the Gospels as to why Peter, James and John were the specially close friends of Jesus from amongst the disciples, nor why out of them all John was the disciple 'whom Jesus loved'. That claim is only found in John's own Gospel (John 13:23; 19:26; 20:2) where he also mentions that he sat next to Jesus, leaning on him, at the Last Supper (John 21:20). Why, I wonder, was the disciple on the other side of him not named – unless of course it was Judas himself?

Jesus may have found in John someone to whom he could relate at a deeper level than most. He may well, even as a young man, have been a very reflective person, someone of a mystical temperament who pondered things in silence, and perceived truth at a depth not matched by any of the other disciples. Certainly his reaction to and behaviour at the empty tomb would suggest that he was able to grasp the mystery of Christ's resurrection before Peter and the others.

In his older years we have evidence of his apprehension of truth through vision, reflection and contemplation. Maybe Jesus was particularly drawn to John for the same reason that he resonated so deeply with Mary of Bethany and loved her for her readiness to sit at his feet in quiet contemplative listening.

John hadn't always been 'of a gentle and quiet spirit' of course – not with a nickname like 'Son of Thunder' (Mark 3:17)! Both he and James appear to have had a hot-headed streak in them; angry at the rejection of Jesus they were eager to call down fire from heaven upon a village. Is there a hint here, that they felt slighted themselves by the non-welcome? And they were ambitious too (or their mother was for them). Moreover they were immature and insensitive enough to let their request for the privileged seats in the Kingdom be known to the others. Not surprisingly, there was angry murmuring amongst the brethren.

Neither of these two latter qualities could have been particularly endearing to Jesus, and yet he singled them out to share with him his most intimate moments – the mysterious experiences of Transfiguration and the last vigil of prayer in Gethsemane, as well as the raising of Jairus' daughter.

Was it that he foresaw the vital leadership they would eventually exercise in the Church – James in Jerusalem, John in Ephesus and Peter in Rome? Was it chiefly for *their* spiritual edification that he took them apart? Or was it his own need for companionship – friends to share his experiences of deepest significance?

Inevitably the term, 'the disciple whom Jesus loved' has led to speculation. Since unquestionably he loved all his disciples, why this mention of a specific love for John? Was there a homosexual attraction between them? 'It has been observed that the homosexual character, if such a thing can be said to exist in its perfect state, is often sensitive to spiritual realities, to beauty, to innerness. . . .'[11], and certainly these qualities could be found in both Jesus and John as they are portrayed in the Gospels. However, for the very reasons he did not become romantically entangled with Mary Magdalen, I believe Jesus did not enter into a homosexual relationship with John, or anyone else for that matter. His acceptance of voluntary celibacy closed the door to any exclusive relationship and paved the way to that communion of hearts on which the Kingdom would be built.

My argument rests, of course, on the belief that, firstly Jesus did feel called to renounce marriage for the sake of the Kingdom, and secondly that the bringing in of the Kingdom and establishing its values as priorities, was his all-consuming desire – one might almost describe it as a 'holy obsession'! Nothing seemed to deflect him from this course – neither deprivation, rejection, misunderstanding, ridicule nor suffering. If in his total dedication to that purpose he could face such hostility, hurt and wounding, any longings for physical intimacy through a clandestine relationship which would hinder his one over-riding passion would have been killed stone dead the minute they began to emerge. He would have regarded them as a precluded form of self-gratification and a diversion of that accessible, all-encompassing love he so wanted to offer to all.

In purely practical terms it would have been difficult, to say the least, to conduct a homosexual relationship under the constant scrutiny of eleven other men with whom they were in close proximity.

Any relationship that could not be openly recognised and mutually honoured, and especially one that would be the cause of jealousy, division and scandal, would have been repellant to Jesus. From the Scriptural injunctions in the Old and New Testaments, we may assume that homosexuality was practised amongst Jews – though the references are sparse (Leviticus 20 and Romans 1:26–7). Jesus himself, it seems, made no particular pronouncement about it.

Whilst he established the precedence of love over law in other respects, it was always love without dissimulation, without deception, without the need of a web of lies to safeguard and surround it.

If Jesus embraced celibacy for the sake of the Kingdom, then he would have been celibate not only in name but in aspiration, intention and in practice. One cannot imagine that he would have cheated – publicly appearing to be single, but privately bonded secretly and sexually to a particular disciple – and I make this claim for two reasons.

Jesus was a man of huge integrity. He could move fearlessly among his critics by virtue of the very fact that he had nothing to hide. He knew neither guilt (for anything he had done) nor shame (for anything he was). Since there is little doubt that the Scriptures as he knew them seemed sternly to disapprove of same-sex sexual activities, Jesus could scarcely have rejoiced openly in a homosexual love for John.

Without entering into a discussion of homosexuality per se, I simply claim that to accept the gift of celibacy with its 'wide angle lens' form of love, but secretly engage in a 'zoom lens' type of love focused on a one-partner, exclusive relationship, would not have been conceivable to Jesus. He lived, I am convinced, in chastity and virginity of heart.

> In Latin, chastity is translated *integritas*. It suggests integrity or single-mindedness. There is a high distraction and destruction quotient in sexuality: it can do violence to relationships, it can ruin careers, it can take one's mind off things on which one's mind ought to be. So, there is always something of a struggle towards integrity, a unity of being between will and heart. It is possible to do the right thing for the right reason; to restrain oneself, not out of fear, inhibition or the wrong kind of God-hauntedness, but because it makes human sense, because there are other things to be done, because life is bigger than sex.[12]

For Jesus there were bigger things in his life than the delights of

sexual pleasure or indeed an exclusive intimacy. There was love –
the deep satisfying love that came from the Father; the nourishing
love of friends with which he was surrounded; and there was the
Kingdom – which required his freedom and availability.

Secondly, in *his* book, it would have been cheating to opt for
celibacy and receive the gift and joys given with that vocation on
the one hand, and then take it back by subterfuge on the other. One
of the possible reasons why people of this age seem bent on marrying
Jesus off to Mary Magdalen or linking him to John in a homosexual
relationship, seems to stem from a belief that celibate life is by its
very nature arid and joyless. It is assumed one cannot live fully and
richly as a virgin. But just as all callings involve renunciation so each
has its own gift. Virginity does not imply an attempt to be asexual.
Sexuality, properly embraced, is one means to wholeness and self-
awareness. It combines an irrepressible longing to love and be loved
with the energy that gives us the very power by which we live.
Sexuality gives us the drive to go beyond ourselves, to communicate,
to build community, to foster relationships of reality and depth and to
be creative. Sex is only one component, and by no means the most
important one in our sexuality. Far deeper is our need for relationships in which there is commitment and security without manipulation or exploitation.

> The objective is to clear a bridge, freed from both egocentric
> distortion and compulsive overadaptation, across which free
> communication may pass and so permit two simple human
> beings to experience themselves, each other and the maximum
> current of life that belongs in the situation between them. In
> this way love and meaning unite in a life experience which is
> not only personal, but also, in a deeper sense, truly religious.[13]

Living as a virgin, I believe Jesus was able to incarnate that life-
creating power of sexuality and show the fearless freedom in loving
that would be the hallmark of the Kingdom. Living as he did, he
demonstrated that celibacy and chastity could be truly fulfilling,
enabling a person to be 'interpersonally unfearful, clearly sexual and
warmly human.'[14] He incarnated his own sexuality in such a way
that showed to his followers for all time that where human love is
concerned, the heart is the central organ; and where the Kingdom
is concerned, love of the heart is the central reality.

Mary Magdalen

The depth of love between Mary Magdalen and Jesus, as the Gospels reveal, is undeniable. It is quite possible that, for a while at any rate, she was in love with him. But, was he in love with her? That question has, of course, given rise to much speculation – indeed even to dogmatic claims.

In her book, *Jesus the Man: A New Interpretation from the Dead Sea Scrolls* (published in 1992 by Doubleday) Barbara Thiering claims (and it guaranteed her book extraordinary and worldwide publicity, not to mention a place amongst the bestsellers) that Jesus was married to Mary Magdalen, that he fathered a daughter and two sons; that they subsequently divorced and that Jesus was then married again – this time to Lydia!

The so-called scholarly 'evidence' is so flimsy and is from such obscure references it lends little credibility to her argument. Another book published in the same year and written by Bishop John Spong of New York[15] also makes the claim that Jesus was quite probably married – to Mary Magdalen, naturally! But again, the reasons for this claim are unconvincing. Both books have been examined critically by Tom Wright and his findings are well worth reading.[16]

Whilst Mary is one of the most colourful characters of the Gospels, we have surprisingly little information about her – though a good deal more, let it be said, than about most of the disciples. What we have is enough to create a vivid and powerful impression of a strong, impetuous, passionate woman. She was healed by Jesus of some form of emotional, psychological and spiritual disturbance or disorder attributed to demonic possession (Mark 16:9, Luke 8:2). She was one of the women who followed from Galilee caring for the material necessities of Jesus and his disciples (Luke 8:3). We know that she was at the foot of the cross out of loyalty, love and her longing to be as close as possible to Jesus for as long as possible (Luke 23:55,

John 19:25). She accompanied the body to the tomb in the garden and sat over against it whilst the Romans rolled the stone into place and sealed it (Matthew 27:57ff.). She joined the other women in preparing spices to take to the tomb early in the morning on the first day of the week to complete the customary burial rituals (Matthew 28:1, Mark 16:2, Luke 24:10, John 20:1ff.).

In Matthew's account Mary and another Mary meet the risen Lord as they return from the tomb (Matthew 28 1–10). In John's account, however, (John 20:1–18) she was at one point alone at the tomb, weeping, when Jesus appeared to her very personally in risen form and commissioned her to break the news of his resurrection to the disciples – which she did, and which has given rise to the Orthodox title for her of 'Apostle to the Apostles'. According to Luke this was not viewed too favourably by the disciples and they refused to believe such an 'idle tale' (Luke 24:11). Tradition has it that she eventually went to Provence as a missionary and ultimately died there.

The part she was able to play in supporting Jesus through his suffering, and in the practical ministrations afterwards, must have been some consolation to her, however little, in her own sorrow. But, elsewhere I have written more fully of Mary's relationship to Jesus.[17] Here, since we are considering *our Lord*'s affective life, it is appropriate to concentrate more on Jesus' relationship with Mary.

In the Jewish culture of that day, falling in love was not the necessary prerequisite or prelude to marriage – though frequently deeply loving and stable relationships could (and still do) grow out of arranged marriages. It was held that there was a certain safety in accepting the wisdom and mature judgement of the family or matchmaker, with clear expectations of fidelity, loyalty and role-fulfillment within the marriage, whereas romantic love which follows the dictates of the heart would be considered precarious. Even if Jesus were in love with Mary, which we need to consider further, it is not evidence that they were married.

I have already argued that Mary and Joseph tried to prepare Jesus gradually and sensitively for his God-ordained destiny and, in order not to put any obstacle in the way of his fulfilling it, refrained from arranging a marriage for him. They recognised his need for total freedom to discern God's will and the way in which he was to fulfil it.

It is not that celibacy is a higher vocation than that of marriage nor that the idea of a married Jesus is shocking. But there are certain callings which require an availability, a freedom to take risks and to love in a particularly inclusive way that precludes an exclusive relationship. From the Gospels there seems to be no shred of real evidence to support the claim that Jesus was married. Surely, so major a relationship would not have gone unrecorded. If the Gospel writers can tell us that Mary, the *mother* of the Lord, was at the foot of the Cross, it would seem strange that they failed to mention that she was accompanied by Mary, the *wife* of the Lord – if indeed Mary Magdalen were that. It is true that in his parables he spoke of wedding feasts, but there is no indication that they refer to his own. Weddings were a normal part of life and everyone loved a wedding feast (after all, they lasted for a week or more and in a country where poverty and hunger were rife, they would have been awaited eagerly and enjoyed to the full. There would have been music and dancing, much fun and laughter, food and drink and the kind of abandoned festivity found uniquely amongst the poor). As we know, Jesus used ordinary, everyday events, local customs and scenes as the raw material of his parables. He would have connected readily with his hearers by mention of a wedding.

When he was criticised for not fasting as the disciples of John the Baptist did, he said, 'Can the wedding guests fast while the bridegroom is still with them?' (Mark 2:18f.). It was an analogy used for teaching purposes. There is no reason to conclude that it is a reference to his own wedding or to his being a literal bridegroom.

It is, of course, always said that one cannot argue from silence either – but it is not total silence. When he spoke of those called to celibacy for the sake of the kingdom, there may well have been personal implications. He wasn't then speaking in parables to crowds, for this concept would certainly not be a norm. Many would have been puzzled by such a statement, especially in view of the obligation to marry with which most would have been strongly imbued. Following his words about the injustices to women of the divorce laws, his disciples said to him – perhaps somewhat gloomily or with a touch of dry sarcasm – 'if such is the case of a man with his wife, it is better not to marry' (Matthew 19:10). But, he said to them: 'Not everyone can accept this teaching, but only those to whom it is given. For there are eunuchs who have been so since birth, and there are eunuchs who have been made eunuchs by others, and there are eunuchs who have made themselves eunuchs for the sake of the Kingdom of Heaven. Let anyone accept this who can' (Matthew 19:10–12).

Although this statement is in no way proof that Jesus felt called to celibacy, it is certainly clear that he saw the renunciation of

have been a particularly comfortable person to be with
ters.

rd of a wife who left her husband, not because her love
gone dead, nor because there was any 'third party'
she wrote to him, 'You are *so* good, I simply cannot
living with you.' Being with people of utter integrity,
dness and purity can, as we know, be very daunting. It
a foretaste of judgement. The light in them shows up
; we feel shabby in their presence, it spotlights our own
people of truth.

ther than Mary, might also have loved Jesus and perhaps
ow him and be known by him more deeply; and yet at
e might they not have feared his powers of perception,
see through masks and smoke screens to the truth and
of a person? There would probably be a sense of never
live up to his standards. No one could ever have been
at. His unpredictability, his single mindedness, his total
is need for solitude, and his fearless challenge to hypoc-
n and hardheartedness must have made them aware,
that he was not only beyond their reach but would be
oo much for them as a daily, intimate companion.

as Mary learned to relax in his most unusual love, her
have been purified and purged of any self-seeking, any
ossess or be possessed. She must have come to realise
could never be narrowed down and focused through the
narriage partnership. Its breadth was such that it could
han embrace the whole world. And basking in the security
her own was able to widen out too, seeking only to give,
ing for herself. If ever any hankerings for Jesus as a
er had obtruded – even if only in her secret areas of
imagination – she would doubtless have recognised that
ongings switched track or did a complete gear-shift, she
g all. To seek him as a lover would have been to forfeit
ninhibited friend. Her relationship with Jesus was so all-
to her, she would not have been prepared to put in
the joy and freedom they found in their love for one
thing was more fulfilling than that.

, the sensitive, intuitive love and friendship of women
f immense importance and surely quite rare in his culture
ccepting celibacy as a gift – with, of course, its renunci-
chiefly as gift – allows unparalleled freedom in relation-

marriage as necessary for some – '*for the sake of the Kingdom*'. And
it seems probable that, in recognising the call of God to some to live
a life which in many ways swims against the strong current of natural
longings, biological urges and social expectations, he felt himself
called to pioneer such a vocation for the sake of the Kingdom, and
so accepted voluntary celibacy. If such a call is given, the grace to
live out that call in joyful fulfilment is also given. For, 'the call is the
enabling gift that fires the life of charity.'[18]

If we accept that Jesus saw celibacy as part of his total vocation
in inaugurating the Kingdom, what then might have been the nature
of his feelings and his love for Mary Magdalen, since his expectations
would obviously not have included marriage?

His first encounter with her must have begun with a love born of
compassion. It would be difficult to heal someone in the way he
healed Mary, with tenderness and sensitivity, without also loving
her. That would be generally true of the many he healed. But with
Mary perhaps his love went deeper, his compassion extended further
than usual, because he saw how much she had been the victim of
circumstances and male abuse. He saw the goodness and potential
beneath the outer shell she had been forced to develop, for her own
self-preservation and sanity. Looking on her, perhaps he loved her
as he loved the rich young ruler, seeing in her as in him, the possibilities, the kind of all-out passionate devotion that could do infinitely
more to bring in the Kingdom than the rectitude of those who stood
on their moral high ground and pointed the finger of judgement at
her. He saw how her extravagant generosity of spirit could be like
fire to the kindling to create a blaze. Possibly he was frustrated
beyond words with the dreary 'do-it-yourself' attempts to live the
good life and 'get it right according to rules' that seemed to be so
prevalent in his day – leading to a dry, unrewarding and loveless life.
Here he saw a person for whom love – utterly unselfconscious,
passionate love – would be the central, guiding light of her life from
now on. He saw someone whose love-longings, born of her deep
experience of forgiveness, were a perfect complement to his own.
Was there perhaps a marriage of minds and hearts, a marriage of
desires and aspirations without a marriage of bodies – a 'love of the
heart rather than the groin' as Ronald Rolheiser puts it?[19]

Jesus' one great passion was 'the Kingdom' and he saw in Mary a
kindred spirit who shared that passion. With one object of their
desire their eyes would both be fixed on that horizon.

Jesus must, of course, have realised the dangers too in such a love.

Undoubtedly, Mary's eyes were not at first always fixed on that shared goal. Whilst he looked for the Kingdom, she probably looked at him. Initially at any rate, she would have been baffled as to what kind of man he was. She had never met his sort before. He seemed to love her without asking anything of her in return. Other men had their pleasure and took all they could get, leaving nothing but a sour after-taste of bitterness and disgust. And she no doubt despised them for it, as most prostitutes despise their clients, joking about them behind their backs in utter contempt. So when, in the musical *Jesus Christ Superstar*, Mary sings 'I don't know how to love him . . . he's a man, he's just a man . . .' (a song which caused considerable uproar in some Christian circles when *Superstar* first hit the West End, because of the implication that as 'just a man' Jesus was only human and not divine), I think we glimpse a true reflection of how she must have felt. He *was*, at that stage, 'just a man' to her, and yet quite unlike any other she had ever encountered. When he looked at her it was with love and not lust – and she scarcely knew how to meet so pure a gaze. He treated her with dignity and respect – as he did any human being. But because it was beyond anything she had experienced before, he broke through her reserves to her woundedness and her craving for deep, genuine love of the heart which went far beyond any desire for sex.

In his presence she felt healed and clean. She grew in proper self-esteem and confidence. Life had a new centre and purpose all of a sudden, and she longed to leave Magdala and all its associations. In her case, it seems, Jesus consented, letting her join his band of followers (amongst the women) whereas with others he healed, he instructed them to stay where they were that their healing might be a sign to their own town or village folk of the breaking in of the Kingdom.

Jesus must have known that he had won the devotion of Mary's heart, but it was crucially important to their relationship that she should learn to trust the love of man without fearing that, at the end of the day, it would not be for herself that she would really be wanted, but for her body. And as Mary gradually came to understand the nature of his non-judgemental, unconditional acceptance, she clearly felt an overwhelming need to express her love outwardly in some way. By its very nature love must always give, but perhaps the last thing she wanted to give or even offer him, was her body which had been used so meaninglessly and wantonly, as anything but an expression of love.

So she conceived the idea [...] precious and very pure, and [...] conventions and doubtless bri[...] very headstrong, take flagrant [...] of folly. Disregarding whatever [...] his guests might feel, she enter[...] feet of Jesus pouring out her lo[...] Completely indifferent to the [...] totally absorbed in Jesus and h[...] contemplation. Having broken [...] Jesus, she began to wipe his f[...] her with very long, beautiful ha[...] that Magdala can mean 'hairdre[...] as a place where dyes were mad[...] almost permanently over the p[...] south west it could pollute eve[...] Galilee. No doubt the women of [...] from which spikenard is made i[...] smell that clung to them. But it [...] of this crushed down brown [...] essential oil.

Jesus must have admired her [...] ably profoundly moved at her un[...] On total and transformed love [...] kind of faith and insight show[...] founded. He saw her love as hav[...] the present and for the future. [...] guests that wherever the Gospel [...] this expression of Mary's love, [...] has its own attraction; total com[...] and a challenge, and Mary's ex[...] see, reverberate down through [...] powerful consequences.

Despite times when Mary mu[...] closer intimacy, for opportunities [...] speak very personally to her in r[...] allowing herself to fantasise abo[...] there must also have been a se[...] Perhaps, though unconscious (on [...] be something that created a cert[...] likelihood it was simply his sheer,[...]

he could nc[...] at close qua[...]
I once he[...] for him ha[...] involved. A[...] bear to go [...] honesty, gc[...] is almost li[...] our darkne.[...] failings to [...]
Women, [...] longed to k[...] the same t[...] his ability t[...] to the reali[...] being able [...] capable of [...] dedication, [...] risy, ambit[...] albeit dim[...] altogether [...]
Graduall[...] own would[...] desire to [...] that his life[...] gates of a [...] do no less [...] of his love [...] asking no[...] sexual pa[...] thought ar[...] unless her [...] risked losi[...] him as an [...] important [...] jeopardy a[...] another. [...]
For Jes[...] was a gift [...] and age. [...] ations, bu[...]

ships. An unambiguous statement is made by the openly avowed acceptance of that calling and the ground is cleared of fears – fears of misinterpreted signals and misunderstood intentions. By flying in the face of the conventions of his day, Jesus points a way forward for us in ours.

'Good, healthy, open, chaste, life-giving heterosexual friendship is rare', said Ronald Rolheiser. 'It is not that we do not crave for it or value it, it is just that we rarely find it.'[20] People complain that it is easier to find a lover than a friend.

Normally speaking it would be true to say that in heterosexual friendships there are likely to be tensions, inhibitions, unspoken agenda, awkwardnesses and coquetry and a certain amount of game-playing. 'Sex is too powerful to allow men and women to be easily honest and upfront in friendship.'[21] And yet there is a desperate need for good heterosexual friendships and friendships in which there is real freedom – freedom from the need to do a balancing act between caution and risk, reservation and abandonment, inhibition and daring vulnerability.

One of the gifts of celibacy can be that very freedom and it was one which I believe Jesus enjoyed in his relationship with women friends and particularly with Mary Magdalen. With them he was able to revel in a rich communion of hearts, a reverential, non-exploitative love, the relief of feeling free to relax fully in mutual understanding and the celebration of the goodness of their friendship. 'The algebra of Christ's virginity is that, among other things, friendship and love, celebration and community, happiness and the Kingdom, lie in the coming together of hearts. Sexuality contributes to the building up and the consummation of this community of hearts only when it helps to lead to the joy and order that come from fidelity and chastity.'[22] It was to the 'consummation' of this 'community of hearts' that I believe the love of Jesus for Mary Magdalen and hers for him witnessed.

Embracing His Sexuality

Whether or not we lead an active sexual life, as human beings we are all sexual beings and every relationship has a sexual component within it. In his full humanity this was equally true of Jesus. As we have already seen, he was not asexual nor necessarily weakly sexed. He had to learn to embrace his sexuality and integrate it in such a way that it led to that wholeness which he longs for us all. It was part of his growth towards individuation – to use Jungian terminology – and it was as much *a process of learning* for him as it is for us. It involved struggle and growth. But what exactly is meant by sexuality?

As I understand it, it is where holiness and earthiness meet and it has a sacramental element within it. Sexuality is a large umbrella term and subsumes our need for relationship, connectedness, unity and wholeness which stems from our being made in the image of God. The same yearning for and fulfilment of that longing for unity which characterises the Trinity, expressing itself in a form of self-giving exchange, lies deep within each of us. 'We feel it is not good for us to be alone. We feel mysteriously incomplete, so all our life is a searching for a remembered unity we have never yet known. Sexuality is one of the modes of our search; it is both a symptom of our incompleteness and a sign of our fulfilment.'[23] That is the holiness part – the part of us that shares in the divine nature.

Part of the search for completion and connectedness may be expressed in actual sexual experience, which only fully yields what it promises when it is both a sign and seal of a covenant bond and a guaranteed mutual commitment. That is the earthiness part, for 'to be holy is not to be heavenly but to know God in one's earthiness and in one's flesh.'[24]

In the whole spectrum of sexuality, between the ideal and what may be the reality, lie many levels of relationship and fulfilled longings. Some barely touch the deep need for connectedness and some are richly satisfying – a foretaste of that completeness we shall one day know in God. The lowest and most dissatisfying of all the levels is that of casual or promiscuous sex. That which is so often held out as a panacea to our inner loneliness, ultimately ends up reinforcing it. It cannot deepen trust or offer lasting security and both are essential to total self-giving. The giving of the mystery of my 'self' to the mystery of another in mutual exchange is the essence of true relationships and mirrors, however faintly, the truth about our relationship with God. Where there are sacred bonds and honoured boundaries, fidelity and stability, there can be the freedom truly to know and be known – which was, of course, synonymous with sexual love in Hebrew idiom.

Within that whole spectrum of sexuality would be found the range of friendships that Jesus enjoyed, and enjoyed to the full with utter freedom because of the absence of ambiguous signals and false expectations. There was mutual attraction in his friendships, togetherness, sharing from the heart, and the risking of vulnerability. There was warmth of companionship with restful silences, the ministry of touch, sight and sound, sympathy, deep affection and trust. And they were immensely important to him – these friendships – with men and women, single and married, young (including children) and old. Despite the fact that they did not include sex, they expressed all the elements of the ideal in sexuality, for they embodied (and I use that word very specifically) the flow and inter-dependence of love within the family of the Godhead. And for Jesus, as has been submitted several times in the course of these reflections, the Kingdom of God was all about loving. In the Kingdom people would be drawn together in love, friendship, celebration, trust, community and playfulness.[25] Love would prompt mutual care and concern; love would be non-exploitative – no one would 'use' another as a 'thing', discarding him or her when no longer needed, without any regard for the trail of hurt feelings left behind . . . what Gerard W Hughes calls 'our "thingifying" tendencies.'[26] In the Kingdom, wounds would be healed rather than inflicted; true communication would lead to communion; fears would be banished and replaced by trust; all would be reverenced and accorded true worth; sex and sexuality would be channelled rightly and joyfully; the ache for wholeness, completion, and consummation would find its fullest satisfaction – but always through mutual love and respect.

This was the Kingdom Jesus believed he had come to inaugurate and incarnate within himself in his own relationships. The signs of that Kingdom would be wholeness – the restoration of the wounded and marginalised, with the blind seeing, the deaf hearing, the lame walking, the leper cleansed. The dead would be raised and the poor would hear the good news . . . and all this because of the infinite worth of each person. Love within the Kingdom would lift those who were made to feel little more than the flotsam and jetsam of society – dispensable and disposable – to a new level of dignity, a new sense of personal worth, a new hope of acceptance, a new halting belief that they might after all be lovable.

The embodying of this vision could only take place through an immeasurable energy of love. That is where Jesus directed the sheer power of his sexuality. I really question whether or not any one human being could have coped with being on the receiving end of such power in an exclusive partnership. Would he or she not always have felt disadvantaged by the paucity of his or her love in comparison? The scope of his love was such that it *had* to take in the whole world.

The integration of our sexuality implies an acceptance of our place as we see it in the complementariness of the man-woman relationship in society as a whole – which is different from accepting a role imposed *upon* us, as women by men, or vice versa! Can we not see Jesus transcending the role-expectations forced upon both sexes of his day, by relating to women freely and valuing their unique contribution to him as a person? We see how the need of an individual took precedence over convention in his encounter with the woman at the well. She was doubly suspect – she was a Samaritan and she was a woman, and moreover, a woman with a highly dubious reputation. His disciples were taken aback if not shocked to return from their shopping expedition and find him calmly conversing 'à deux' with such a woman (John 4:4ff.). It was almost unheard of in his day.

When the woman in the crowd touched the hem of his garment, Jesus' only concern was to meet her personally and assure her of the healing her faith had made possible. There was no hint of condemnation for the liberty she took, or for thereby having rendered him ritually impure without his consent – for to have direct contact with anyone with a discharge or menstrual flow (whether normal or, as in this case, abnormal) would have done just that (Mark 5:32).

He made no protest or attempt to halt the ministrations of Mary when she poured out the perfume of her love in holy extravagance as a fragrant offering to him – touching him, wiping his feet with her hair, defying 'good taste' and propriety (Luke 7:38).

Did he break through accepted norms in his tenderness and physical expressions of affection towards John, his beloved disciple? In his loving, as in so much else, he would not allow the social dictates of his day to define his behaviour if they made it less than fully loving. Perhaps he felt protective towards him as the youngest member of his group. Or possibly he realised something of his vulnerability in a way that the other disciples failed to appreciate. Nothing in the Gospels indicates that his love for him was uninhibited in ways that raised eyebrows at the time. Even John's 'leaning on the bosom' of Jesus at the Last Supper seems not to have provoked any adverse comment. I have not met any serious suggestion that the expression 'the disciple whom Jesus loved' is in any way a technical one, meaning a gay relationship.

Maybe in his heart of hearts, Jesus would have liked to go even further and draw the band of women followers more closely into his chosen group. But he would certainly not have exposed them to the criticism and shame that might have been meted out to them by the public at large had such an invitation been accepted. Nor would he have wanted to subject them to the physical hardships he and his disciples often had to endure – rolling up in their cloaks and sleeping under the stars with nowhere else 'to lay their heads'.

Jesus appears to have had few if any 'hang ups' about women. He dearly loved his disciples but was sometimes frustrated by their slowness to understand him, whereas the women whose friendship he cherished were often able to enter with greater intuitive powers into his feelings, his hopes, his longings and his vision for the Kingdom. Despite the limitations of what was proper and permissible in his day and culture, there seems to have been a real meeting of hearts.

Beyond his driving passion to establish the Kingdom as the ultimate loving community, must there not have been those times when as a human being he ached for completion? Did he ever find it difficult at times to handle normal, biological urges? Even to be as strongly motivated as he was by his sense of destiny would not have ruled out the natural instincts. All relationships, as we have noted, are coloured by the fact that we are sexual beings; and simply because we are sexed, there are many levels at which we experience ourselves as incomplete and lacking in wholeness. The very word 'sex' comes from the Latin word *secare* which means literally, to cut off or divide.

But the answer to that sense of incompleteness is not necessarily sex. It can never just be, as the poet Margaret Atwood puts it, '. . . a dentistry, the slick filling of aches and cavities.' Sex by itself will not cure our loneliness, for 'our deepest hungers are for heterosexual relations beyond having sex. The ache is for men and women to come together as more than lovers.'[27]

Jesus, by pioneering for his generation the possibility of good heterosexual friendships, and in many ways being ahead of his time in his attitude to women, went a long way to satisfying some of the deepest hungers that loneliness can create. And, any sense of incompletion would surely, for him, have found abundant comfort in his one-ness with the Father.

Where he did experience sexual longings might he not simply have given thanks for them as evidence of normal maleness and virility? After all, these are good longings, all part of God's design, who knew that it was 'not good for men (or women) to be alone.' Jesus spoke of a man leaving his mother and father and cleaving to a wife in a one-flesh union, as something right and proper, a relationship for all-round rejoicing. Would he not have given thanks that there was within him the potential for something so good and God-ordained, even though it was not something he was free to realise or fulfil within his particular calling?

At a conference for religious which I attended, we were actively encouraged to explore within ourselves the qualities of parenthood we each had. As those vowed to celibacy, I questioned whether or not this was looking back over our shoulders at the 'might have beens' in a dishonest way. The leader assured us, however, that there was nothing improper about owning our inbuilt qualities of motherhood or fatherhood, as perfectly good potential which could have been drawn out to the full had our vocation been to marriage. More than that, however, the exercise was designed to enable us to see how those gifts of mothering and fathering, that are all part of our make-up, could be channelled into our present vocation.

Jesus may well have pondered his own fatherly instincts as he watched children and entered into their games. Perhaps as he dwelt upon all that side of his nature which could not be directly brought into play, including his sexual potential, he saw such reflections as a way of quite deliberately channelling sexual energies into gentleness, tenderness, reverence for women and insight about their feelings. For by choosing virginity he was not denying the goodness of sex and certainly not implying that there was anything inherently wrong in it.

The very thought of Jesus fantasising in these areas could be extremely offensive to some people, but I believe any fantasies would have been such that there would have been no cause for shame before God – nothing dishonouring to anyone, nothing sordid or lustful.

Martin Scorsese's film *The Last Temptation of Christ* based on the book by Nikos Kazantzakis caused an enormous furore when it was released, largely because Jesus was portrayed as fantasising on the cross about Mary Magdalen and the home and married life he had spurned in order to do his Father's will as he perceived it. On the cross, however, he feels he has failed so utterly that his sacrifice may have been all for nothing. He might just as well have married, settled for a life of domesticity, and lived his full three score years and ten.

Even those who had never seen the film were up in arms at such a suggestion. Just the thought of it outraged them.

Was it Dr Johnson who wrote, '. . . when a man knows he is to be hanged in a fortnight, it concentrates his mind wonderfully'? It is hard to imagine anyone being able to fantasise about anything when suffering the kind of excruciating torture that we know Jesus endured in crucifixion. Even with much lesser pain, experience tells us that it has the power to fill our horizon and banish almost all other thoughts. And, after all, fantasising requires a certain degree of leisureliness. So, for that reason alone it could be argued that it was highly improbable that Jesus' imagination had any free rein.

However, the outcry was not only about Jesus fantasising on the *cross*, though that was offensive enough to many. I strongly suspect it was because of the suggestion that Jesus fantasised about marriage or sex at all. But as a fully sexed being, it would have been impossible and quite unnatural had he never thought about sex, particularly in his earlier years. Indeed, he could not have spoken about lust, adultery and fidelity as he did, had he not thought about them and the principles involved. With maturity, however, there is a change in sexuality that takes us beyond the ache for sex in any genital connotation to our longing for intimacy and creativity, both of which can be fulfilled without sex. Our sexuality needs to give birth to *something* and for Jesus, it was the Kingdom. As a sexual celibate, his fantasies would have conceived and helped bring to birth the new community which would be a life-enhancing, healing agent in a wounded world. Fantasies are the fruit of sensitivity and imagination, but they are not necessarily erotic or narcissistic. They can 'be fruitful' and can 'multiply' in giving birth to new vision. All great art begins in this way as Chaim Potok shows:

> The cascades of colour and form, the images that had possessed me: I would gaze at them inside myself, watching them grow from the empty point of their beginnings, from the void of non-being, to amorphous, shapeless lumps, and then simmer slowly into a moulded nucleus of life, fragile, tender, frightened, incomplete. The constant wide-eyed looking at the shapes inside myself. That strange sense of being possessed by the other.[28]

God calls to the artist in each of us to give space to that creative instinct in which he can inspire vision. He invites us to enter imaginatively into his heart to know, too, that 'strange sense of being possessed by the Other' in a fearless intimacy in which we experience fulfilment and completion.

Overdependent Relationships

◇◆◇◆◇◆◇◆◇◆◇◆◇◆◇◆◇◆◇◆◇◆◇◆◇◆◇◆◇◆◇◆◇◆◇

How might Jesus have handled difficult relationships? Was he, for example, ever irritated by histrionic, clinging types of people? Needs are needs and can make a person very greedy and demanding, and downright manipulative if those needs are not met to their satisfaction. This 'clinging ivy' syndrome is a fairly common phenomenon for clergy to have to cope with, and often it is very difficult to know how to discourage and terminate such a dependency without being rude or dismissive.

It would be most unlikely that Jesus never had to meet such a situation, given his attractive personality and single status (though it is by no means always single men or women who have to extricate themselves from an emotionally entangled relationship). How might he have acted?

As we have already noted, Jesus never allowed himself to be put on a pedestal: he never wanted to be there. Other people were anxious to put him there, and that can, of course, be very seductive. It was vitally important for Jesus that he didn't get sucked into traps of that kind. His freedom of heart was paramount to his mission.

If, in its early stages, his relationship with Mary Magdalen had been one of over-dependence on her part – and it would have been wholly understandable had it been so, in view of the emotional void her previous lifestyle must have created in her, and the overwhelming joy of the sudden replacement of lust by love – Jesus must gently have weaned her from the clinging to a proper detachment. Clearly it would have been an ongoing process culminating in the garden at his resurrection when she lapsed once more into her old fear-filled, clinging pattern of relating. He had to reassure her, gently encourage her to 'let go' and 'free fall' in his love so that she could discover 'the voice that calls us beyond the limits of human togetherness.'[29] He would have longed for her to know the freedom of a non-possessive, maturely independent love which could expand and deepen without his actual physical presence. That kind of love would enable her to fulfil the apostolic calling which he foresaw for her. The prospect of the loss of Jesus, who alone gave meaning to her life, was too awful to contemplate. So, in that resurrection encounter in the garden, he had to say to her for the last time, tenderly and compassionately, 'Don't cling to me. There is no need to be afraid. Don't cling to your projections of me. Don't cling to your preconceived expectations. Let me go, and set me free to go forward with you into a hitherto unsuspected and unimagined dimension of relationship'.

For Jesus, his protection always lay in the quality of his loving. With his attractive and accessible personality, he must always have been at high risk where dependent, insecure, attachment-seeking people were concerned, but he would surely have wanted to remain properly detached without being unkind or downright hurtful. That is far from easy! But he does leave us some clues.

There was never any self-seeking in his love. He never 'used' people to fulfil his needs. He asked his friends for help; he gratefully accepted hospitality from them and borrowed from them; he cherished the friendship of his disciples and wider circle of friends – indeed he recognised and acknowledged his wholly proper need for human love and companionship. But his friends never ended up feeling they had been exploited or used solely to meet his needs.

The only dependency he would actively encourage would be a total dependency upon the Father such as he himself practised. Probably because that was his only dependency, childish dependencies in others didn't pose too much of a problem. He could wean people away from them without being sucked into any kind of collusion. The Gospels give us a picture of someone who was almost 'cling-proof' in the sense that he himself had no need of adulation or devotion or self-gratifying relationships. Just as he wouldn't take on other people's guilt, he wouldn't take on their responsibilities either. If, for example, any of 'the women who followed them from Galilee and who provided for them' (Matthew 27:55) had begun to cling to him, weave improper fantasies around him and constantly angle for attention or engineer situations where they could be alone briefly, I am sure he would have reckoned it to be entirely their responsibility – not his. He would never buy into their need.

It is essential for those who become the object of obsessive and possessive relationships to have space – emotional as well as physical – if they are going to be able to cope with the feeling of a cloying, suffocating 'crush'. Jesus, as we know, made that need for space a priority in his life – albeit at the cost of sleep. His inner freedom was nurtured by his nights of solitude and prayer on the hill slopes of Galilee. There he was able to rest fully from the pressures laid on him by others. There he discerned the traps into which it would have been all too easy to fall. There he fostered that solitude of heart through which alone we are able to 'enter into the silence of our innermost being'.[30] There he ensured that his aloneness was protected, an aloneness in which he could commune with God who was his 'All'. There he could relax in blissful freedom from other people's projections and fantasies.

How might Jesus, then, help us to see the right approach to take in unsought hysteric or dependent relationships?

The histrionic person needs someone to idealise. That idealised person or indeed, idol, becomes the centre of the hysteric's world. Through identification his or her whole *raison d'être* becomes lodged in that one idol. But since that is an impossibly heavy burden to put on another human being, there will always and inevitably be a mighty crash when the 'idol' manages to topple him or herself exposing the feet of clay. Along with the idol, the hysteric's world is shattered. This is a recurring and devastatingly painful pattern in the 'clinger's' life.

It is the kind of dilemma in which it is not uncommon for spiritual directors to find themselves, and admittedly it has not always been sufficiently discouraged in the past, if it ministered to the director's need for power.

For example (and I use fictitious characters for the purpose of illustration), James was a priest. He was celibate (but not by vow), clever, much sought-after as a confessor, gentle, courteous, prayerful, Christ-like and fun. In the course of his retreats Isabel met him, went to him for counsel, found it very helpful and asked James if he would act as her spiritual director. Perhaps he was flattered or perhaps it fed into his need to be needed. Who knows? We are barely aware of our own true motives, let alone anyone else's.

Before long, Isabel was absolutely besotted with James – not primarily sexually, as she was considerably older than he. But it was an inevitable component in the sense that, as sexual beings, it is there in all our relationships. As time went by, Isabel's whole world began to revolve around James, to the extent that no matter who was celebrant at the Eucharist, it was James she saw behind the altar, James who administered the host, James with whom she conducted imaginary conversations. Or was it?

In actual fact, what she really saw was her fantasy, her projection of who James was. He became the son she had never had. She began to weave so many fantasies around him that eventually she became incapable of seeing the real man. Maybe without realising what he was getting into, perhaps not being sufficiently perceptive as to Isabel's true needs (though as an experienced director he should have been), James allowed her to pursue this course.

She was generous, kind, always remembered his birthday and ordination anniversaries, and showered him with gifts at Christmas, Easter and on any other occasion she could – all given so lovingly and with such obvious delight, he couldn't bring himself to refuse them. He was essentially a loving, kind person and hated to hurt anyone, let alone Isabel. And so the two of them got deeper and deeper into a relational quagmire.

He was unable to see that the gifts were not free gifts. They had a heavy price tag attached – and that price tag was Isabel's huge need. Isabel was ministering primarily to herself in these gifts – not to James.

He was an elusive and very private person which made him all the more ideal. Surrounded by an air of mystery as he was, he became the perfect blank screen for Isabel's projections – and that of a number of other people too. For there were others, amongst them a good many women, who competed for first place in his affections surrounding him in a network of jealousies and rivalries dressed up with spiritual labels that fooled no one . . . except James, it seems.

Perhaps he dismissed all this devotion as 'their' responsibility and walked away from each one not having given too much of himself. But it *was* his responsibility to know what mechanisms were at work, to check those who were projecting their fantasies on to him and bring them to a necessary disillusionment in so far as it was possible.

Through his lack of awareness and insight, James had made a fatal mistake. He had bought into Isabel's projections and then began to feel cheated because he wasn't allowed to be himself. It was impossible for him then to extract himself from the tentacles of Isabel's 'love' that had become so tightly entwined around him.

Finally, in desperation, he tried to have a heart-to-heart with Isabel – to suggest that perhaps she should draw back a little, be a little less dependent and leave more distance between them. She, of course, was utterly devastated. She had moved in too close and now

he wanted to back off – only to find his back was to the wall.
Suddenly the blank screen was blank no longer. It was filled with a
terrifying 'writing on the wall' that seemed to predict the death of
their relationship.

She wept and wept and made herself ill through worry and misery.
She expected James to come, cap-in-hand, and beg her forgiveness
for making her ill. He didn't. He was too busy enjoying a blessed
breathing space.

Suddenly for Isabel the centre of her world had dropped out and
her life collapsed around her in a heap. Her lovely dreams were
shattered. For James, his solitude of heart had been invaded and
seriously eroded, he had become trapped and now he felt guilty that
he was partially responsible for Isabel's distress. Her intense clinging
had led to what felt like total loss to her, and picking up the pieces
in that kind of bereavement is a complex matter.

Henri Nouwen's words, some of which have already been alluded
to, are very applicable and worth quoting in full.

> Without the solitude of heart, the intimacy of friendship . . .
> cannot be creative. Without the solitude of heart, our relation-
> ships with others easily become needy and greedy, sticky and
> clinging, dependent and sentimental, exploitative and parasitic,
> because without the solitude of heart we cannot experience
> others as different from ourselves but only as people who can
> be used for the fulfilment of our own, often hidden, needs.
>
> The mystery of love is that it protects and respects the alone-
> ness of the other . . . In this solitude we can strengthen each
> other by mutual respect, by careful consideration of each other's
> privacy, by a reverent understanding of the sacredness of the
> human heart. In this solitude we encourage each other to enter
> into the silence of our innermost being and discover there the
> voice that calls us beyond the limits of human togetherness . . .
> we can slowly become aware of the presence of him who
> embraces friends and lovers and offers us the freedom to love
> each other, because he loved us first (1 John 4:19).[31]

Much of Jesus' ability to discern what was going on beneath the
surface in a relationship was directly due to the solitude of heart he
so assiduously guarded. As far as we know, he never once invited
any disciple (not even John) to accompany him in his nights of
prayer. That all-important aloneness with the Father not only put
him in touch with the divine wisdom he needed in order to penetrate

to the truth of relationships, it also replenished the divine love which poured out through him responding unerringly to people's needs without ever getting trapped by them. It was pure love without any conditions or price tags. It was a love that set people free and left them free.

Woe to any counsellor, pastor, director or priest who believes and is flattered by the one who claims, 'You are the only person I have ever been able to talk to – you are the only one who has ever really listened to me.' We buy into that at our own peril. We can guarantee that he or she is talking to several other confidants and will have said much the same to each of them. When conflicting advice is given, and is relayed back from one counsellor to another, it creates a tangled set of reactions – envy, desire to retaliate, annoyance if not real anger. Perhaps they made us feel, 'I'm a wonderful counsellor', but if we needed them to make us feel good about ourselves, then their semi-rejection would be bound to leave us feeling depleted.

Jesus wouldn't have got drawn into all that stuff, for the simple reason that above and beyond all human relationships – even the richest – ultimately he looked to one source alone for his energy, for confirmation or affirmation. He never needed it from anyone else, whether women or men, *in order* to feel of worth or good about himself. Always and only he looked to the Father to minister to his personal need for affirmation. There was no fear attached to that sole dependency, for it was the fruit of perfect love.

Jesus' example points us to the need for solitude of heart to give us right discernment; for inner freedom from the need to be needed; for the wisdom and far-sightedness to disappoint people's expectations at an early stage if they are going to become 'sticky and clinging'; for the discipline to turn resolutely from all flattery. 'Why do you call me good?' he asked the rich young ruler (Mark 10:18). Here was someone he could love deeply. It was as though he was saying to the young man, 'Don't spoil the relationship by flattery'; for a burning desire that in all relationships, whether friends or lovers, the mutual love should be of the kind that draws both into a closer relationship with God. That is ultimately the greatest safety and no one has expressed it more beautifully than Temple Gairdner in the prayer he wrote on the eve of his wedding, a prayer the *sentiments* of which can be translated into other relationships.

That I may come near to her, draw me nearer to Thee than to her; that I may know her, make me to know Thee more than her; that I may love with the perfect love of a perfectly whole heart, cause me to love Thee more than her and most of all. Amen. Amen. That nothing may be between me and her, be Thou between us, every moment. That we may be constantly together, draw us into separate loneliness with Thyself. And when we meet breast to breast, my God, let it be on Thine own. Amen. Amen.[32]

5

'THROUGH A MIRROR
DIMLY'

The Unconscious

One doesn't have to dig very far below the surface in any one of us, so we are told by the psychoanalysts, before we reach some pretty murky depths. What is more, those depths are the common property of the human race. Jung himself proposed this in his theory of the 'collective unconscious', claiming that we are all inextricably bound up with the past as well as the present. The unconscious contains an archetypal inheritance that is passed from generation to generation, is global and cultural, and encompasses a collective memory. (The word 'archetypal' refers to those patterns of psychological functioning latent in the collective unconscious which are universal in content and meaning and are as powerful in the psychological realm as are instincts in the physiological.)

There are even early stirrings of this in very primitive cultures. Archetypal symbols have emerged which are common to myths, folklore, fairy stories and wisdom literature of all ages and peoples. They are found, for example, in the native wisdom of African, Aboriginal, North and South American Indian myths, the themes of which cluster round such figures as the Great Mother, the Wicked Witch, the Giant, the Wise Old Man, the Crone, the Beggar. They are universal symbols repeated over and over again and imbued with deep significance.

Sometimes our dreams are peopled by these archetypes; sometimes they convey rather horrifying evidence of the kind of muck there is in our depths, which mostly we experience as beyond our control to change or discharge.

If that is true, and of course Jung's theories do not go undisputed (but nor should we simply dismiss them because we find them unpalatable), the question we must consider is, 'Did Jesus, since he was fully human, share in that collective unconscious? Did he also have to wrestle with his "Shadow"? (In her book *Knowing Women*,

Irene Claremont de Castillejo writes: 'The "shadow" is that part of the psyche which could and should become conscious, yet of which we are unaware. It contains bright undeveloped potentials as well as dark, unpleasant, repressed elements – painful memories etc.')

Did Jesus find unbidden thoughts, instincts and urges surfacing from the depths? If so, did he own them as part of his personal responsibility or regard them simply as part of the collective junk he was obliged to accept as a member of the human race? Was he in some exceptional way able to exercise any control over his unconscious? Was he aware of a collective memory being formed out of some kind of evolving chaos? One thing we do know – he escaped nothing of what is involved in being human. And that would inevitably mean grappling with his unconscious – without which he could not have lived. All of us have whole areas of our being that are hidden from our consciousness and Jesus, too, had to have something unavailable to himself to work on, if he was to *grow into* maturity, rather than reach it unnaturally without effort – which would have rendered him a freak.

This recognition of his unconscious and his shadow was essential in order to be truly incarnate. He could not avoid the inescapable suffering and struggle involved in being human.

It has been suggested that our personalities are like four windows.[1] The first window reveals that part of us that the public sees. The second window represents what other people who really *know* us see, and are prepared to reflect back to us; the third is what *we* know of ourselves; and the fourth is the part unknown to ourselves or anyone else. It is this fourth window that represents the unconscious. Perhaps this was in part what St Paul meant when he said, 'For now we see through a glass darkly, but then face to face'. And it isn't the 'darkened glass' of that fourth window that alone limits our understanding. From our own personal perspectives, too, everything becomes distorted and we are not even aware of it.

St Paul expresses it very differently from Jung, and yet, in his own way, is he not pointing to the same truth – that the window on to the self that *we* know, only demists little by little and will never reveal us to ourselves fully in this life? However, the Christian belief is that, after death, all *will* be revealed. 'Now I know in part; then I shall understand fully, even as I have been fully understood' (1 Corinthians 13:12). Meanwhile, the ongoing challenge in this life is to befriend our Shadow trying to meet and embrace these hidden aspects of ourselves as and when they are gradually brought to light.

For the Shadow is made up of all sorts of unborn and unloved bits of ourselves – parts that we have never allowed to come to birth, and others that have been pushed away, disowned and rejected.

One writer has suggested that the story of Jacob at Peniel could well symbolise his wrestling with his unconscious – with what he really didn't want to know. And yet, Jacob refused to let the stranger go until he revealed his identity. There was an ambivalence in Jacob – not wanting to yield to that Unknown Being yet desperately needing to name him. Could he have been encountering his Shadow, wrestling with some part of it only just coming into focus as it were, needing to name, own and reclaim it as part of himself? In order to do that he had to be able to make that identification.

Don't we all have that experience in dreams? There are times when we are very near recognising the people we meet in them, very near grasping some truth . . . but it eludes us and we are left struggling to give shape and expression to something strange yet familiar, emerging from the mists of the unconscious.

What evidence, if any, is there that Jesus neither denied nor repressed his Shadow? First and foremost, since he had the ability to help others to befriend theirs, he must have had the power to do so for himself.

Perhaps one of the areas which he had to explore in depth was that of prejudice. Throughout the Gospels he seemed always to be working through the Jewish-Gentile dichotomy. Within himself he carried cultural attitudes and racial memories – a special sense of being one of the Chosen People of God. That choice has often been the cause of pride and prejudice among Jews in the past – their claim to privilege. To enter into that particular shadowland of prejudice therefore would, normally speaking, constitute a huge hurdle to any Jew. It is not, of course, peculiar to the Jewish culture. David Lloyd George in a speech at Cambridge (1927) said: 'Every man has a House of Lords in his own head. Fears, prejudices, misconceptions – these are the peers, and they are hereditary.'

In his encounter with the Syrophoenician woman, Jesus seemed to be wrestling with that very area and working through to a place of personal freedom from attitudes dictated by his Jewish culture and tradition – especially those concerned with racial distinctions. He was able to disentangle himself from the influences that had helped shape his own assumptions and freely choose his course of action based solely on love – a love in which fear, the great enemy, had been cast out.

The Samaritan woman at the well could, in the normal course of things, have posed a threat to Jesus. She was Samaritan, she was female and she had a bad reputation. Any one of those factors would ordinarily have been a barrier to any contact for a male Jew. Yet Jesus could relate to her with complete ease. He was far more of a threat to her. Whereas in the matter of racial taboos he had come to terms with his Shadow and reached a place of personal freedom and integrity, she was still stuck in hers: 'Do you, a Jew, ask water of *me* – a woman of Samaria?'

In that context, we need to remember that the Rabbis taught that the water of Samaria was more unclean than the blood of swine.[2] Yet here was a Jew so thirsty and uninhibited by religious and social customs, he could ask for it. The Rabbis had also decreed that it was 'improper to address a woman publicly, even one's own wife in the street or one's sister or daughters in an inn'. It would aggravate the scandal if a true and pious Jew were to address a heathen woman in Samaria. 'But it was neither the first nor last time that Jesus calmly broke traditional conventions which, however honoured they might be, were really only manifestations of the worst of Jewish exclusiveness.'[3]

Again he broke through racial barriers in ministering healing to the Centurion's servant – a Roman – albeit from a distance. 'Legion' came from the region of Decapolis – but he was a human being in desperate need. That was the only qualification needed for Jesus' healing. In giving it he exposed himself to further criticism – and it didn't all come from the owners of the pigs!

Just as members of the National Front and neo-Nazi movements lump groups together calling them 'wogs' or 'Pakis', because they feel threatened by their presence, so Jesus recognised that same fear which lay behind the racial hatreds of his day. He understood, too, the naïveté of those who were hostile to him, recognised the limitations to their understanding and acceptance of those who were different from themselves. He didn't challenge them, but nor did he collude with them. He accepted that in their fear-filled ignorance, they cast people in stereotypes.

One of the areas of our Shadow that we all have to come to terms with in different ways is our own sense of omnipotence. Even as tiny babies we have a deep sense of being able to control our entire world by dictating our wishes through recognisably manipulative behaviour. Part of our maturation is learning what powers lie within us and where we are actually power*less* – differentiating between omnipotence and impotence, for the one can all too readily be mistaken for the other!

Jesus had a profound understanding of the nature of power. He must surely have been deeply in touch with this part of his Shadow, fighting and overcoming the fear that gives rise to a feeling of powerlessness – a fear which can be very manipulative, individually or collectively. He was always conscious of his power's origin. His exchange with Pilate is one clear example. To the question: 'Do you know that I have power to release you, and power to crucify you?' Jesus replied, 'You would have no power over me unless it had been given you from above . . .' (John 19:10–11).

Divine power was the only true power and all that had been vested in him was, he knew, of God. Those final words to his disciples (whether or not there are question marks over their authenticity, I nevertheless believe they reflect the mind of Jesus) make it abundantly clear. 'All authority (and power) in heaven and on earth has been given to me', he said (Matthew 28:18).

St Paul, writing of the 'mind of Christ' in his great Christological hymn, reiterates this thought, for though Jesus was in the form of God, he did not 'regard equality with God as something to be exploited . . .' (Philippians 2:6). (In other versions, 'exploited' is translated as 'grasped', 'grabbed at', 'seized'.) Or as Janet Morley writes: 'You emptied yourself of power and took upon you our unprotected flesh. . . .'⁴

Equality in that context implies equality of status and power. Jesus did not seize power – ever. It was given him, bestowed on him by God and, in some respects, accorded to him by human beings. For we do empower people – sometimes by election or delegation; sometimes by colluding with them, by playing into their hands; sometimes by co-operation. It was such co-operation that enabled Jesus to exercise healing power. He was power*less* in the face of unbelief for he would never violate another's freedom of choice.

He knew himself to be imbued with divine power but he never abused it, never used it to force, dominate, terrorise, subdue or manipulate anyone. He never flaunted it in order to feel powerful, to ensure that he remained undisputed leader in control. His authority lay in his own person and it was rooted in truth. Even Pilate dimly apprehended that.

That truth gave him highly perceptive insights into the games people play with one another, the power struggles and machinations that operate – within the 'inner society' of an individual, and within groups. Without any knowledge of modern psychology or group dynamics he could see where manipulative tactics had come into play, where fear and insecurity were spawning cruelty, oppression, ruthless domination or, indeed, wholesale swindling in order to gain the universal currency of power that money is.

He was deeply aware of the power of self-sacrifice, fully persuaded of the true power of love – the only power that is ultimately able to triumph. It didn't need history to teach him that all earthly powers finally collapse – without exception – because absolute power corrupts absolutely.

'Now is the judgement of this world; now the ruler of this world will be driven out', said Jesus. 'And I, when I am lifted up from the earth will draw all people to myself' (John 12:31–2). Sacrifice had an unrivalled drawing power.

He realised that *seized* power is always limited – in scope and in time. What is stolen can just as easily be snatched away. Treachery has a way of rebounding back on its perpetrator.

Power was one of the things the Evil One offered Jesus in the wilderness. Showing him the kingdoms of the world he said, 'To you I will give their glory and all this authority/power; for it has been given over to me, and I give it to anyone I please' (Luke 4:6).

In his novel, *The Hidden Years*, Neil Boyd brilliantly portrays Jesus puzzling over this temptation. Why was the Tempter offering to hand over power? Where was the flaw? With astonishingly plausible arguments he tries to coax and persuade Jesus that by receiving all power totally, he, the Tempter, will atone for his past and could step off the world scene to leave it for the Kingdom of God to come in with unrivalled dominion.

Something was wrong. Something had to be wrong.

Then, to Jesus' needle-sharp brain, there came a massive illumination.

This temptation was itself proof that only through trials and tribulations can God ever be served. When Jesus saw this, the last shreds of plausibility were also torn from the other two temptations he had endured.

God would not be better served if Satan left the world. He would not be served at all. Service of God cannot be had on the cheap. It requires the overcoming of evil; there is no other way.

Evil, Jesus saw, will never be banished, but all the while it is being contained and often mastered. The rule of good is to suffer and absorb evil and, by so doing, to redeem it. . . .

Without a contest, without a possibility of losing, there is no victory.

A world good through and through, without trials, without temptations, is a milk-sop world, a world of happy children who never grow up. It would have no cowards but no heroes; no sinners but no saints; no failures but no triumphs; no hazards and no ecstasy. It would be boring, tepid, monochrome. In such a terrible world, there would be no way for people to prove their love.

No wonder the Tempter prefers to leave the world. It would then revel in its own mediocrity; now it threatens him. He would far sooner slip away than fight battles which, however bloody, he could never ultimately win.

To evil there are no victories. Only if Satan were permitted to leave the world would he triumph over creation. Final victory would be assured him, when he saw goodness unassailable, unthreatened – minuscule.

Jesus finally saw the temptations for what they were: a huge deception, a marvellous piece of effrontery. He laughed at the Tempter for posing as God's rival, as his equal. When really God has no rivals and Satan is nothing. Satan has no final victory; he only contributes desolately to the final victory of good.

No wonder Satan saw that his best hope was not to haunt the world and make it even messier but to clear out. . . . His greatest punishment is knowing he is necessary to the glory and greatness of God's world.[5]

Neil Boyd is making an important point here for, if the Tempter in the wilderness was the projection of Jesus' own Shadow, then it could not just be denied by letting it 'step off the world scene'. Always it needs to be redeemed – not escaped.

Our unconscious provides the key to our compulsions and why we behave as we do under pressure. Do the 'oughts' and 'musts' dictate to us? Are we driven by people's expectations of us, or more likely, parental hopes and ambitions which, as we reach adulthood, become those of the internalised, finger-wagging, judgemental parent governing, in hidden ways, so much of our attitude and response to life?

There were times, as we can discover from the Gospels, when

Jesus was under considerable pressure. He didn't always respond to requests or needs immediately. Not that he gave help reluctantly or grudgingly, but it would seem that it was only when it could be given freely that he acted. He did things because he wanted to; he could not be coerced into doing them.

When we behave in that way, only doing what we want to do, it can be a case of sheer pig-headedness. With Jesus, I believe it had to do with that freedom of choice which to him was sacrosanct – a freedom which then demanded full, personal responsibility for one's actions. Where such freedom does not exist, we can always shift the responsibility, and therefore the blame, on to our upbringing, our social deprivations, the conditioning of home, school and religion, or some traumatic childhood experience. Jesus, however, was constantly calling people to take mature responsibility for themselves, rather than allow themselves to feel kicked around like a ball in play.

He himself needed that second 'window' [cf. p. 170] on to his personality. The third one that opened on to what he knew of himself was already large and clear. But he needed other people's perception of him, too. 'Who do people say that I am?' he asked his disciples at Caesarea Philippi. Sometimes it was the self-knowledge others gave him that in times of pressure shifted him. We can pinpoint, perhaps, times when he did not respond immediately to needs which clearly put him under certain pressure. There was a delay, for example, before he changed the water into wine at the wedding in Cana. Bartimaeus called out several times before Jesus ministered to him. When Jesus was receiving hospitality in Peter's home, there could have been pressure to heal Peter's mother-in-law. But his inner freedom meant that when he acted, it was solely out of love and concern. When he and the disciples were pressed by the size of the crowd which had come to listen to Jesus, and felt trapped by their reluctance to leave, he chose to feed them. On other occasions he had refused to use divine powers to supply food miraculously – for himself or others. Here, however, he was moved by compassion not simply at their physical hunger, but more by their lack of spiritual sustenance.

We all of us have considerable ability to repress areas of consciousness. Jesus was concerned only to open up, to release from imprisonment and set free, constantly bringing to light the hidden things of darkness. He was in touch with reality and always sought the truth (i.e. the heart) of any matter.

Unlike the visionaries for whom the real world hardly seems to exist, who live on the edge where dreams and experience merge (and where madness also lies in wait), Jesus had his feet firmly on the ground. His parables were rooted in daily life, indeed, his teaching always related to people in their life-situations. His vigorous realism and capacity for plain speaking were signs of a sane, well-balanced personality.

In view of his realism and earthiness, could we venture to say that Jesus had a 'mystical temperament' asks Daniel Rops? 'If we do, we must first be careful to strip from the term all that dubious accumulation of confused and equivocal traits', which have become associated with the term, 'remembering that the highest mystics have been men and women who were perfectly sane, endowed often with superior common sense and powers of action; not the distracted creatures lost in ecstasies with whom they are too often ranked. In the hierarchy of true spiritual values, the ecstasy is an inferior phenomenon which serves chiefly to denote the subject's weakness; beyond all this lies that "dark night" where the approach of God may be felt.'[6]

It is extraordinarily refreshing to meet someone who is 'real', who has no pretence or sham, speaks with a directness and sanity that brooks no sentimentality, and whose love is genuine and transparent. It must then have been quite mind-blowing to meet someone as real as Jesus, and at the same time a deeply searching experience.

Jesus was indeed that Word of God 'living and active, sharper than any two-edged sword, piercing until it divides soul from spirit, joints from marrow'; a Word 'able to judge the thoughts and intentions of the heart',[7] many of which lie within the unconscious. For when everything is 'naked and laid bare to the eyes of one to whom we must render account', it is because he looks through that first window.

It seems very clear then that Jesus went down into the unconscious more than any other human being and made it accessible to himself in a way most of us neither have not nor could not. His fearless passion for truth meant that he didn't resort to the kind of defence mechanisms which most of us use to protect ourselves when truth and reality become too painful or threatening.

He lived out of his unconscious uniquely in the sense that he looked into motives more searchingly than has anyone else. The Sermon on the Mount with its quite terrifying moral demands, is one powerful example. In those collated gems of teaching it is clear that he was able to recognise how the Law itself had become one such block – a form of bondage in which obedience for some could be an excuse to opt out of the responsibilities of mature choice – in, for example, their handling of different situations, in their freedom to discern priorities and exercise necessary flexibility for the sake of love. He himself was able to respond with freedom and maturity to the needs of others, with insight into his own motives, in ways that broke the letter of the Law but fulfilled its spirit. He accepted the accusations made by hostile critics as the inevitable outcome of his choices. When they protested that he was a Law-breaker and a Sabbath-breaker he pointed to the deeper demands of love that always, for him, took priority over the Law. No wonder Paul cried out to the Galatians, 'For freedom Christ has set us free; stand firm therefore and do not submit again to a yoke of slavery' (Galatians 5:1).

Was part of his 'harrowing of hell' a descent into those unexplored depths of the collective unconscious to set free some of what is imprisoned there, and to redeem some of its terrors? As part of the mystery of redemption was he able to tackle something of the seeds of violence, cruelty, deceit, treachery and indifference which are there in our unconscious and which flourish under certain conditions? Did he accept that the potential of all such evil was in himself – seeds which he never watered and which therefore lay dormant but waiting for redemption?

In the unconscious is all the potential for heroism too, of course – for self-sacrifice, nobility and greatness such as we cannot imagine ever attaining. They are there just as surely as the vile things. It was out of that part of the unconscious that it seemed Jesus was able to live and so 'redeem the world'. Redemption did not come simply through his death but by the way he lived his entire life.

In much mythology, the hero (or heroine) meets from time to time with figures such as an old crone, a beggar, an ugly beast – red queens, wise old men, dragons, witches, 'hobgoblins and foul fiends' – and has to befriend them in order to move on in his or her journey and search for the ultimate goal. These figures, often somewhat frightening at first, usually turn out to be fairly benevolent on closer acquaintance. They represent aspects of our Shadow that we all encounter from time to time on our life's journey. We need to pause, acknowledge, question, dialogue with and 'hear' what they are saying to us. At times we meet up with an innate wisdom which surprises us. At others we are confronted by a beast we need to kiss into life – some part of ourselves we dislike intensely, of which we are ashamed, but which as a part of our being we must not disown; a part which has a valid and valued gift within it if only our perceptions could be sufficiently cleansed to recognise it. Having befriended these emerging aspects of our shadow, we are able to continue our journey with greater insight, self-knowledge and therefore freedom.

What is true for us must also have been true for the fully human Jesus. In a sense the Tempter in the wilderness was such a figure presenting Jesus with challenges and choices, forcing him to sort and sift motives, to grapple with the bias to rebellion and the urge to grasp and seize power with which all human nature is tainted and which it must needs overcome in order to be free.

When the people of Nazareth expressed astonishment at the wisdom that poured from the lips of their local carpenter's son, and began to ask one another, 'Where did he get it?', they had unwittingly put their finger on one of the ways in which Jesus had exceptional access to his unconscious. Even at that stage, it would seem, he had encountered, confronted and owned the wisdom of God within him which was slowly emerging into consciousness. He had already begun to distinguish, select and own that wisdom from among the other shadowy figures that lurked in the unconscious.

'O the depths of the riches and wisdom and knowledge of God!' cried Paul. 'How unsearchable are his judgements and how inscrutable his ways! For who has known the mind of the Lord?' (Romans 11:33-4).

Through access to his own inner depths, Jesus was discovering the extent to which he knew that mind! But part of those depths surely lies hidden in all God's creatures who bear his image? *Our* lives are 'hidden with Christ in God' (Colossians 3:3). This truth is demonstrated for us supremely well by the One in whom the divine likeness was unflawed. Hidden in the shadows, the depths of the unconscious, for him, were the unique riches, wisdom and knowledge of his Father, waiting to be discovered, owned, appropriated and set loose upon the world.

I have found myself asking: Does the way we live consciously ever have any redeeming effect upon the collective *un*conscious? Or are we so dominated and imprisoned by its influence that it determines to a very large degree our conscious behaviour? Jung would say that the only sin is not to be as conscious as we are able, and that is to reject the freedom that can be ours if we confront our own depths. To what extent does free will operate to govern our choices? Do we really *have* the freedom to take personal responsibility for our actions? Would the purity and sheer holiness of Jesus have had any power over our collective murkiness? And have the saints and sages also contributed to the cleaning up operation?

Jesus, who could perceive the thoughts and intentions of the hearts of others, and who had such remarkable self-awareness himself, knew only too well what seeds of horrific evil lurk in that unconscious which humanity shares. He was equally aware, however, of all its potential for good. His earthly ministry was a continual encountering of the 'Beast' and of love's awakening in it the latent beauty, the potential goodness, courage, compassion and power of self sacrifice. In the seed bed of the unconscious he was mightily selective in what he watered. Even if the wheat and tares had to grow together, he knew within himself the power ultimately to separate them and to choose life rather than death. It is the secret he shares with us for abundant life.

Dreams

It is perhaps somewhat tantalising that in a culture that took its dreams so seriously, we have absolutely no record of any dream that was given to, or had influence upon, Jesus. The Old Testament world held it as a fundamental belief that dreams were one of the ways by which the speaking God communicated with human beings – sometimes in warning dreams, at other times in reminder dreams, predictive dreams, troubling and recurring dreams, or indeed, nightmares. We are told that God communicated with Moses in direct speech (obviously exceptional), as opposed to the dreams and dark speech (riddles) by which he spoke to others (as the norm) (Numbers 12:8).

Job came to believe that when God addressed the heart – but was not heard – he then spoke 'again and again, in dreams, in visions of the night when deep sleep falls upon people as they lie in their beds. He opens ears in times like that, and gives them wisdom and instruction, causing them to change their minds, keeping them from pride, warning them of penalties of sin, and keeping them from falling into a trap' (cf. Job 33:14–18). But if the warnings went unheeded, then they might well take on the form of nightmares. 'Then he opens the ears of men, and terrifies them with warnings . . . When I say, "My bed will comfort me" . . . then you visit me with dreams and terrify me with visions' (Job 33:16; 7:13–14).

Synesius of Cyrene, Bishop of Ptolemais, wrote in the fourth century:

> The time that nature has ordained for us to repose, brings us, with sleep, an accessory more precious than sleep itself; that natural necessity becomes a source of enjoyment and we do not sleep merely to live, but to learn to live well . . . Then let us

deliver ourselves to the interpretation of dreams ... it is an oracle always ready to be our infallible and silent counsellor.[8]

These views are not so far off the insights of some modern psychologists. In his book, *The Primal Scream*, Arthur Janov concludes that there are many people in psychiatric care today because they refused or failed to pay attention to their dreams and especially their nightmares.[9]

Perhaps where Jesus is concerned, there is silence on the matter of dreams partly because their importance was taken for granted, partly because dreams, as Jung maintained, are 'an integral, important and personal expression of the individual's consciousness'.[10] It is not always appropriate to share such self-knowledge, firstly because it takes time to absorb the inherent wisdom in a dream. (In the Old Testament, wisdom and the ability to understand one's dreams were very closely connected (Daniel 1:17).) Secondly, perhaps, in Jesus' case, the nature of what was revealed to him in dreams could not be disclosed prematurely.

In twentieth-century Western society, dreams have been well described as 'God's forgotten language', or the 'dark speech of the spirit'.[11] We have our dream psychologists, it is true, and increasingly people are being encouraged to note and record their dreams on waking. Maybe then, our generation is rediscovering the immense importance of dreams and their interpretation and beginning to acknowledge them rather more as a source of great wisdom for, as one dream psychologist put it, 'We neglect them at our peril'.

That Jesus did dream is certain because the process of dreaming is a normal human experience and essential to health. If, too, he was in touch with his own (and the collective) unconscious – much more than most of us – then he *must* have dreamed. There are those like Dr Francis Crick who view dreaming as the 'brain's dustbin' and sleep as giving the opportunity for flushing out of our systems all sorts of undesirable junk. Experience would suggest that, if that is the dream's prime function, it is a manifest failure. Far more important to wholeness than the discharging of rubbish, is the ability to be in touch with our repressed unconscious; to attend to that material brought to us in the dream which we have largely ignored in our waking life; to receive insights into our own problems and situations which elude us in conscious moments, and in that receiving, we often find the answer hidden within ourselves; to perceive truth – about ourselves and others – in a way that may demand a total volte-face of attitude; to deal with the unfinished or unfaced business of life; to be in touch with deep sources of creativity, wisdom and potential energy within us; to avail ourselves of healing – of past wounds, of distorted views and mistaken perceptions – for, as Ann Faraday suggests, 'There is indeed a greater degree of honesty to be found within the dream material than in the waking awareness we display of our self-understanding.'[12]

She does not believe that the key to this understanding lies solely in the hands of the specialist. It is a door which can be unlocked by regaining an awareness of our dreams and what they are saying, of all they reveal to us of what we really believe and the world view we hold.

Did Jesus, in his dream life, ever draw on memories of his pre-existent glory, I wonder? Did he, in the substrata of our conscious thinking, ever 'pick up' hints of the evil intentions others had towards him? 'In sleep we are one', said one dream researcher to me. We are unable to erect barriers to protect our separateness. We are inescapably exposed to what others will towards us for good or ill. It is said that Abraham Lincoln, Martin Luther King and John F Kennedy all had nightmares for two weeks or more before their assassinations. Somewhere in the realms of the unconscious it would seem, they had 'picked up' the willed evil planned by their assassins so that it surfaced in their dream life in the form of nightmares.

If that is true of evil intentions, how immeasurably more so, in that mishmash of images, symbols, ideas, motives and intentions – the inhabitants of our dream world – may good also be willed towards others and a feeling of well-being similarly be communicated. Our dreamlife can thus be an important element in and extension of our intercession, the loving intentions of our hearts being transmitted in sleep.

In one of his poems Tagore cries:

Love, my heart longs day and night for the meeting with you –
for the meeting that is like all-devouring death.
Sweep me away like a storm; take everything I have;
Open my sleep and plunder my dreams. Rob me of my world.
In that devastation, in the utter nakedness of spirit, let us become
one in beauty.
Alas for my vain desire! Where is this hope for union except in
Thee, my God.[13]

Since Jesus in his perfect love willed only the highest good for anyone, how much, we may wonder, did that cross thresholds and penetrate the dream lives of others to surface in them as feelings of security, joy, peace or comfort?

Was this how the love of Jesus bore in upon the subconscious of those he encountered? Perhaps this was why Claudia was sufficiently troubled to try and warn Pontius Pilate that he was dealing with no ordinary criminal. Had the love that Jesus embodied somehow reached into her dreams to disturb her?

Dreams sometimes give an unbidden disclosure of truth about another person, and, for the first time, we see them as they really are rather than the monster of our conscious projections or the idealised but false persons we have foisted on them.

Jesus' discernment and powers of perception were such that he could penetrate to the truth of a person even in his waking life. He may well not have needed the kind of illumination dreams can give, for since he lived permanently in the truth and was Truth, he could not help but be aware of sham and pretence. He was like a living 'lie detector' who, without seeking to test or intrude on others in an investigative way, nevertheless saw through the masks, the projections, the pitiful attempts to 'hide behind fig leaves', to the inner reality of a person. Hence he was able to love people, whoever and whatever they were, for, beyond the shame they sought to cover, the insecurities that forced them to pose and pretend, he saw the lovely beings God intended them to be. He saw the unrealised depths of goodness, beauty, courage and holiness, which far outweighed the ugliness.

He may, possibly, have seen the truth of others through predictive dreams – a kind of rehearsal before even meeting them in the flesh. Was this how he first saw Nathanael under a fig tree . . . in a dream? Nathanael was certainly taken aback by what seemed to be Jesus' psychic powers. And Jesus was genuinely astonished at Nathanael's reaction. 'You think this is remarkable', he said. 'I tell you, you will see far greater things than these.' 'Very truly, I tell you, you will see heaven opened and the angels of God ascending and descending on the Son of Man' (John 1:51).

Is there any significance, I wonder, in Jesus' speaking of Nathanael's eventual discovery of the truth about his divine nature, in terms of Jacob's well-known and highly symbolic dream?

Fantasies

Closely akin to dreams are fantasies and daydreams. Fantasy has been so linked to unreality, untruth and all that we project on to others, that we would probably hotly deny that we are given to 'fantasising'. Even if we know it is true, most of us would be reluctant and even ashamed to admit it. There is, however, a sense in which fantasies are very good and healthy and, let it be stated openly, we *all* engage in them – without exception. It is an acceptable and normal use of our imaginative faculty. Like any other gift, we can misuse it: by perpetually plunging into fantasy as an escape from reality, we reach the point of no return where we live and act out our fantasies in a life that has lost touch with reality. But despite this risk of misuse, there is no reason to banish entirely the fantasies that take shape and form in our minds. Life would be very much the poorer without them and some escapism is harmless – no more than a relaxation from the sheer intensity of life or a counterbalance to overly stressful situations.

'There is something so nice about daydreaming', says Ronald Rolheiser in his book, *Forgotten Among the Lilies*.

> There our dreams can come true and we attain that one-in-a-billion specialness that we ache for. In our daydreams we are the superstars: we write the songs, score the goals, dance the ballets and are so successful, beautiful, great and impressive that all our critics are silenced and all the persons we desire fall in love with us.
>
> It is no accident that we so often escape into the world of daydreams, because there we can live life without tears, without limits and without failure. In fantasy we achieve salvation, consummation and vindication.[14]

Why is it that though we may be prepared to share our dreams and seek some interpretation of them, we feel desperately reticent, and even coy, about our daydreams? Maybe it is the egoistical nature of them – self is usually at the centre and it is a self that can achieve successes at every level, a self that is much sought-after and loved. We would be appalled if others could tune in to those kind of fantasies!

However, I repeat, up to a point it is healthy and relaxing to escape into our daydreams:

> There is little difference between a tired person inserting a musical cassette tape into a stereo and sitting back to forget life's problems and another tired soul inserting her favourite daydream into her imagination and sitting back to relax. Both can be a healthy escape from over-intensity and there should be no more shame in one than in the other. Moreover, a healthy fantasy life can positively help spawn creativity because our daydreams put us in touch with the goodness and potential that is inside us.[15]

Personally, I prefer to call this latter aspect of fantasising 'holy wool-gathering'. In our daydreams we can think big. We can dream great dreams for the future. Possibly the best known example of that is seen in Martin Luther King's, 'I have a dream . . .' speech. There, in his daydreams, he articulated his hopes and aspirations for the black people of the USA. He had a vision of the day when there would be equality of opportunity for all people, regardless of colour, class or creed; he saw the gift that his people could be to the nation as a whole. There he envisaged a time when there would be no wars or bloodshed, no oppression of, or injustice to, the marginalised. There he saw, ached and longed for what could be. Such dreams are not out of touch with reality. They accept it as it is in the present but, through good will and a faith that sees beyond the now to the possibilities that could be, they begin to bring their dreams to birth and make the transition from wishful thinking to vision, from potential to actual reality.

Our daydreams and fantasies can, of course, be about self-aggrandisement, a massive compensation for feelings of inadequacy; they can be a rehearsal of all manner of evil which makes the implementation of it that much easier; but they can also be part of our life hidden with Christ in God – if we constantly offer our imaginations to God for consecration and cleansing. Then all our fantasising can, if we so desire and ask, be under the control of and indeed prompted by the Holy Spirit – a Spirit who in meeting our request rejoices to allow us a very long rein to explore and enjoy the fun of this gift, but a rein that stops short of the kind of unbridled liberty where the gift becomes like a runaway horse leading us into areas of total confusion and inability to distinguish truth from untruth.

The focal place that the Father had in all of Jesus' thinking and desiring makes one wonder if the Father was central to his fantasies too. Could it have been that instead of his own ego, as in so much human fantasising, it was the Father he saw being acknowledged, extolled and glorified, the Father taking central stage, the Father winning victories?

Most people, at some point, dream of what it would be like to be great, possibly famous, and the steps they would take to achieve that end. That has to be followed by a sifting process in which what is pure nonsense is discarded, and what has within it the seed of truth and potential is consciously chosen and assimilated.

One of the agonising things for Jesus in his period of testing in the wilderness was this necessary sifting – distinguishing the fantasies that held possibilities for the fulfilling of God's will from those that might have led to self-aggrandisement, or even held the potential for downright evil within them. And it must have been an ongoing spiritual exercise for him throughout his life. But there, in the inhospitable environment of the Judaean wilderness, with its vastness and capacity to induce hallucinations, the struggle to be true reached a peak. There, with the insistent, 'If . . . if . . . if . . . you are the Son of God', forcing him to examine his heart, his mind, his thoughts, his motives and imaginings, he had to rehearse the choices which would present themselves to him again and again throughout his ministry, between one form of greatness and another.

Was it there in the wilderness, through his fantasies, that once more and ever more deeply he grappled with the true nature of power? Now, on the threshold of his mission, did he see the options of power that could bring greatness overnight and achieve his goals – all without suffering?

His dreaming would undoubtedly have been of the Kingdom and how, in practical terms, it was to break in upon the world. Perhaps he dreamed about ways of helping the starving, the orphans and widows who had no social benefits or income support; the lame, dumb and blind who could only make a living by begging. Did he dream of how those who were marginalised could be drawn into the life of the community as valued members of it? Did he, as Martin

Luther King did later, dream of a time when justice would flow down like a river, and righteousness like an ever-rolling stream? Did he foresee in his imagination the sifting of national motives, the sifting of religious motives, taking the scribes and Pharisees back to their original charism, giving them the opportunity to start afresh on that path which could lead their people into a deeper faith and trust in God, a way that would imbue discipline once more with joy and gladness, instead of the dreary duty it had become?

Did he dream about the kind of men and women he would select to support him in his ministry, mulling over in his imagination the many possibilities – examining his own motives for his choice?

Did he dream of ways in which Israel would fulfil its vocation – to be a light to the nations? At present he could only see how arrogant, self-righteous and exclusive she had become. There was precious little welcome for the stranger at their gates. He couldn't see much possibility of, for example, the Romans tugging at the sleeve of a Jew and saying, 'Let us go with you, for we have heard that God is with you' (Zechariah 8:23). What kind of a light were his people to the Samaritans when they had no dealings with each other? Did he dream of opportunities – in very small and practical ways – of breaking down some of those barriers? Was he *only* sent to the lost sheep of the house of Israel, or might God intend him to throw the net of the Kingdom wider? Under what circumstances might he be able (as part of that light to the nations) to assure, for example, the Phoenicians, the Samaritans and the Syrians, of God's all-embracing love? Did he dream of a time when women would be treated more fairly and valued for their special qualities of perception and sensitivity?

How was he to prevent people from getting the wrong idea about him? How would he handle situations where they would want to make him a king – an attempt which would only lead to ruthless suppression by the Romans?

Was it as he dreamed and reflected in this way that he began to realise, with awful clarity, how easy it would be to use his divine power to manipulate situations to achieve his own ends? And was it there, in the isolation, the heat, the hunger and the thirst of the desert that he became aware, in ways he had never faced before, of God's estimate of greatness – an estimate in direct opposition to worldly notions – one in which 'human greatness is not achieved on the backs of others but at their feet'?[16] Was this insight so firmly lodged in his understanding from that point on that, at the last, he was able to give his powerful and poignant demonstration to his own disciples in their need to understand true greatness, by, quite literally, being 'at their feet' – to wash them?

If we are not careful, our daydreaming can prevent us from being present to the present moment, and can dull our appreciation of what is good in our immediate situation. It can leave us fixated in our fantasies so that we wind up overly preoccupied with ourselves, and too centred on our own agenda and obsessions. But, rightly used, they can help us see below the surface to the hidden potential in others. That in turn will influence the way we treat them and enable us to draw out the best in them so that they become the people they have it in them to be. Gerard W Hughes tells the story of a religious superior of whom it was said that his communities were always outstandingly good. After his death, the superior's biographer commenting on this wrote, 'The goodness of his communities existed, at first, solely in his pious imagination'![17]

Jesus surely dreamed of what Israel could become and longed for that 'becoming'. His confidence and trust in what he saw of her possibilities must, at the same time, have opened a way to making them realities. We cannot calculate just how much psychic and spiritual energy is released in others through that kind of faith. There would, of course, be no automatic bending of wills. Jesus always recognised that he could never make people change. Hence he asked the man at the pool of Siloam, 'Do you *want* to be made well?' (John 5:6). It had to be his choice and his responsibility. Whatever dreams Jesus may have had of the new life that could be his if the man were healed, in the last resort, it had to be the man's own decision and his alone.

He would never override the personal freedom of others nor encourage an abdication of responsibilities. 'He could do no mighty work there because of their unbelief' (Matthew 13:58). Sad though he must have been, he totally accepted the situation without feelings of rejection or rancour at the ingratitude of those he had been willing to help. They had made their choice and he respected it.

Some present-day family therapists have moved towards 'Brief Solution Focused Therapy'. One of their techniques is to ask the 'miracle question', which is basically, 'If you could have a wish that would be granted what would it be? If you could have, be, or do anything in the world, what would that be?'

In this way they try to get people to project where they think they *could* be, when they are stuck in the morass of the here and now.

Jesus also asked Bartimaeus the miracle question, 'What do you want me to do for you?' He would never subvert what people wanted. He worked for healing to keep a balance between disintegration and wholeness. But if people couldn't respond to the miracle question, he would never force it. Mostly people would say quite simply, 'I want to be healed', or, 'Lord, I believe. Help my unbelief'. This made it possible for momentous things to occur. Jesus still goes on working that way now – with or without human agencies – and people's real desires and attitudes still govern what can or can't be done.

Take for example a contemporary illustration. If someone with a drug problem is referred for counselling by a social worker or the courts, or is dragged along reluctantly by a relative, absolutely nothing can be achieved unless the client says authentically (and not because of others' expectations), 'I want to stop taking drugs.' That is the only way forward. If he or she is under pressure from family and friends, or threatened with some kind of punishment (e.g. the husband will leave, the children will be taken into care), without that true, 'I want to come off drugs', all they are really requesting is outward compliance. And that is all they will get. It is impossible to take over another's power of choice without their feeling pushed and pulled about, like booty being fought over.

When people came to Jesus he would encourage them to identify their needs, to say from the bottom of their hearts what it was they really wanted, no matter how improbable it seemed. We use a colloquialism, 'He never dreamed that could happen', or 'She never dreamed she could do this', pointing to the fact that we all have our dreams, but sometimes events exceed even our wildest dreaming.

Probably the paralytic (John 5:2 ff.) never dreamed that he could be healed instantly. After 38 years of infirmity, all he could hope for was enough money from his begging to support himself. If his hopes and dreams had been more expectant and believing, he would have done far more much sooner to get himself to the water 'when it was troubled'. His reply to Jesus was both pathetic and apathetic, so Jesus had to ask him, 'Do you really *want* to be healed?' Although it wasn't *called* Brief Solution Focused Therapy, that was the way Jesus often worked, getting people to project their dreams to where they *could* be, with faith and hope.

Parents quite naturally dream dreams for their children, and in and through their fantasies they build up high hopes. During his long nights of prayer did Jesus do the same for his disciples? 'Simon, I have prayed for you . . .', he said (Luke 22:32), indicating that he probably focused on individual disciples as he communed with his Father, and expressed his longings for each one.

The difficulty comes when others do not match up to the dreams we have for them. They may, to our great disappointment choose to go in a totally different direction. But the example of Jesus is one in which individual freedom was always respected. He neither imposed his dreams nor his will on others, but left them to become themselves – unlike the father in the film, *Dead Poets Society*. Here we see the reverse of Jesus' way of standing back, giving others space to develop and become their own person. In the film, a dominating, ambitious father rules and over-rules his artistic son, Neil. He has sent Neil to the school he himself would have loved to attend. Vicariously he enjoys through Neil all that he was denied in his own education. But to live one's dreams through a son or daughter is to trap them in one's own fantasy, leaving them tragically unfree. Unable to break from his fantasy, Neil's father forces him into the mould of *his* choosing, following the subjects and career *he* had coveted (regardless of Neil's particular gifts), enjoying through Neil the successes that might have been his. He creates a fantasy world which countenances no contradiction or reasoning – and ultimately his heartless domination drives his son to suicide.

The Christ-figure in this situation – the highly original and unorthodox English master who, as a true educationalist, has tried desperately (by breaking the pattern of robot-like note-taking and parrot-like repetition) to make the boys think for themselves, take responsibility for their choices and find the freedom to mature and individuate – is 'crucified'. He is made the scapegoat onto whom the parents, the headmaster, the governors and staff, all project their terrible weight of guilt. In this projection, they seek in vain to absolve themselves.

'For freedom, Christ has set us free!' cried Paul (Galatians 5:1), and whilst he spoke of freedom from slavish subjection to the minutiae of the Law, it could aptly be applied to freedom from others' projections and fantasies about us.

I have suggested that Jesus may have dreamed his dreams for each disciple as a form of prayer for them. Sometimes the dividing line between dreaming and praying can be very thin. But daydreams and fantasies are of our own creation – reflecting *our* hopes and longings – whereas prayer is opening ourselves to glimpse those of God. In prayer the focus of attention shifts away from ourselves and the fruits of our imaginations, to what is given – the vision of God's viewpoint. 'Contemplation is an awareness without manipulation', and that, we are assured by the mystics, is prayer. 'It is enjoyable to daydream but it is ultimately more enriching to pray.'[18]

If we agree with this as one definition of contemplation, then perhaps we could say that in his ability to be non-directive, non-manipulative, leaving others free to fulfil their own dreams, Jesus was a true contemplative.

The Divided Self

◆◇◆◇◆◇◆◇◆◇◆◇◆◇◆◇◆◇◆◇◆◇◆◇◆◇◆◇◆◇◆◇◆◇◆

Jesus came into Gadara and there met a man who was possessed of demons, and he asked him his name. 'Legion' came the reply, 'for we are many' (Mark 5:9). In this confused, broken human being, we have a vivid picture of almost total disintegration. The man was like the separated pieces of a jigsaw puzzle – utterly fragmented mentally or personality-wise.

Whatever the cause of the conflict within him – whether we view it as mental or physical illness, personality or behavioural rather than organic disorders, or demonic possession – temporarily it gave him an exceptional strength that he was turning on himself in terrible self-destruction. So violent was he that no one could constrain him, control him or safely get close enough to help him. Thus he continued relentlessly to tear and gash himself, snapping chains like twigs and ripping his clothes in pieces.

When Jesus approached him, however, there was a remarkable response. 'Legion' ran to him – almost as though he sensed in Jesus the wholeness and integration he so desperately longed for and without which there was no hope. Conversely and simultaneously, there was a repulsion: 'What do you want with me, Jesus, Son of the Most High God? Swear by God that you will not torture me!' (Mark 5:7).

Do we not perhaps see, in this stricken man, a reflection of some of our own inner chaos? Have we not also known that double movement of longing for healing on the one hand and shrinking from it on the other?

There is a sense in which if Jesus were to ask any of us, 'What is your name?', we could well answer, 'Legion – for we are many.' The healing of 'Legion' is the healing we all need in varying degrees. We have a 'cast of thousands' which needs to be integrated. We, too, are fragmented, broken people with a Humpty Dumpty desire to be 'put together again'.

Jigsaws are regarded as harmless leisure pursuits, a mindless relaxation suitable for retreats, holidays or convalescence. But beware! They can become compulsive. Jesus himself seemed to be motivated by an inner compulsion to unite the broken pieces of people's lives, fitting them together to give the whole picture, or perhaps more significantly, the picture of wholeness. But he only yielded to that compulsion of love when there was a movement towards him, however tentative, by the many 'Legions' he met. Only when he could assure them that it was their faith, and not his own inner need or compulsion, that had made them whole, would he act. His respect for individual freedom – to choose wholeness or not – prevented his ever forcing healing or crashing the barriers of another person's inner reserve.

We need to ponder the richness of the essential complexity we call 'self'. For our 'self' can be 'Legion', with all its inner chaos and confusion – sub-personalities, as J W T Redfearn calls them.[19] Or it can ultimately be a community – a community of love in which our different and separated selves are welcomed, accepted and bound together in a respect such as we see symbolised for us supremely in the Trinity.

> The range of human experience which we see on a grand scale in society and the world is present in miniature, so to speak, within ourselves. My self is not merely the personality I cultivate for public presentation. There are a host of other selves which just as truly belong to the whole me.[20]

The different 'pieces' of our personality jigsaws disclose themselves to us from time to time in dreams when they may appear in personified form under animal, as well as human, guise. We can come to identify the stresses, diversities, tensions, compulsions, conflicts, rivalries and polarities manifested by our moods and behaviour as 'stemming from clashes and power struggles going on in our inner society, within the community of the self. The image of the self as microcosm, world in miniature',[21] is no new device of modern psychology, nor the product simply of recent theological reflection. It is found in ancient philosophy and the myths of many cultures.

Jung encouraged the view of the human journey towards maturity and personal wholeness as one of 'individuation'. 'This is the process of maturation through which the obscure and excluded elements of the self are brought at last into integration with the rest.'[22]

In his book *Insearch*, James Hillman, himself a Jungian psychologist, speaks of our need to meet, recognise and embrace within ourselves, 'a host of shadowy, unpleasant figures and discover an ability to love even the least of these traits'. He asks us to consider just how much charity and compassion we have for our own inner weaknesses and brokenness. How far are we able 'to build an inner society on the principle of love, allowing a place for everyone?'[23]

That personal, inner, inclusive society is in microcosm what the Christian community, the Church, should be – including all, allowing a place for all, welcoming the unlikely – a society based on the principle of love. In the words of Martin Smith: 'It is illuminating and helpful to think of the Holy Spirit making a church-in-miniature out of the many elements, the many persons, the conflicting and various selves we have within us. Grace does not achieve peace and unity in the heart by rejecting and annihilating inner selves. It heals, blesses and brings them into harmony with one another through love. The Spirit brings all of the selves into relationship to Christ, in whom they can come together',[24] and upon whom he may pronounce with authority, 'Your faith has made you whole'.

Since this is the human condition and 'Legion' is a name with relevance for all of us, there must have been a sense in which Jesus himself could have said *his* name was 'Legion'. His own maturation involved the steady, deepening integration of his many selves. Was there, then, any power struggle in his inner society? It would seem that in an extraordinary way, surpassing any other human being, he was 'at unity in himself' (Psalm 122:3). He was not the house divided against itself of which he spoke in his parable (Matthew 12:25). Indeed, it would appear that his own 'community of being' enabled him to offer wholeness to others by his encounter with them, and, by his healing word or touch, somehow to absorb their brokenness. He could give, instead, a love which awakened in them a new self-respect – a self-love which acted as generous host to the rejected, despised areas of their being, the banished and forgotten selves, the wounded and buried selves. Love alone could bring them together in a celebration of truly healing, holy communion. True self-love is always the fruit of knowing oneself to be loved and lovable.

Although Jesus experienced himself as loved – fully by his Father, and deeply by Mary (despite her human inadequacies) – his own 'community of being' could not have grown without any conflict or struggle. What, then, might some of his different 'selves' have been that he had to learn to welcome and accept?

Like all of us, he must have had his 'inner child'. It is testimony to Mary's good mothering that everything in the Gospels points to that inner child being a very secure one. It didn't clamour for attention or make itself felt by inappropriate childish outbursts. The child neither dominated nor diminished the adult Jesus. Mary and Joseph had so consistently attended to and delighted in Jesus that, from the outset, he began to have a sense of his own intrinsic goodness and worth. Despite the intense anxiety that his coming gave to both Mary and Joseph – from the Annunciation through to the return from Egypt – there is no indication that Jesus felt apologetic for his existence. Rather he seems to have had a developing sense of destiny and purpose in his life. Whatever traumas he suffered as a child, they were so well integrated into his present, he could choose to relive them, re-experiencing homelessness, rejection, disfavour with the ruling authorities of the day, and bearing the death threats hanging over him. If the repetition in adult life of these traumas re-awakened memories and their attendant fears, he was sufficiently in charge of his emotional life to isolate and deal with the present fear rather than allow it to be compounded by the past, until the 'floods [of fear] overwhelmed him'.

In Jungian terms, like every human being, he contained within himself an animus and an anima. Despite the gender distinctions of first-century Judaism being even greater than those of twentieth century Western society, Jesus was in touch with 'the woman in himself' and was seemingly at ease with her amongst the other selves in his inner society. As much at ease, it would seem, as with 'the man in him' – his masculine self. He could blend his intuitive faculties, his receptivity and gentleness with the more assertive, incisive and authoritative side of his nature without contradiction or disjunction.

Physical hardships brought out a toughness in him together with astonishing qualities of endurance – as happened during his lengthy time in the wilderness without food or shelter. Yet he could also acknowledge his disappointment that arriving tired and dusty, Simon the Pharisee had provided no water for the washing of feet before a meal. He, too, greatly appreciated simple, creature comforts and welcomed the ministrations of a woman who provided what his male host had neglected to give.

I think it unlikely that it was an aggressive male 'self' in Jesus that so strongly attracted women to him. Rather they could respond to, and relax in, his finely balanced masculine-feminine polarity that enabled him to operate fully and richly without ambivalence. He did not exclude, starve or suppress the feminine aspect that was so essential to the fullness of his being. Passion, sensitivity, feeling, nurturing and caring qualities flowed through him, till not only was he mature (in the sense of *teleios* – fulfilled and fulfilling his true functions as a human being), but in the words of Peter, he 'adorned the doctrine of God' (Titus 2:10). A rare beauty shone through him – the beauty of Proper Man as opposed to disintegrated 'Legion'.

Jesus must, like us, have had a 'Wounded Self'. In fact, a sensitive spirit such as his would have suffered deeper wounds than most. Instead of being a self turned in on itself, withdrawn, self-pitying, barricaded against further hurt, his 'wounded self' was baptised – totally immersed in a love that forgave, accepted, offered second chances and made itself vulnerable again and again. Up to seventy-times-seven? No – countless times. His 'wounded self' did not hide behind a 'stiff-upper-lip' mask or a macho image. It opened its arms wide in ever greater risk of further and deeper wounding, at the same time creating a refuge and a place of comfort to others who were similarly afflicted. More even than that, his 'wounded self' embraced in compassion and incredible love the perpetrators of the wounds – those who denied him, those who rejected him, those who persecuted him . . . even those who betrayed him. It was so during his earthly life. It is so still.

The Union of Opposites

The highest individual peak, the greatest good a person could achieve was, in Jung's view, total individuation – to be fully oneself in every respect. In order to reach that point, for each of us there has to be the union of opposites. This, in his view, was wholeness and growth towards it is always a struggle. Marion Milner (herself a Freudian) speaks of 'facing the psychic pain of recognition of the opposites in ourselves.'[25]

When we look into the Gospels, and discover from the Epistles some of the memories and impressions of Jesus circulated by the Early Church, we have perhaps a picture *par excellence* of a truly integrated human being – which in Jung's terminology *is* an individuated person.[26] But the union of opposites could no more have been for him a facile achievement than it is for us. It does indeed involve psychic pain.

What were some of the opposites which Jesus sought to unite in himself on his journey to individuation?

In embracing his sexuality he came to terms with the anima in himself, uniting it comfortably with his animus. His gentleness and sensitivity, his intuition and love of beauty, his vulnerability and capacity to be deeply hurt were not denied or camouflaged as being unworthy in a man. Nor were they in such stark contrast to his animus, so untypical, that he became two people. He combined his aggression and compassion, his tenderness and toughness, his disturbing silence and his provocative speech, his humble submission and authoritative pronouncements, moving with freedom from one facet of his personality to another.

In terms of contemporary insights into personality traits,[27] we might observe a very fine balance in him between the introvert and the extrovert. He who was in many respects a very private, contained person and drew tremendous energy from his inner world, yet greatly enjoyed being with people, loved socialising and was energised by his outer world.

He was highly intuitive, experienced life with intensity and reflected very deeply. Yet so much came through his senses too, and became the raw material of his teaching. In addition to his penetrating sense of sight, his touch was diagnostic not merely ministering healing but at times discerning the cause of the disorder. As Martin Buber once claimed, ultimately it is touch that will break through when all else fails. We can imagine his immense gratitude for and intense pleasure in his faculties of smelling and tasting – as he appreciated to the full the scent of the flowers of the field and the perfume poured over him, the taste of grapes and figs, freshly baked bread, corn plucked by hand from a field and fish baked over a charcoal fire on a beach early in the morning.

Being vibrantly awake to his environment and aware of so much unspoken communication in the human and animal world, he would have picked up far more than most of us are ever capable of hearing, his understanding of all creation becoming increasingly profound by all that he received from without and all that he encountered within.

His incisive exchanges, his thoughtful questioning, his penetrating insight into minds and hearts, his sharp-witted responses and repartee with those he encountered on the hill slopes and in the villages of Galilee, in the synagogues and Temple, indicate a well-developed rational faculty. Whereas the many references to his being 'moved with compassion' show how strongly he was in touch with his feelings.

He appears to have been a person who could be spontaneous and flexible, preferring to keep his options open and boundaries fluid, and yet he also had a very strong sense of purpose and of moving forward in obedience to a destiny.

It would be very difficult indeed to categorise the personality of Jesus in the way that is now possible in our attempts to understand ourselves – using the tool of the Myers-Briggs Personality Type Indicator (which like any tool has its limitations). Whatever his 'dominant' and 'auxiliary' traits were, the margin of difference must have been narrow, so that he could operate in both with an apparent ease, and embrace them all as being part of his God-given human nature. That is true integration.

There was in Jesus' day a split in Judaism between religion and everyday life, motive and action, fear and devotion, law and love –

as there had been down through the centuries.* Again and again
prophetic voices had been raised in judgement and warning against
the inconsistencies and hypocrisy in the lives of many worshippers.
It is a split found in most religions, including Christianity. In the
context of his own life, Jesus sought to heal those divisions and live
in inner harmony. Perhaps a good deal of energy went into uniting
the split that arose out of being a man of his time and a 'man for all
seasons'; a man of Jewish faith and culture and yet the Proper Man
who reflected a God for whom there are no distinctions, a God of
all generations and cultures whose particular people were called to
proclaim his universal love. His extension of parameters in relations
with Gentiles and outcasts made him not only misunderstood and
unpopular, but the kind of threat that could not be tolerated.

Throughout its history the Church – the continuing Body of Christ
– has been torn by a split spirituality of one sort or another. If Jesus
were incarnate among us today, he would still be directing his psychic
energy towards the healing of such splits and the uniting of opposites;
and he could and can only do so because he himself achieved individuation. The Psalmist spoke of Jerusalem being 'at unity in itself'
(Psalm 122:3), and that could aptly describe the kind of peace which
emanated from Christ as a result of his wholeness.

Writing of the contemporary split in spirituality, Gerard W Hughes
points to some of the inconsistencies in every branch of the Church.
He says, 'The division has deep roots in our religious vocabulary of
grace and nature, natural and supernatural, terms which can be easily
understood to support the split. The division does not allow God to
be God who became one of us in Jesus: it keeps God at a safe distance
from our everyday behaviour and from our individual and national
attitudes, values and policies'[28] – the very criticism that echoes so
strongly in the prophecies of Amos, Micah, Isaiah and Jeremiah.

One of the most deeply-entrenched splits in spirituality from early
days to the present is that between flesh and spirit. Spiritual writers
through the centuries, from Paul and Augustine to the present day,
have seen them as warring factions within each individual. In earlier
centuries the answer was to reinforce the split by pronouncing it
totally irreconcilable, and such views led to harsh self-inflicted disci-
plines, untold anguish, tormented guilt, deep-seated shame,
emotional damage and unhealed inner division.

* I should like to acknowledge that in much of what I have read of Hasidic
sects, I am deeply impressed at the extent to which religious practice and
daily life are impressively closely integrated – externally at any rate.

One of the saddest commentaries on such split spirituality comes from that disillusioned ex-monk, Nikos Kazantzakis, who wrote, in his prologue to *The Last Temptation of Christ*,

> My principal anguish and the source of all my joys and sorrows from my youth onward has been the incessant, merciless battle between the spirit and the flesh.
>
> Within me are the dark immemorial forces of the Evil One, human and pre-human; within me too are the luminous forces, human and pre-human of God – and my soul is the arena where these two armies have clashed and met.
>
> The anguish has been intense. I loved my body and did not want it to perish; I loved my soul and did not want it to decay. I have fought to reconcile these primordial forces which are so contrary to each other, to make them realise that they are not enemies but, rather, fellow workers, so that they might rejoice in their harmony – and so might I rejoice in them. . . .
>
> The struggle between God and man breaks out in everyone, together with the longing for reconciliation. . . . The stronger the soul and the flesh, the more fruitful the struggle and the richer the final harmony. God does not love weak souls and flabby flesh. . . .
>
> Struggle between the flesh and the spirit, rebellion and resistance, reconciliation and submission, and finally – the supreme purpose of the struggle – union with God: this was the ascent taken by Christ, the ascent which he invites us to take as well, following in his bloody tracks.[29]

Kazantzakis could see the goal towards which he was struggling – that union of opposites, that reconciliation of inner splitting, which Jesus had achieved – but he was clearly still locked into an appalling battle when he wrote the above, an either/or situation. Whereas, Jesus was never stuck there. Freud regarded the libido as exclusively sexual energy, Jung saw it as total energy. For Jesus, this libidinal energy was embraced as good and God-given, to be released and harnessed for the establishment of the Kingdom. It was not a source of shame. The 'immemorial forces of the Evil One' were the primordial darkness within. The 'luminous forces . . . of God' were the primordial and external light.

Within his internal world, Jesus seemed to have embraced the darkness, the shadow stuff, in such a way that it had been integrated, absorbed and overcome by the light. So much so that, in Jesus, we glimpse God (whose privilege it was to *dwell* in thick darkness because he created both light and dark) as, in himself, all light in whom there is no darkness at all (1 John 1:5). 'In him [Jesus] was life, and the life was the light of all people. The light shines in the darkness, and the darkness did not overcome it.' Through him 'the true light which enlightens . . . everyone' was coming into *their own inner world* (John 1:4–5,9; my italics).

The split Kazantzakis describes is one that has dogged Christians of every generation – very particularly in the West – despite Jesus' own attitude and freedom, and the teachings of such mystics as Julian of Norwich who wrote:

> Our sensuality is grounded in Nature,
> in Compassion and in Grace.
> In our sensuality God is.
> God is the means
> whereby our Substance
> and our Sensuality
> are kept together
> So as never to be apart.[30]

Writing later in the fourteenth century, Mechtild of Magdeburg said:

> Do not disdain your body.
> For the soul is just as safe in its body
> as in the Kingdom of Heaven.[31]

What a pity Nikos Kazantzakis had apparently not come across this wisdom and been able to assimilate it in his own struggle!

Some of the ambivalence still felt by Christians towards the body has been transmitted via the Old Testament with its taboos and purity rituals, which have somehow lingered on to surface in what Bishop Richard Holloway calls the 'pollution theory'.[32] Sex becomes equated with smut and dirt. Certain vital body fluids, under the Levitical code, rendered a person ritually unclean, and *something* of that attitude has persisted, reverberating throughout Christianity, creating an artificial split between purity and pollution.

It is particularly intriguing that we have carried this pollution theory of sexuality over from ancient times, because our Lord seems to have challenged and overturned it by his words and actions. He ignored most of the pollution taboos . . . Presumably, this was not because he had anything in particular against washings and ritual cleansings, or lacked physical fastidiousness, but because he had penetrated to the heart of the matter, which was access to God and the Holy . . . he internalised value and virtue. He replaced an objective, ritualistic ethic of purity and pollution with an ethic of the heart and mind that demystified access to God.[33]

Although there is much sexual licence and moral confusion as we approach the twenty-first century, amongst Christians and indeed many who would make no claim to any kind of religious allegiance, there is a desire for a more holistic approach to life. Holiness has to do with connectedness and recognising wholeness. This concentration on wholeness, which I believe is prompted by the Holy Spirit and is wholly in keeping with Jesus' *modus operandi*, is slowly bringing healing to all sorts of splits that unconsciously divide us – from one another and within ourselves.

We have in many ways reclaimed the body's part in worship and healed the split between the cerebral and emotional strands in it. We feel greater personal responsibility for our health. Health food shops, dieticians and health farms are big business and we spend nearly as much on slimming aids and diets as we do on defence, so obsessive are we about our weight. We are more in tune with the body's rhythms, more conscious of the need for exercise and alternative medical treatment, than was perhaps true in the last few decades.

With marriage encounter groups and psycho-sexual consultation on offer today, couples are encouraged to talk about their problems at all levels rather than shrouding them in secrecy and living in misery. Bodies are not viewed as enemies to a healthy spirituality as they once were.

It is all part of Christ's ongoing work of building bridges of integration rather than walls of division. He is our peace and breaks down the walls of partition at every level of our lives to bring us to that openness where we can receive the love of God, allow it to be shed abroad in our hearts and poured out in abandoned generosity upon others.

In Jesus we see the balance and the tension of nature and grace, power and powerlessness, weakness and strength, light and darkness. Yet he was as whole as any human being has ever been.

In the book of Job he asks: 'Am I the sea?' (Job 7:12). The question in that context implies the answer, 'No', but in many ways it is a brilliant analogy of total integration, a vivid picture of our own contradictions and paradoxes. In the sea there are the extremes of raging anger and deep peace; its changing colours and moods are all part of what Gregory of Nyssa called 'the landscape of paradox'. Yet the sea is one and indivisible (eg. at what precise point does the Atlantic become the Indian Ocean?); it is always itself – predictable and yet unpredictable; wild and elemental yet gentle and comforting; it invades every crevice and niche, yet withdraws, exposing mysterious rockpools, sandy wastes and unsuspected beauty.

The sea is fearsome, commanding our utmost respect, yet so often it is inviting, affording pleasure and relaxation; destructive yet healing; but it is always the sea, always there; changeable yet immutable; a unity in itself; obedient to natural laws yet free at times to override them. In its mighty strength it is no respecter of persons, yet buoys up and gently carries the weak. There is a sea in each of us. We *are* each a sea and none is more sublimely so than Jesus.

It was because he pushed back the frontiers to venture into this landscape of paradox harmonising it within himself that he so threatened his contemporaries.

Scholars claim that we cannot build any picture of Jesus from Pauline theology. Nevertheless, I do not think we can dismiss all that Paul received through the oral tradition (which, even in the countries where it survives today, is invariably very reliable). There must have been so much more of Jesus' teaching that has not been recorded in the Gospels but which nevertheless was handed down by word of mouth to inform and influence the first Christians as they came to understand, through the eyes of faith, more of his person and work. I would want to acknowledge the weight of 'received tradition' in Pauline writings, which may not be verifiable through ancient texts and manuscripts – exciting and valuable though these are. Even so, they too rely heavily upon individual selection and interpretation of facts. All history comes through the individual, and not unbiased, filters of the historians.

In the Epistle to the Galatians, Paul says that all those who are baptised into Christ have thereby clothed themselves with Christ (and so with his unity and wholeness), for 'there is no longer Jew or Greek, there is no longer slave or free, there is no longer male or female; for all of you are one [integrated] in Christ Jesus' (Colossians 3:11).

Might we not also see something of Christ's power to unite

opposites in the letter to the Ephesians (2:14ff.)? 'For he is our peace; in his flesh he has made both groups into one and has broken down the dividing wall, that is, the hostility between us [i.e. Jews and Gentiles]. He has abolished the law with its commandments and ordinances, that he might create *in himself* one new humanity in place of the two thus making peace, and might reconcile both groups to God in one body.'

That was the impression he left. That was the extraordinary reputation he had. Only he who was in the process of putting to death any hostility within himself, any inner civil war, could offer peace and harmony to others. Only he could speak to us in our fragmentation and, as it were, declare that we need no longer be 'strangers and aliens' to our own selves (cf. Ephesians 2:19). For what was true of his unifying work in the society of his day as a whole, was and is true for all time of his reconciling work in our inner society.

6

'A NEW THING'

A New Dimension of Love

Jesus was very plainly a man of destiny, but he was by no means a fatalist. He had one passionate, over-arching purpose in his life and increasingly, as he discerned the direction he should take to fulfil it, he recognised the possible consequences. But he knew that in following this path the Kingdom would take root and grow – small at first as a mustard seed but in time flourishing and developing into a mighty tree.

The glory of his life was so much more than simply being one which was without sin, as though he had been able to walk through life without picking up any dirt. It was far more that at every point along the way, in every situation, a love streamed out of him that broke down hardness, unbelief and fear, broke through the most impenetrable barriers and broke up the complacency and false security of the righteous.

His life was not 'the unfolding of a pre-arranged set of events all neatly shaped to point towards the passion'.[1] It was not as though all chance and randomness had been eliminated from it. He was not 'speaking the lines of a script or obeying the directions of an invisible producer',[2] he was living with the same unpredictability and uncertainties that we face day by day; the same need for choices; the same submission to muddled decision-making of earthly authorities with all the frustration and injustice that can entail.

Nor did he come preaching and teaching the good news of the Kingdom 'in order to get himself executed, as though he was stage-managing his own execution – a peculiarly sick idea, though one which many Christians seem willing to accept'.[3] Nor was this a terrible tragedy scripted by God in which each of the protagonists was forced to play out his or her part without choice or freedom to deviate from the script. Each one, from Pilate to the crowds that roared for Barabbas, from Caiaphas to Judas, from Herod to the disciples was presented with choices. They could no more escape those choices than could Jesus. They were not programmed like computers in order that the script should 'work' and come to its author's appointed end. Right up until the moment of his death Jesus was free to choose.

A God who exacted that kind of inexorable, predesigned suffering – more in the nature of a pagan sacrifice – would not have won hearts by the extraordinary quality of his love. It was because Jesus embodied the kind of love God really has for all his people and creation as a whole, that 'it was necessary that he should suffer', or rather, inevitable that he did, for such love demands a response. The Kingdom which was none other than God's kingly rule, was a Kingdom centred on and surrounded by divine love. In ushering in God's reign, Jesus wasn't simply introducing people to that love, nor reminding them of the history of God's loving, saving acts in the past. He *became* that love – in all his encounters, in all his actions, in all his relationships. In Jesus, for the first time, people could reach out and touch God's love with their fingertips, see it in his eyes and be seen by it, hear it in his voice and be heard from their innermost depths. And it was all too much for his opponents. This was a love which excluded no one and recognised no outsider, and that was intolerable. To get rid of the source of such love was the only answer – hence it was indeed 'necessary' and expedient that Jesus should suffer.

The prophets of Israel had repeatedly emphasised that there was only one God: 'I am the Lord, and there is no other' (Isaiah 45:5). They had seen that he was concerned for all his creation. His rain fell on the just and unjust, he could use a Persian king – an outsider – to bring about the deliverance of his people, and he had a bias towards the strangers, the outcasts, the off-scouring of society, the widows, the orphans and the aliens.

As John Barton has put it, however:

> People who belong to a religious tradition are in effect defining themselves as forming a larger family, but distinguishing themselves from the 'strangers' who make up the rest of the human race. A religious commitment becomes a kind of tribal allegiance, and religions often develop ways of policing the frontiers of the religious community to make sure that only the real insiders are inside, and that people cannot get in by stealth if they do not really believe in what the religion stands for, or practise

what it teaches. Judaism and Christianity, as they have developed down the years, are no exceptions to this rule. Both are deeply concerned with identity, with authority and with initiation rites that make it possible to decide without doubt who is in and who is out.[4]

The Jews constantly forgot their own past, when they themselves had been strangers and aliens in the land. They fixed their racial and religious boundaries and hardened the distinctions that preserved a 'them' and 'us' situation, hoping to protect their purity and isolate themselves from 'sinners' and all contamination.

Jesus, who moved beyond the boundaries, ignored the distinctions and demonstrated God's impartial love, caused deep offence to them. His kind of loving was a sharp protest against all the defence mechanisms, individual and corporate, that kept the unacceptable safely 'out there'. The love of God in Christ challenged all their securities, for to let down the drawbridge and welcome all and sundry would be altogether overwhelming.

This was the threat of the Kingdom to the Jewish authorities. The love, the mercy, the healing and the hope were all being offered indiscriminately – and to people who, far from having earned them by good works, had actually, as they thought, disqualified themselves by profligate, intolerable behaviour.

Jesus' whole ministry was living witness to the fact that the Kingdom of God was not an exclusive club that debarred all sorts of unwanted, undesirable rejects of society. Indeed, he made it clear that some of them would go in first to the Kingdom before those considered respectable and religiously correct. He came along upsetting and reversing all their notions of greatness, superiority and importance.

His preaching, teaching and healing ministries were all worrying enough, but his loving simply could not go unchecked. It was the disturbing nature of his love that led to his own exclusion. And it was that love – undiminished and undefeated even through all the horrendous events of the Passion – that was the true triumph over evil and the baptism of the Kingdom. 'Can you be baptised with the baptism with which I will be baptised?' he asked his disciples (Mark 10:38). They answered, 'We can.' Jesus was referring not simply to suffering and death, but to the establishment of a community of love that would be his dynamic agent in the world to break down walls of hostility and barriers of exclusion. He knew, as his disciples did not at that stage, what that baptism would involve.

A New Moses

◇◇◇◇◇◇◇◇◇◇◇◇◇◇◇◇◇◇◇◇◇◇◇◇◇◇◇◇◇◇◇◇◇◇◇◇

Jesus is often referred to as the 'New Moses' who gave a New Commandment, but how far did Jesus see himself as that? He was certainly quite categorical in his support of the Mosaic Law. He disputed hotly – it seems – the claim made by the scribes and Pharisees that he had come to destroy the Law. 'I have not come to destroy the Law, but to fulfil it.' In other words, to fill it full with new meaning and, without diminishing it in any way, to apply it more deeply, more searchingly; to rid it of some of the burdensome accretions that had made the Law so inaccessible to many ordinary Jews. I believe Jesus wanted to restore the Law to the one in which the Psalmist was able to delight: 'Oh how I love Thy Law. It is my meditation all day long' (Psalm 119:97).

For many the Law evoked not love but fear – and possibly anger at the injustice of a religious system which marked out many of its adherents as failures. Jesus looked at the Law which often in practice had become reduced to innumerable regulations, and longed to recover it as the gift it was intended to be. He wanted to get behind the letter of the Law and release its spirit amongst his people, a spirit that had been trapped beneath layers and layers of explicit detail. He longed to call it forth from the tomb in which it had been imprisoned and raise it from the dead. For ideally, Torah was not a string of duties but an expression of love. Torah was meant to be cherished.

There were, of course, very devout Jews living in Israel – Jews for whom the Law of Moses was still a blessing. The Ana'wim were such people and Simeon, Anna and even Mary, mother of Jesus, were among them. But where legalism had superceded love, Jesus wanted to initiate a reversal so that God could be worshipped 'in spirit and in truth' and not by the observance of certain externals which inculcated a very *self* conscious form of ritualism.

There are certainly many remarkable parallels in the lives of Moses and Jesus. Both were children whose lives were threatened by ruling powers and had to be hidden in order to escape death. Both were survivors amongst the many babies who were slaughtered.

Both grew up with a gradually perceived sense of destiny – to save their people. Both spent preparatory years in ordinary jobs – Moses in shepherding and Jesus in carpentry. Both apprehended their call through a vision of God – the one in the burning bush and the other at baptism.

Both became threats to the political leaders of their day and challenged them face to face. Moses led his people out of slavery by passing through the Red Sea. Jesus identified with his people's longing to be set free from the slavery of sin and spiritual exile, by being baptised in the Jordan – symbolising a new exodus, a passing through death to life.

Both introduced 'Last Suppers' – the original Passover meal, and a subsequent one which would spread far beyond the bounds of Judaism.

Both were transfigured on mountains. Both shone with such glory that others were afraid.

Both gave Commandments to Israel – the Ten Commandments, and a New Commandment of heart-searching love.

Both were greatly misunderstood, even by their followers. They had to suffer 'the murmurings' of the people – so much harder than face-to-face confrontation.

Both brought saving power through a 'lifting up' – of the bronze serpent by Moses, of himself by Jesus in his crucifixion. 'I if I be lifted up will draw all humanity to myself.'

Moses tapped the rock to provide his people with sweet water in the desert.

Jesus *is* the Rock from which living water flows. And, in that curious imagery of Paul (1 Corinthians 10:4) is the Rock which followed the Israelites in their wilderness wanderings.

Moses gave his people manna from heaven in the wilderness.

Jesus fed thousands with supernatural food, but in a moment of self-disclosure declared himself to be the Bread of Life.

Both died saying, 'It is finished', yet not seeing the fulfilment of their work in this life, but believing that 'they would one day see the travail of their souls and be satisfied' (Isaiah 53:11).

Moses appeared to Jesus (together with Elijah) in his Transfiguration. We are told that they spoke to Jesus of his 'ἐξ όdos' (Luke

9:31) his exodus, his departure. It was a confirmation that he was on the right course, that he had been fulfilling the Law and the Prophets and that fulfilment would be culminated in his Passion. And from that point onwards Jesus resolutely 'set his face to go to Jerusalem' (Luke 9:51) with the inner certitude which had come in the experience of Transfiguration. Flanked by the chief representatives of the Law and the Prophets, he had heard God repeat the affirmation and vocation given him in baptism. 'This is my beloved Son: listen to him,' (Mark 9:7; Luke 9:35). He was assured that his movement towards death was a right one and 'his hour' was very near.

After his death, the three disciples who had been with Jesus in that experience, obviously shared it with the others. Were they able then to see how consistent his teaching and his new Commandment were with the Law of Moses? 'Loving one another', included all that Moses had taught about respect for all that another has and is.

Moses had delivered the Commandments to his people with the authority of God. And it was because God's authority had been flouted that, in anger, he smashed the tablets of stone.

Jesus fleshed out the Law of Moses through his own authority given him by God. He was able to say, 'You have heard it said from old times . . . but *I* say to you . . .'. No other person had dared to make this claim.

In his anger he scourged the Temple, and in his death ripped apart its mystique and thereby its power. In the death of Jesus, the glory departed from the Temple.

Amongst the Kabbalistic Jews there is the belief that the Shekinah glory still wanders endlessly in exile over the face of the earth, separated from her 'lord', and that 'she will be reunited with him only in the hour of redemption'.[5]

Christians believe that reunion has already taken place and the 'light of the knowledge of the glory of God shines in the face of Jesus Christ' (2 Corinthians 4:6). The hour of redemption has come.

A New Baptism

━◆━◆━◆━◆━◆━◆━◆━◆━◆━◆━◆━◆━◆━◆━◆━◆━◆━◆━◆━

'Then Jesus came from Galilee to John at Jordan to be baptised by him' (Matthew 3:13).

But why? There was nothing new in baptism. Proselytes were baptised into the Jewish faith. In total immersion they were symbolically reborn and from then on were treated as babes in the faith, having to learn all that concerned Jewish belief and practice in the same way that Jewish children growing up would be instructed. Normally, such a baptism would not draw a crowd. It would be administered privately in one of the immersion pools used for ritual cleansing. In coming for baptism, the convert not only came forth symbolically from the waters of the womb of Judaism into a new birth as a Jew, but was at the same time cleansed from all the impurities carried over from his/her Gentile life.

It was not required of a Jew to be 'drowned' (literal meaning of baptism) in order to die to an old life and be raised from the water to a new one.

John's preaching, however, was drawing crowds of people to the part of Jordan called Bethabara where most unusually he was baptising those who were born and bred Jews! What had wrought this change and given people the humility to undergo a rite normally reserved for those who were not by birth 'sons of Abraham'?

Perhaps initially people came out of plain curiosity. Rumour got around that a rather weird, eccentric character, dressed in a garment of camel's hair, who seemed to live chiefly in the desert on a self-sufficient, eco-friendly diet of locusts (rich in protein) and wild honey, was preaching an extraordinary message calling people to prepare the way for the Messiah by repentance – and to demonstrate the sincerity of their intention publicly in baptism.

Having allowed curiosity to prompt them, a great number who went out to hear this wild-looking man (for under Nazarite vows he never shaved or cut his hair) found him compelling. Many of them were so heart-smitten, they stepped into the river and submitted to baptism on the spot.

When Jesus heard about John's baptism and the reason for it, he wanted to find out more for himself. I imagine he felt a sudden inner quickening, a kindling of hope and excitement. Was this the sign he had long awaited? And perhaps he was additionally struck by the fact that, not since Elisha made the Jordan a source of healing and wholeness, had anyone used it to show people the way to repentance.

All that he heard of John's preaching must have resonated so strongly with his own thinking and longing that he was eager to meet this kindred spirit. Whether or not he realised that the man the Jews called 'John the Baptist' was John, son of Zechariah the priest, his own relative, is unclear. Nor do we know if he was surprised that John had rejected his own priestly future in order to exercise a preaching ministry. It certainly seems that they recognised one another when they met.

Surprisingly, Jesus does not appear to have sought a personal audience with John – to discuss with him further and share his own vision for Israel. He simply went down into the water and asked for baptism. We are very familiar with John's deference to Jesus. We know that this experience of baptism marked a turning point in Jesus' life. It gave him God's seal of approval with which he was to start his own ministry. His 'hour' had come.

Even so, it does not answer the question, why – if he was without sin – did he submit to baptism in which he was publicly declaring his repentance?

We need to recall the Hebrew understanding of corporate person-ality to see what Jesus was about here. As the people listened to John, they did not become ashamed simply of their individual short-comings. They began to see how Israel as a community had failed again and again to fulfil the obligations laid upon her by her particular Covenant relationship with God. They were all part of a great national rebellion which would be visited by the judgement and wrath of God. For they had been called to be a light to enlighten the nations, 'but the light was turned in on itself. Israel was called to be the peacemaker, but she was bent on violent revolution. Israel was called to be the healer, but was determined to dash the pagans to pieces like a potter's vessel. Jesus saw the judgement coming, and realised that it was not just from Rome, but from God.'[6] He had felt a burning compulsion to tell people that they needed to repent – as the People of God – and here he found John doing the very same thing. It affirmed his own thinking. It excited him to realise that John's preaching was receiving such a massive response. This was a heart-warming Renewal Movement within Judaism and he wanted to identify with it fully. He longed for Israel to be true to her calling, to be the people God had intended her to be. The moment of vision which he received as he came up out of the water was his Confirmation. The Holy Spirit descended upon him in power (as he is more than willing to do at any Confirmation) but also, symbolically, as peace ('Let me hear what God the Lord will speak, for he will speak peace to his people, to his faithful, to those whose hearts are turned to him' Psalm 85:8). For all those coming to receive John's baptism there had to be a radical 'turning of the heart'. The prophets had continually stressed the need to 'turn to the Lord' (e.g. Jeremiah 25:5; 31:21; Lamentations 3:40), and Jesus stood squarely in the prophetic tradition seeing this as the basic step in a renewal of the Covenant relationship of Israel with her God, as his parable of the Prodigal Son well illustrates.

After this climactic incident, one imagines John continued his mission, still calling people to repentance and baptism, until his arrest, imprisonment (with that deputation of disciples sent to Jesus to ask him if he really was 'The Coming One') and ultimate execution. The disciples of Jesus also began to baptise, though Jesus did not (John 4:1–2). But, somewhere between the baptisms in the Jordan and those in the Early Church, an enormous shift of emphasis had occurred. It is true that baptism of proselytes had been part of the initiation into the Jewish faith, and baptism beyond Pentecost was a sign of initiation into the Christian Church. But at some point it became an outward sign of an inner identification with the whole story of the Community of God's people in its bondage, exodus and deliverance; its exile and restoration – the final mark of which had been the death and resurrection of Jesus. The corporate story of Israel became the personal story of each member of the new Community of God's redeemed people as, being buried and raised in baptism, he/she passed through the waters from death to life, from personal exile to restoration.

It has been suggested in earlier chapters that Jesus may increasingly have become troubled by the inadequacy of the sacrificial system and the injustice of it as a sole means of outward assurance of forgiveness – chiefly because it meant that those who lived too far from Jerusalem to go up for more than one feast in the year, and those of the

Diaspora who might only get to the Temple once in a lifetime, were largely excluded from the joy of such assurance. Despite the fact that, for them, Torah had to replace Temple and their Covenant God was encountered in the study of it, they may have been left carrying all manner of burdens – of guilt and shame – for lengthy periods.

Jesus always longed for people to be free from inappropriate loads of guilt and fear. Was this the point at which he wanted to challenge the monopoly on forgiveness that the Temple had come to hold? Did he question the sheer power the Temple officials had over the people, by their insistence that forgiveness could only be mediated through them? He was aware, of course, how it benefitted the financial resources of the Temple, so any challenge to the system would scarcely be welcomed. Yet since, in his view, the Temple itself needed cleansing – from the corruption that had set in not only in the usage of the building but in the power politics and condescension of the priests and officials – it was hardly a fit channel for dealing with sin anyway.

Had the baptism of John heralded a new way of coping with the fact of sin? Was he, in the Jordan, offering an alternative to the Temple? This could surely be a way by which radical change, a 'turning of hearts', could save Israel from utter decay.

There were, of course, and still are, purity laws and regulations whereby people underwent cleansing (as laid down in the Levitical code). And these largely took place in the widely distributed immersion pools, which archaeological excavations have uncovered. The large number of them would indicate that the purity laws were generally obeyed by ordinary Jews as well as Pharisees and rabbis. In fact, a good many Palestinian Jews were sufficiently devout to accept more purity laws than were actually laid down in the Scriptures. The substantial remains of these pools that have been discovered show that they were usually about seven feet deep with a surface area of seven – ten feet. Steps led down into the pool right to the bottom and often had a dividing line or rail to separate the right from the left.[7] So the worshipper entered the pool down the steps on one side – until completely submerged – and then returned up the other side. It symbolised the entry into the water as unclean, and the rising up out of the water as ritually cleansed.

It is worth noting that even today it is customary in churches that practise baptism by total immersion to have two sets of steps in the baptistery to indicate a passing *through* the water and out the other side. In the Church of which I am an associate member, written in mosaic on the top marble step by which the Candidate enters the water are the words, 'Buried with Him', and on the top step as the Candidate leaves the pool, 'Raised with Him'. In between those two flights of steps a mighty covenant is made, the implications of which take a lifetime to appropriate.

We know that the Essenes at Qumran had replaced animal sacrifices with lustrations. Remains of their pools have been discovered and photographs give us a clear idea of their size and depth. They were not used for bathing, nor as storage tanks for water – either for domestic use or for drinking. Separate cisterns provided for the day to day needs.

Did Jesus perhaps try to bridge a gap between Jewish tradition and Essene practice? The Essenes administered baptism as an outward symbol of cleansing from sin, not just from ritual impurities. Did Jesus see a possible merging of the baptism of repentance with lustrations for the forgiveness of sins? And not simply for private sins, but to restore the Community of God's people to its rightful, covenantal relationship?

We know that, at Passover, a river of blood flowed from the Temple to the brook Kedron. As Jesus pondered the failure of the sacrificial system to bring Israel back into relationship with God *as a community*, did he, I wonder, recall the prophecy of Ezekiel who saw in vision not blood flowing from the Temple, but a river of water?

> Then he brought me back to the entrance of the temple; there water was flowing from below the threshold of the temple toward the east . . .; and the water was flowing down from below the south end of the threshold of the temple, south of the altar . . .
>
> Going on eastward with a cord in his hand, the man measured one thousand cubits, and then led me through the water; and it was knee-deep . . . Again he measured one thousand, and it was a river that I could not cross, for the water had risen; it was deep enough to swim in, a river that could not be crossed . . .
> (Ezekiel 47: 1–6)

Could not be crossed, that is, except by total immersion in it.

If this is felt to be too speculative, I would ask for tolerance, for is it not a powerful picture of what happens in baptism (or ritual cleansing)? In vision Ezekiel enters the water little by little, feeling the water creeping up his body as he goes in deeper and deeper, until at last he is out of his depth. The alternatives are to swim, be submerged or turn back.

At that point in his vision, Ezekiel is unable to 'cross over' completely – the equivalent of not being able to rise out of the immersion pool by way of the second flight of steps. He simply turns round and retrieves his steps, going back the way he came until he is back on the bank. But as he walks along that bank, he sees many trees on either side. Where the river is flowing, it changes stagnant water into fresh. Everywhere it flows it gives life. The leaves on the tree will not wither nor their fruit fail – in fact, there will be a continuous supply each month, 'because the water for them flows from the sanctuary. Their fruit will be for food and their leaves for healing' (Ezekiel 47:12).

It is a picture of fresh, life-giving water touching what is stagnant. And, of course, it is the picture which John takes up in the Apocalypse: 'Then the angel showed me the river of the water of life, bright as a crystal, flowing from the throne of God and of the Lamb . . . On either side of the river, is the tree of life . . . producing its fruit each month; and the leaves of the tree are for the healing of the nations' (Revelation 22:1ff.).

Did that vision of Ezekiel – of the river which would bring new life, new fruit, freshness to what is stagnant and widespread healing – have any influence upon Jesus in his longing for renewal to come into and from the very heart of the Jewish faith with consequent healing and restoration? For Ezekiel, the river flowed from the sanctuary of God in the temple; for John, from the throne of God. But since the Holy of Holies was often spoken of as the throne of God, the shrine of the Mercy Seat, there is no discrepancy in the pictures.

Did Jesus reflect on the possibility of it being a river of water, not blood, flowing from the very belly of the Temple that would be the means of new life, a new covenant and a new commitment for the people of God? Would baptism and its radical 'turning' replace sacrifices as the life-giving force in Israel? As and when the Temple crumbled, what would replace it as the centre of renewal and restoration? Surely it would have to be a living human temple in which the renewing presence of the Spirit, the Shekinah glory, could take up residence; a hollowed out space in a human heart to become the new Holy of Holies. At his own baptism, the Holy Spirit descended upon Jesus and indwelt him – a sign and foretaste of his promised presence within the believing community. And so Jesus could also claim, 'Out of the *believer's* heart shall flow rivers of living water'

(John 7:38). From the very belly of the community of the new humanity would flow, by the power of the Spirit, life where there had been decay, freshness where there had been sterility, and healing where there had been separation. So, on the day of Pentecost when the Spirit's presence in his community was initially made so manifest the call was, 'Repent and be baptised'. Did Jesus see himself completing what Ezekiel was unable to finish, in his vision? Where Ezekiel turned back, in baptism Jesus entered fully into the watery depths, always redolent of chaos to the Jews, was totally submerged and rose to a new relationship with the Father as the true representative of a restored Community of Israel.

It would surely have rejoiced Jesus' heart when Nicodemus sought him out to talk to him about the Kingdom – the community of the new humanity. After the many expectations with which people came to him for healing, and the careful scrutiny and barbed questions of the scribes and Pharisees, it must have been pure joy to have so sincere and earnest an enquirer come to discuss with him his all-consuming passion – the Kingdom. It mattered not that Nicodemus was an eminent figure in Israel. To come to Jesus was as levelling an experience then as it is today. Worldly labels and reputations fall away as we stand before him simply as those who need him and long for him to unfold the wisdom of God.

Though probably considerably older than Jesus, Nicodemus nevertheless addressed him by the courtesy title of Rabbi. 'Rabbi, we know that you are a teacher who has come from God; for no one can do these signs that you do apart from the presence of God' (John 3:2).

Jesus needed no further prompting. 'That is true', he replied [my paraphrase]. 'No one will have the perception to see the breaking in of the Kingdom of God without being born from above.' When Nicodemus appeared almost deliberately to evade the implications of this by suggesting that rebirth would be a physical impossibility, Jesus went on to say, 'No one can enter the Kingdom of God without being born of water and Spirit.' There was no mention of entering the Kingdom by means of blood sacrifices.

In his novel, *Jeshua*, Moelwyn Merchant depicts this encounter between Nicodemus and Jesus very vividly. Earlier in his book he has named Nicodemus as one of the doctors of the law who had been present when the 12-year-old Jesus had questioned and discussed with them, and amazed them by his remarkable wisdom and maturity.

'Rabbi! I know that you are of God. Never shall I forget those hours in the Temple, when I, with wise and holy men, and Joseph who always sought for truth, listened with awe and some fear to a boy from the hill-country who in his young Galilean accent asked such questions that our souls were searched. Now, as the years begin with stealth to creep upon me, I hear not the questions but such strange answers. I hear of a progress through the wilderness in which the blind see, the deaf hear and the paralysed walk. What, in this power, will you do to our tradition? What in God's name will you require of us?'

'The tradition may shatter – the sound, the smell of corruption assails you even in the Temple itself. We need re-birth; yes, man must be born again.'

Before the intensity of these words Nicodemus recoiled into a defensive raillery.

'Born again! And must I enter once more the darkness and the preparation of my mother's womb and be born again?'

'That is the answer of flesh, Rabbi. Would that man could know even that re-birth. But much more he needs the harsher birth by water and the breath of God.'[8]

That 'harsher birth by water and the breath of God' was what Jesus came to see would be the outward sign of entry into the community of the redeemed. It was a baptism that incorporated the essential 'turning' in repentance from darkness to light, and a repudiation of all the evil that darkness symbolises, by entering into the chaos of the waters and passing through them. By its power to cleanse and purify it could bring about deep 'bonding' within the community. It offered the possibility of new birth and radical conversion. In other words it encompassed John's baptism of repentance, the Essene immersions of purification and community identity and the proselyte baptism of rebirth. More than that, however, it carried within it the particular gift to the new community – the gift of the Holy Spirit, the gift Jesus had himself received in fullest possible measure at his baptism.

A river of life flowing from the heart of their faith, seemed to be the insight that seized Jesus. Ezekiel's vision had been of what could be, the future Temple worship, when Israel was set free from the exile and restored to Jerusalem. Jesus saw how the new community of redeemed Israel would be brought back from the exile of a failed

Covenant to a restored relationship with her God by entering again into the life of God through the Covenant of baptism.

The Early Church came to see that all who were subsequently baptised would be immersed into Jesus, into his death and resurrection, restored to new life and hope, to become one with the new humanity. Thus they would enter into the story of the new Covenant people – the community of the redeemed – and would spend the rest of their lives assimilating the significance and grace of such an act.

A New Temple

In his very moving novel *The Hidden Years*,[9] Neil Boyd tries, as we have already seen, to capture something of the inwardness of the temptations against which Jesus struggled in the wilderness. Speaking of the second of them, he writes of the Tempter's wily approach:

> 'In the long nights you spent on the hills around your home and here on Olivet, you felt about the Temple a certain . . . apprehension? Why not then leap from this pinnacle and float down into the Temple precincts like a bird? Like a dove of peace? Then', whispered the Tempter, 'they will listen to you and believe in you, and you will be able to rid the place of all the things that anger you so much – like hypocrisy, heartlessness, injustice, greed, corruption and irreligion.'[10]

There was nothing he wanted more than to see the Temple freed from excessive trappings. He longed that the building should not dictate the worship which, after all, existed only for the glory of God and to minister to human souls, not to burden them or keep them trapped in lavish, fussy rituals of the cultus and a pandering to its officials.

It was true that, if he were Son of God, he *could* help the Temple shed its false godliness – a godliness which somehow enabled people to pray most devoutly whilst at the same time ejecting widows and orphans from their homes and leaving their fellow human beings to die, bruised and battered, by the roadside.

> 'You can put an end to this, Son of Man', whispered the Tempter. '[You could] send away these priests in their purple and fine linen, religious leaders who betray God's name . . . Rid religion of its trivialities, its long spiritual decay . . . I beg you, float down and sweetly purify religion . . . Alas, Israel forgot its

origins in the wilderness. Israel put up a building and God was no longer the God of the heart but of the building . . . God is worshipped here . . . as if his people needed to make a special journey to meet him. As if he were not already present everywhere, before they lift a foot or speak a word, or their hearts awake. Look down, Son of Man. What are they admiring? God or the building? . . . Can you not hear them chanting, exactly as Jeremiah heard them chant, "The Temple, the Temple, the Temple? . . ." You must concede that the so-called sacredness of this place destroys the sacredness of the rest of God's world . . . End the costly priestcraft, the flamboyant Levitical ministrations . . . [Because, greedy and jealous as the religious authorities are] they cannot tolerate that a holy man, a *genuinely* holy man, should instruct and purify the people *free of charge*.'[11]

Even if Neil Boyd has caricatured to some extent the life of the Temple, he has also captured vividly the sheer scale of Christ's temptations. Each of them was, quite literally, diabolically subtle – so easy to interpret as the voice of God prompting and guiding. Most certainly Jesus wanted to see worship, and particularly that of the Temple, rid of all that negated true worship of the heart, all that made it difficult for the marginalised to have access to God and find in him a loving, merciful and compassionate God who didn't demand extortionate, financial remuneration for his love and forgiveness. But how? How could this longing become reality?

Not through theatrical showmanship or circus stunts – of that Jesus was sure. Purification could not begin with the kind of sensation that would bring people running with a desire for entertainment . . . a desire that would become insatiable. Somehow, the cleansing of the Temple had to start in the heart, in consciences newly awakened to the extent of Israel's failure to be the true Israel. He wanted people to know that God is Spirit, and those who worship him must worship him in spirit and in truth. It would be through deep repentance, a turning to God with all their hearts, and a genuine desire to fulfil Israel's vocation, that the changes would come – the very reason why he had welcomed John's baptism. The renewal of the Temple would begin in the individual temples of the heart – an insight which became an imperative as, over the years, he began to grasp that the Temple on Mount Zion was doomed to destruction.

Perhaps it was there in the wilderness, as he wrestled with the implications of a new, purged Temple that Jesus saw very clearly how his ministry would have to start with the common people – not with the hierarchy and religious authorities. He needed to initiate this renewal at the grass-roots level before he was silenced by scribes, Pharisees, Levites or Rome.

As he began his ministry, keeping away from the bigger towns where it could have been interpreted as inciting another revolution, or, at any rate, encouraging a military resistance like that of the Zealots, Jesus found himself faced with people – good, honest, sincere people – struggling under the 'system', religious and political. There were so many sick people who couldn't afford doctor's fees, so many people forced into prostitution or begging – simply to stay alive. There were those who felt the dead weight of guilt, fearing that unwittingly and unknowingly they had broken some of the numerous laws. Others were not unduly worried. The Law had for them become arid and the endless commentaries on it, expounded in the syna-gogues, no longer ministered to the deep hunger in their hearts so they did not seek anxiously to obey it in its every detail. They had given up as hopeless any such attempt. These were the people who heard Jesus 'with delight' (Mark 12:37). He was like a fresh wind blowing on the dry bones of rabbinical teaching and quickening them to new life.

His emphasis was on a God who cared about individuals – like one lost lamb, or an errant son. He spoke to their hearts of God's compassion and love even for the sinful – in fact, Jesus seemed to indicate, God was not particularly interested in those who were without any sense of sin, the proud and haughty ones. It never occurred to such people that in accusing Jesus of mixing with sinners it inevitably included them!

He spoke to a God who looked on the heart, on the motives of people, rather than outward observances. He knew the Law and *loved* it, but was able to redefine it, so that it became at once both less sterile and yet more demanding, in one sense more accessible, yet in another, always beyond human power to fulfil. He stretched them by his teaching as well as comforting them. He talked of celebration more than sacrifice. There was something so compelling about him that, despite their need to work and earn money to support families, men were prepared to 'down tools' and run after him – sometimes great distances – just to hear him speak in ways that truly touched the heart and with a personal authority that they had never experienced before, utterly unlike that of the scribes.

Somehow he made not just the Law but God himself so much

more accessible, so interested in *them* as people rather than in all the 'paraphernalia' of religion. He healed on the Sabbath because it was a loving thing to do. It was not work, or a burden (as defined by the Law), but a delight. He saw it as God coming among his people in very particular mercy on their day of rest, of sharing with them in compassionate solidarity – for love cannot be shut off for one day in a week or even one moment in a day.

Until this time, the Temple had been the place not only of worship but of mediation. If people rendered 'unclean' because of some ritual impurity wanted to be cleansed, they went to the Temple and performed appropriate rites. If they wanted assurance that their sin was forgiven, they sought it through Temple sacrifices. If someone wanted to celebrate and give thanks for God's restoration of his people 'and the hope of restoration still to come, he or she would normally go to the Temple.'[12]

The Temple formed in principle the heart of Judaism, in the full metaphorical sense: it was the organ from which there went out to the body of Judaism, in Palestine and in the Diaspora, the living and healing presence of the Covenant God.[13]

When, I wonder, did it consciously dawn upon Jesus that, in his preaching, healing and restoring people to wholeness, he was fulfilling functions that rightly belonged to the Temple but which it neither did satisfactorily nor could do because of its geographical distance from many in Judaism or its spiritual paralysis brought about by much corruption and many compromises? As he responded in love to the desperate need and longing he found in people all around him, he himself was increasingly becoming what the Temple was intended to be – a locus of encounter with God.

The Jews looked back to the destruction of the Temple at the time of their exile into Babylon as one of the major disasters of their history. Herod the Great had built their present Temple – the crowning achievement of all his building projects. But after 46 years it was still not completed. The Jews yearned for the day when the Temple would be fully restored and even more resplendent than it already was. Although, not a few were irked by the bitter irony that *their* Temple, the present shrine of the Lord God, 'was built in ostentation by the unseemly Herod, and was still a-building as he fraternised with the Roman powers'.[14]

The Romans had learned through bitter experience that whatever else they did as the occupying power, they must maintain a 'hands off' policy where the Temple was concerned. They kept a wary eye on events in the Temple from the fortress Antonia adjoining it, but they knew that to interfere would court disaster. Hence the Zealots felt able to use the Temple precincts as a safe place to gather and lay their plans. They traded on the protection of these sacrosanct precincts, thereby putting many lives at risk. That rightly angered Jesus, for it showed that Israel was worshipping a caricature of her own God. Her God was a God of mercy and forgiveness, of healing a:d restoration; and the Temple in Jerusalem was being used as a symbol of military resistance, speaking of a God who wants to obliterate the world in order to rescue Israel alone. Jesus' agenda was the exact opposite of this. Believing that Israel's destiny had devolved on to him and him alone, he came to believe that 'it was his task to be obliterated, in order that the world might be healed.'[15]

The slogan of the day was 'No king but God', and the place where God would set up his throne and from which he would rule, would of course be the Temple – the focal point of the nation's life. Others may have looked for this to happen in literal or materialistic ways. Jesus knew that God's kingly rule was already breaking in upon the life of Israel – through people's hearts changing and turning to the way of life the prophets had advocated passionately centuries earlier.

If we had been first-century Jews under Roman domination, we should doubtless have shared the popular beliefs of the day. Kingly rule would have implied armed resistance to, and victory over, the Romans. The whole nation waited expectantly on tip-toe for the Messiah to come and bring release from oppression and humiliation. Not surprisingly, people were beginning to build their hopes around Jesus. Could he be the King so long awaited?

Jesus was increasingly coming to understand that, staggering as it may sound, he was not only to inaugurate God's kingly rule (or Kingdom), he was not only to cleanse the Temple in order that it should be a worthy throne for the King, but that Temple was to be a flesh and blood one – a living seat of mercy! He himself was to incarnate the Temple, to be the 'temple–in–person'.[16]

> He was, in that very claim, confronting the pagan powers of the world with the news: this is where Israel's God is now becoming King! Here is the rallying point around which the true people of God will gather, so that they might be delivered from the powers of darkness! No wonder the crowds flocked to him. This was what they wanted to hear and experience.[17]

Understandably, the Temple officials were distinctly troubled. If Israel's God was establishing his Kingdom in the hearts of people and if the Temple prerogatives of healing, forgiveness and restoration were being ministered to people through Jesus, what would become of *them*, their jobs, their living, their status and immense power over the ordinary people? What if the whole infra-structure of the Temple were to collapse? What would be the future prospect of the cultus with all its rights, the revenue which paid the wages of as many as two thousand employees, the place of privilege and spiritual power it held in the nation? What would happen to the building?

It was a case of what had already happened to it. The axe was already laid to the root of the tree. Jesus could see that the spiritual foundations of the Temple were already crumbling. Maybe as he wept over Jerusalem, a major part of his sorrow centred around the Temple – after all, it would have dominated the skyline from almost any viewpoint. Did he weep because he already perceived its destruction? Coming away from the Temple once, his disciples commented on the magnificence and size of the blocks of stone used in the building. Jesus said to them, 'Truly I tell you, not one stone will be left upon another; all will be thrown down' (Matthew 24:2). The disciples had every reason to feel shocked, for there was nothing like the Temple anywhere else in their country, or indeed, in the ancient world at that time. It was built of white marble plated with gold which so shone and glinted in the sun, it became almost unbearable to look at.

The Temple area itself was surrounded by great porches – Solomon's Porch and the Royal Porch which were upheld by pillars cut in one piece out of solid blocks of marble. They were 37-and-a-half feet high and so thick that three men stretching to link hands with one another could only just get their arms round them. At the corners of the Temple, angle stones have been discovered measuring 20–40 feet in length and weighing a hundred tons. How they were cut, transported and placed in position is a mystery and one of the greatest feats of Herod's architectural, engineering genius. No wonder the disciples were awed by the size and splendour of the building. And clearly, their previous visits to the Temple had not diminished their wonder. They were appalled at Jesus' ominous prediction of its destruction.

So, when they were alone, they asked him to explain it. When was this terrible destruction going to take place? And he began to warn them of the Day of the Lord which would be a time of cosmic upheaval and moral chaos when wars, violence and hatred would be commonplace.

After his dramatic scourging of the Temple, he was challenged by the Jews to declare his authority. 'What sign can you show us for doing this?' (John 2:18ff.) Then Jesus disclosed to them what he had inwardly discerned: 'Destroy this temple and in three days I will raise it up.' They did not understand, of course. He probably got the response he expected. 'This temple has been under construction for forty-six years, and you will raise it up in three days?' To his hearers it was manifestly absurd – just another example of how crazy this megalomaniac could be. But Jesus had not only perceived the destruction of Herod's Temple. All his reflections on that enigmatic suffering servant figure with whom, it would seem, he identified, would have led him to believe that he himself would be 'despised and rejected . . . a man of sorrows and acquainted with grief' (Isaiah 53:3). His ultimate obedience would be through oblation and death. The Temple was, above all, the place of sacrifice. And somehow he came to see himself as both the Temple and the sacrificial lamb – Temple, Priest and Victim all in one!

The original enticement in the wilderness had been to purify the Temple by jumping from a pinnacle and landing miraculously unharmed. His mission, as Jesus came to perceive it, was to be the exact opposite. It was not simply to purge the existing Temple but to become a new one. Not to do his purifying work without any personal harm – but rather *through* pain and the way of destruction. No longer would it be the place where year by year thousands upon thousands of innocent lambs were slaughtered – but one perfect Lamb would become the guilt-offering and provide a full, perfect and sufficient sacrifice for the sins of many (cf. The Book of Common Prayer, Prayer of Consecration). It would be the sacrifice to end all animal sacrifices. It would be a new and *living* way to God; it would be the only truly, acceptable and pleasing offering to God – for it would be a self-willed offering of total love and obedience 'costing not less than everything', an offering with the potential to bring all people to the Father.

A New Thing?

◇◇◇◇◇◇◇◇◇◇◇◇◇◇◇◇◇◇◇◇◇◇◇◇◇◇

'Behold I am doing a new thing; now it springs forth, do you not perceive it?' (Isaiah 43:19) are words which Jesus could have applied to his own ministry. But how new? Was Jesus' teaching truly radical? Indeed it was in the sense of going to the very root of things. But in many respects he was drawing out what had been foreshadowed by the prophets and fulfilling it in ways which startled his contemporaries. Much of what he taught of God's forgiveness and compassion, his demands for justice and mercy, acceptance of the marginalised and protection of those without financial support (such as widows and orphans) had been an explicit part of the prophetic message. Jesus was uncovering and exposing once more what was firmly established and deeply embedded in the Law, the Prophets and the Writings – truths which had become obscured and at times overlaid by the pedantry of scholarly debate, engaging as it did the mind but not necessarily the heart.

Just as in carpentry, working with wood, he knew its grain, its growth, its thrust upward and around its core; and just as he felt for the knot and its pattern[18] in order to carve with the wood and not against it, to follow its natural curves rather than twist its shape and distort its proportions, so in much the same way he skilfully brought forth truth – never bending, twisting or distorting it. But feeling its 'grain', he probed gently for the thrust upward and around its vibrant, penetrating core and with great sensitivity exposed it, at the right moment, in the right way and from different angles, to reveal its many-faceted beauty. He presented truth as something living and to be lived.

Hence the scribes and Pharisees who could see truth but often only in limited, dry and very rigid ways, regarded him with horror as a Sabbath breaker, a deviator from the Law – someone with scandalous priorities. Yet, in effect, Israel had never had a truer Son of the Law. They failed to see how the core of truth, its spirit, is alive and quick, giving freedom and openness to explore its depths of meaning further – not a commitment to one irrefutable and immutable interpretation. Where truths of God were concerned, Jesus wanted to take people to the very 'heart of the wood' where it was green and growing and the life-force could be felt – that life-force which was of course love and compassion. Indeed, very literally, he took them to the 'heart of the wood' as he hung nailed to it in unfaltering love.

The totally new thing which broke upon the world with the coming of Jesus was the true humanity to which we were all destined. This new humanity was not just a better, vamped up version of humanity. It was an entirely new creation – something of a totally new order. What happened in the Christ event was no mere *evolution* of Israel's past history – it was a breaking into history of something qualitatively new. Not a better creation, but a new creation. And Paul's claim is that all those who are drawn into the new humanity of Jesus become themselves a wholly new creation (2 Corinthians 5:17).

This book has explored, through reflection, the ways in which Emmanuel, the God-with-us God, became one with us in flesh and blood form with all the normal human emotions, uncertainties, temptations and opportunities. It has raised questions as to how God in Jesus experienced full humanity and the guiding stars by which he steered through the muck and mess of the world – namely, love, compassion and his vision of the Kingdom.

The last 'new thing' which completed his incarnation, was the Ascension. When Jesus returned to his place 'at the right hand of the Father', there to dwell in glory, he was not in one sense the same Jesus who was conceived in the womb of Mary. 'Manhood had been taken by the Son',[19] but at the Ascension, manhood or humanity was taken for the first time right into the Godhead. Humanity, redeemed and perfected through obedience and suffering, was received back with the Son in his exaltation, and from then on the Godhead too was different.

Our humanity is there, an assurance that in union with Jesus we shall 'ascend' by faith into that same realm amongst all the redeemed.

> Thou hast raised our human nature
> In the clouds to God's right hand;
> There we sit in heavenly places,

There with Thee in glory stand;
Jesus reigns adored by angels,
Man with God is on the throne.
Mighty Lord in thy Ascension
We by faith behold our own.[20]

Nowhere in the Gospels do we have a description of the facial features of Jesus. We know only that the light of the knowledge of the glory of God shone in his face – very particularly at the Transfiguration, where we see how humanity would have been had sin not marred it and caused dehumanisation. But we also see how redeemed humanity, and we as part of it, *will* be, if we gaze in contemplation on that face. If our ongoing stance before Jesus is one of loving gaze, his hidden face will one day be reflected on our own, for 'all of us, with unveiled faces, seeing the glory of the Lord as though reflected in a mirror, are being transformed into the same image from one degree of glory to another' (2 Corinthians 3:18).

EPILOGUE

Blowing through heaven and earth, and in our hearts and in the heart of every living thing, is a gigantic breath – a great Cry – which we call God. Plant life wished to continue its motionless sleep next to stagnant waters, but the Cry leapt up within it and violently shook its roots: 'Away, let go of the earth, walk!' Had the tree been able to think and judge, it would have cried, 'I don't want to. What are you urging me to do! You are demanding the impossible!' But the Cry, without pity, kept shaking its roots and shouting, 'Away, let go of the earth, walk!'

It shouted in this way for thousands of aeons; and lo! as a result of desire and struggle, life escaped the motionless tree and was liberated.

Animals appeared – worms – making themselves at home in water and mud. 'We're just fine here', they said. 'We have peace and security; we're not budging!'

But the terrible Cry hammered itself pitilessly into their loins. 'Leave the mud, stand up. Give birth to your betters!'

'We don't want to! We can't!'

'You can't, but I can. Stand up!'

And lo! after thousands of aeons, man emerged, trembling on his still unsolid legs.

The human being is a centaur; his equine hoofs are planted in the ground, but his body from breast to head is worked on and tormented by the merciless Cry. He has been fighting, again for thousands of aeons, to draw himself like a sword, out of his animalistic scabbard. He is also fighting – this is his new struggle – to draw himself out of his human scabbard. Man calls in despair, 'Where can I go? I have reached the pinnacle, beyond is the abyss.' And the Cry answers, 'I am beyond. Stand up!'[1]

If only Nikos Kazantzakis had known – and believed – that humanity has no need to draw itself out of its human scabbard. We were never meant to be detached from or ashamed of it. Christ ascended not *out* of that scabbard but taking it with him, fully redeemed, into the Godhead ('Yes angels tremble when they see how changed is our humanity'[2]) – not as some kind of centaur but as Proper Man.

As Jesus reveals more and more of his hidden face to us, we see in him that to be fully human is to be truly holy.

NOTES

INTRODUCTION

1. Nikos Kazantzakis, *The Last Temptation of Christ* (New York, Bantam Books, 1958), prologue.

CHAPTER 1: 'FULLY HUMAN'

PRE-NATAL INFLUENCES

1. Thomas Verny and John Kelly, *The Secret Life of the Unborn Child* (London, Sphere Books, 1982), p. 2.
2. G Florovsky, 'The Ever-Virgin Mother of God', in E L Mascall (ed.) *The Mother of God* (Dacre Press, 1950), pp. 51–63.
3. Hymn, 'The Angel Gabriel from Heaven Came'.
4. Verny and Kelly, *The Secret Life*, p. 5.
5. This is the view of a former Professor of Paediatrics, Linguistics and Anthropology at the University of Miami. Cf. Verny and Kelly, *The Secret Life*, pp. 6–7.

BIRTH AND BABYHOOD

6. Daniel Rops, *Jesus in His Time* (London, Eyre and Spottiswoode/ Burns and Oates, 1955), p. 110.
7. Ibid.
8. M Scott Peck, *The Road Less Travelled* (London, Century, 1978), p. 35.
9. The use of the term 'Galilean' may have been a loaded one. A movement under the leadership of Judas the Galilean had led to an uprising in AD 6 when Jesus was still an adolescent. It was quelled violently by the Romans.

BOYHOOD

10. Cf. John Marsh, *Jesus in His Lifetime* (London, Sidgwick and Jackson, 1981), pp. 89–90.
11 E P Sanders, *Judaism: Belief and Practice* (London, SCM, 1992), cf. pp. 119–120.
12 Sanders, *Judaism: Belief and Practice*, from Spec. Laws 1. 133, 136, p. 120.
13. Sanders, *Judaism: Belief and Practice*, from Legat 16 (115).
14. I am indebted for much of this factual information to Emil Schurer, *The History of the Jewish People of the Age of Jesus Christ, Vol. 2*, revised and edited by G Vermes, F Millar and M Black (Edinburgh, T & T Clark, 1979), pp. 417–421.
15. A N Wilson, *Jesus* (London, Sinclair-Stevenson, 1992), p. 8.

THE EMERGING VISION

16. Sanders, *Judaism: Belief and Practice*, p. 129.
17. N T Wright, *The New Testament and the People of God* (London, SPCK, 1992), pp. 229, 163.
18. Charles Lamb, *Essays of Elia*, cited in *Dictionary of Religious and Spiritual Quotations* (London, Routledge, 1990), p. 139.
19. George Bernard Shaw, 'Everybody's Political What's What', cited in *Dictionary of Religious and Spiritual Quotations*, p. 139.

ADOLESCENCE AND PUBERTY

20. Wright, *The New Testament*, p. 236.
21. Melanie Klein, *Psychoanalysis of Children* (London, Virago).
22. R Stoller, *Sex and Gender*, Vol. 1 (Maresfield Reprint, 1968).
23. Richard Holloway, *Anger, Sex, Doubt and Death* (London, SPCK, 1992), p. 50.

THE WAITING YEARS

24. W H Vanstone, *The Stature of Waiting* (London, Darton, Longman and Todd, 1982), cf. pp. 1–33.
25. From a prayer attributed to Gregory Vlastos.

CHAPTER 2: 'TEMPTED IN EVERY RESPECT?'

FULLY HUMAN, FULLY DIVINE

1. James Finlay, *Merton's Palace of Nowhere* (Notre Dame, Indiana, Ave Maria Press, 1978), p. 27.

ANGER

2. Walter Brueggemann, *The Prophetic Imagination* (London, SCM, 1992), p. 84.
3. Ibid.
4. Mark 8:12 (my paraphrase).
5. Henri J M Nouwen, D P McNeill, D A Morrison, *Compassion* (London, Darton, Longman and Todd, 1982), p. 53.
6. Brueggemann, *The Prophetic Imagination*, p. 85.
7. I acknowledge my debt to Walter Brueggemann for chapter 5 of *The Prophetic Imagination* which has prompted some of the thinking in this section.
8. Thomas Merton, *The Sign of Jonas* (London, Burns and Oates, 1953), pp. 325–6.
9. Ibid.
10. Hymn for Vespers of the Feast of the Sacred Heart in the *Daily Office, Part 1*, copyright CSMV.

LUST

11. Gerard Hughes, *Oh God, Why?* (London, BRF, 1993), p. 67.
12. Nicholas Peter Harvey, *The Morals of Jesus* (London, Darton, Longman and Todd, 1991), p. 11.

ENVY

13. Stewart Henderson, 'God Gives You This Day', taken from *A Giant's Scrapbook* (London, Spire, 1989), p. 81.

COVETOUSNESS

14. Bernard O'Connor OSA, *The Human Face of Jesus* (CTS, 1986), p. 23.

PRIDE

15. Harvey, *The Morals of Jesus*, p. 56.
16. Bianco da Siena, 'Come Down O Love Divine', *New English Hymnal*, no. 137.
17. Harvey, *The Morals of Jesus*, p. 99.
18. Ibid.
19. Ibid.

JEALOUSY

20. Gerd Theissen, *The Shadow of the Galilean* (London, SCM, 1987).
21. Harvey, *The Morals of Jesus*, p. 57.
22. Ibid.
23. Ibid. p. 104.

240 NOTES

CHAPTER 3: 'MADE PERFECT IN WEAKNESS'

A SENSE OF HUMOUR
1. Michael Quoist, *Prayers of Life* (Dublin, Gill & Macmillan, 1963), pp. 3–4.
2. My paraphrase.

SENSITIVITY
3. *Godspell*, musical based upon the Gospel according to Saint Matthew. Music and Lyrics by Stephen Schwartz (1971).
4. Andrew Elphinstone, *Freedom, Suffering and Love* (London, SCM, 1976), p. 110.
5. Ibid. p. 99.
6. I am indebted to Tom Wright for this point. See his *The Crown and the Fire* (London, SPCK, 1992), p. 15.
7. William Shakespeare, *King Lear*, Act 1 Scene IV.
8. Elphinstone, *Freedom, Suffering and Love*, p. 108.
9. Ibid. pp. 108–9.
10. Lewis B Smedes, *Love Within Limits* (London, Lion, 1979).
11. Hughes, *Oh God, Why?* p. 113.
12. Elphinstone, *Freedom, Suffering and Love*, p. 137.
13. Ibid.
14. Ibid. p. 138.

PSYCHOLOGICAL EVALUATIONS
15. Winfred Overholser in Albert Schweitzer, *Psychiatric Study of Jesus* (Boston, Beacon Press, 1958), p. 15.
16. William Hirsch, *Conclusions of a Psychiatrist*, p. 126.
17. Ibid.
18. Schweitzer, *Psychiatric Study of Jesus*, pp. 33–4.
19. Shirley du Boulay, *Tutu* (London, Penguin, 1989), p. 194.
20. Janet Morley, *All Desires Known* (London, SPCK, 1992), p. 17.

CHAPTER 4: 'LOVING AND BEING LOVED'

RELATIONSHIPS
1. O'Connor, *The Human Face of Jesus*, pp. 21–2.

WITH MARY, HIS MOTHER
2. Wilson, *Jesus*, p. 120.
3. Wright, *The Crown and the Fire*, pp. 7–12.
4. Ibid.

5. B Wharton, 'The Hidden Face of Shame', *The Journal of Analytical Psychology*, vol. 35, no. 3, July 1990.
6. Harvey, *The Morals of Jesus*, p. 60.
7. Christina Wieland, 'Beauty and the Beast', *British Journal of Psychotherapy*, vol. 8, no. 2, Winter 1991.
8. Matthew 8:21–2 (my paraphrase).

THE HOUSEHOLD AT BETHANY
9. Rops, *Jesus in His Time*, p. 282.
10. N T Wright, *Who Was Jesus?* (London, SPCK, 1992), p. viii.

JOHN
11. Holloway, *Anger, Sex, Doubt and Death*, p. 48.
12. Ibid. p. 59.
13. Eleanor Bertine, *Human Relationships*, cited in D B Phillips, E Boyden Howe and Lucille M Nixon (eds.), *The Choice is Always Yours* (Illinois, Re-Quest Books, 1982), p. 348.
14. Ronald Rolheiser, *Forgotten Among the Lilies* (London, Spire, 1991), p. 68.

MARY MAGDALEN
15. John Spong, *Born of a Woman* (London, Harper Collins, 1992).
16. Wright, *Who Was Jesus?*
17. Margaret Magdalen CSMV, *Transformed by Love: The Way of Mary Magdalen* (London, Darton, Longman and Todd, 1989).
18. Hymn for First Vespers of a Religious in the *Daily Office, Part 2*, copyright CSMV.
19. Rolheiser, *Forgotten Among the Lilies*, cf. p. 65.
20. Ibid. p. 33.
21. Ibid.
22. Ibid. p. 67.

EMBRACING HIS SEXUALITY
23. Holloway, *Anger, Sex, Doubt and Death*, p. 35.
24. Stephen Verney, *Water into Wine* (London, Fount, 1958), p. 180.
25. I am indebted to Ronald Rolheiser for this thought.
26. Hughes, *Oh God, Why?* p. 145.
27. Rolheiser, *Forgotten Among the Lilies*, p. 67.
28. Chaim Potok, *The Gift of Aster Lev* (London, Penguin, 1990), p. 29.

OVERDEPENDENT RELATIONSHIPS
29. Henri Nouwen, *Reaching Out* (London, Fount, 1980), p. 44.
30. Ibid.
31. Ibid.
32. Constance Padwick, *Temple Gairdner of Cairo* (London, SPCK, 1930), p. 92.

CHAPTER 5: 'THROUGH A MIRROR DIMLY'

THE UNCONSCIOUS
1. Referred to by psychologists as 'Jacobson's Window' – a classic 4-square model of self-awareness.
2. Rops, *Jesus in His Time*, p. 168.
3. Ibid. p. 169.
4. Morley, *All Desires Known*, p. 46.
5. Neil Boyd, *The Hidden Years* (London, Hodder and Stoughton, 1984), pp. 234–5.
6. Rops, *Jesus in His Time*, p. 248.
7. Hebrews 4:12–13.

DREAMS
8. Russ Parker, *Dreams and Spirituality* (Nottingham, Grove Books Ltd, 1985), p. 2.
9. Arthur Janov, *Primal Scream* (Abacus Books, 1976), pp. 264–5.
10. Carl Jung, *Man and his Symbols* (Picada, 1978), p. ix.
11. John Sanford, *God's Forgotten Language* (Harper & Row, 1968).
12. Parker, *Dreams and Spirituality*, p. 21.
13. Rabindranath Tagore, *The Gardener* (London, Macmillan and Co Ltd, 1917), p. 87.

FANTASIES
14. Rolheiser, *Forgotten Among the Lilies*, p. 121.
15. Ibid.
16. O'Connor, *The Human Face of God*, p. 35.
17. Hughes, *Oh God, Why?* p. 105.
18. Rolheiser, *Forgotten Among the Lilies*, p. 123.

THE DIVIDED SELF
19. J W T Redfearn, *My Self, My Many Selves* (London, Academic/Routledge Press).
20. Martin Smith, *The Word is Very Near You* (London, Darton, Longman and Todd, 1989), p. 97.

21. Ibid.
22. Ibid.
23. James Hillman, *Insearch* (London, Hodder & Stoughton, 1967),
     p. 69.
24. Smith, *The Word is Very Near You*, pp. 98–9.

THE UNION OF OPPOSITES
25. M Milner, *The Suppressed Madness of the Sane Man* (London,
     Tavistock, 1987).
26. For Jung, 'integration' was the first stage – our task in youth.
     He recommended building up the ego through recognising the
     shadow, anima, persona – all those legion or sub-personalities,
     and bringing the opposites together. 'Individuation' he saw as
     a later stage in life, which eventually leads to surrendering the
     ego (the small conscious bit) in service of the self or Self, which
     embraces all we are and more. He saw the self-image as very
     near to the God-image – neither could be comprehended except
     in images (cf. D I Berkley Phillips).
27. Cf. Myers-Briggs Personality Type Indicator and Enneagram Per-
     sonality Types.
28. Hughes, *Oh God, Why?* p. 22.
29. Kazantzakis, *The Last Temptation of Christ*, pp. 1–2.
30. Matthew Fox, *Original Blessing* (Sante Fe, Bear & Co, 1986),
     p. 58.
31. Ibid.
32. Holloway, *Anger, Sex, Doubt and Death*, pp. 32ff.
33. Ibid.

                    CHAPTER 6: 'A NEW THING'

A NEW DIMENSION OF LOVE
 1. John Barton, *Love Unknown* (London, SPCK, 1990), p. 14.
 2. Ibid.
 3. Ibid. p. 3.
 4. Ibid. p. 8.

A NEW MOSES
 5. Martin Buber, *Hasidim and Modern Man* (New York, Harper &
     Row, 1958), p. 81.

A NEW BAPTISM

6. Wright, *Who Was Jesus?* p. 101.
7. Sanders, *Judaism: Belief and Practice*, pp. 224ff.
8. Moelwyn Merchant, *Jeshua* (Swansea, Christopher Davies, 1987), p. 163.

A NEW TEMPLE

9. Boyd, *The Hidden Years*, pp. 218ff.
10. Ibid. p. 176.
11. Ibid.
12. N T Wright, *New Tasks for a Renewed Church* (London, Hodder & Stoughton, 1992), especially p. 68.
13. Wright, *The New Testament*, p. 226.
14. Merchant, *Jeshua*, p. 33.
15. Wright, *New Tasks*, p. 69.
16. Ibid.
17. Ibid.

A NEW THING

18. Cf. Merchant, *Jeshua*, p. 72.
19. John Henry Newman, 'Firmly I believe and truly', *New English Hymnbook*, no. 36.
20. Christopher Wordsworth, 'See the Conqueror mounts in triumph', *New English Hymnbook*, no. 132.

EPILOGUE

1. Nikos Kazantzakis, *Report to Greco*, cited in Dorothy Berkley Phillips (ed.), *The Choice is Always Ours* (Illinois, Re-Quest Books, 1982), p. 32.
2. Hymn for First Vespers, Ascension Day, *The Daily Office*, Part 1, copyright CSMV.